S0-BSP-603

Road to Bo[...]

Bowry Lane

M.<sup>r</sup> De Lancey

De Lanceys
or
Great
Square

Street

Division Street

M.<sup>r</sup> Jones

Salt Meadow

CROWN P.<sup>T</sup> or COENTIES HOOK

T OR SOUND RI[...]

M.<sup>r</sup> Rapalie

PART OF LONG OR NASSAU ISLAND

Ramfens Mill

# ALEXANDER McDOUGALL
## AND THE AMERICAN REVOLUTION
### IN NEW YORK

# Alexander
# McDougall
## and the
# American Revolution
## in New York

## Roger J. Champagne

LIBRARY
SEMINOLE COMMUNITY COLLEGE

REC. DEC 21 1976

SANFORD, FLORIDA
32771

The New York State
American Revolution Bicentennial Commission
*in conjunction with*
Union College Press
Schenectady, New York
1975

Copyright 1975 by Roger J. Champagne. All rights reserved. Design and production services by David May at the Ithaca Office, Ithaca, New York. Composition, printing, and binding by Vail-Ballou Press, Inc., Binghamton, New York. Manufactured entirely in the United States of America.

Published in 1975 by Union College Press, Schenectady, New York 12308, U.S.A.

Distributed by Syracuse University Press, Syracuse, New York 13210, U.S.A.

International Standard Book Number 0-912765-05-5

Library of Congress Catalog Card Number 74-81986

**Library of Congress Cataloging in Publication Data**

Champagne, Roger J
    Alexander McDougall and the American Revolution in New York.

    Bibliography: p.
    Includes index.
    1.McDougall, Alexander, 1732–1786. 2.New York (State)—History—Revolution, 1775–1783.
I.New York State American Revolution Bicentennial Commission. II.Title.
E207.M12C47     973.3'092'4 [B]     74-81986
ISBN 0-912765-05-5

*Frontispiece:* Alexander McDougall, from a miniature on ivory by John Ramage. Courtesy New-York Historical Society.

*Endpaper maps: Front,* from "Plan of the City of New York," by Bern⁴ Ratzer, Lieu⁴ in the 60th Reg⁴, 1767. Reproduced from *History of New York during the Revolutionary War,* by Thomas Jones. New York: The New-York Historical Society, 1879.

*Back,* from "A Chorographical Map of the Province of New York in North America," by Claude Joseph Sauthier, Esq., engraved and published in London by William Fadden, 1779. Reproduced from *The Documentary History of the State of New York* by E. B. O'Callaghan, M. D. Albany: Weed, Parsons & Co., 1850.

TO MY WIFE

# Contents

# Foreword

Alexander McDougall has long deserved a full-length biography. The son of a milkman on a Manhattan Island farm, he rose to be a ship's captain, a privateer, a wealthy merchant, a leading radical agitator and revolutionist, an important political leader, a general in the Continental army, and ultimately one of George Washington's advisors and strongest supporters. Much of McDougall's historical significance, however, lies not in his actual role as a revolutionary leader but in the way he reflected a constantly changing American attitude toward civil war and revolution. The way McDougall viewed the world in 1783, after the war was over, was very different from the way he had seen it in 1770, when few had yet thought of rebellion. The story of how that change occurred provides important insights into how many Americans gradually came to feel about their revolution.

It is with a great deal of pride, therefore, that the New York State American Revolution Bicentennial Commission is acting as co-publisher with Union College Press of this, the first biography of Mc-Dougall to be published. Part of the Commission's publishing aim is to encourage and, when possible, to aid in the publication of significant new works on New York's role in the American Revolution. The Commission is particularly pleased to work jointly with university and college presses in the state in order to give these valued educational institutions a role in the bicentennial commemoration. This book represents a truly cooperative effort between Union College and the Commission in everything from editing to funding. The Commission is proud that it is to be the first of several jointly published works on New York and New Yorkers in the American Revolution.

JOHN H. G. PELL
Chairman
New York State American Revolution
Bicentennial Commission

# Preface

My interest in Alexander McDougall began years ago in graduate seminars on the American Revolution at the University of Wisconsin. The result was a dissertation on "The Sons of Liberty and the Aristocracy in New York Politics, 1765–1790." That early work furnished background material for this biography of McDougall. From that time to this, friends and colleagues provided me with encouragement and assistance during various stages of the project. I am indebted to the keepers of manuscripts at a number of libraries: New-York Historical Society, New York Public Library, City Museum of New York, Special Collections of Columbia University, New York State Library at Albany, William L. Clements Library at Ann Arbor, U.S. Military Academy Library at West Point, and Schaffer Library at Union College, Schenectady, New York. All extended courtesies far beyond reasonable expectation, for which I am grateful. The staff of Milner Library, Illinois State University, was particularly helpful, and Edwin K. Tolan of Schaffer Library and John L. Hawkes of Dorset, Vermont, generously allowed free access to the W. Wright Hawkes Collection of Revolutionary Documents at Union College. I owe a special debt to Bernard R. Carman and William A. Polf, whose editorial skills have made this a far better book than when first drafted. They have my thanks. Any remaining slips are my own. The Graduate School at Illinois State University provided research support and the National Endowment for the Humanities financed a leave of absence. Above all, I am indebted to Merrill Jensen, who first introduced me to Alexander McDougall and to my wife who patiently allowed McDougall into our family life.

ROGER J. CHAMPAGNE

*Illinois State University*
*1974*

# Introduction

The political and military career of Alexander McDougall of New York embodied much of the politics and spirit of rebellion among Americans who declared their independence of Great Britain and then went to war to defend it. Unlike a George Washington, a Thomas Jefferson, or a John Adams—historical giants whose thought and action dramatically and profoundly influenced their own time—McDougall was clearly a secondary figure in the American Revolution, one of a number of local leaders noted for political resourcefulness, militancy, and ceaseless effort in the cause of independence. He was a self-made and self-taught "man on the make," like many men in eighteenth century America in which he lived. He was recognized in his own time as one of New York's leading coffee-house politicians and one of George Washington's most dependable generals. Dedicated to the public interest as he saw and felt it but personally ambitious and jealous of his achievements, he was a canny Scot who calculated the need for change as carefully as he did the risks of rebellion.

Alexander McDougall was one of a larger group preoccupied with the local politics of the American revolutionary era. Appearing on the scene in the years following the French and Indian War, McDougall and others like him stood at the forefront of the opposition to Britain, participating in demonstrations against and leading the public attacks upon parliamentary power and royal authority. McDougall was of modest wealth and middling social rank, as were most other popular leaders, including Isaac Sears and John Lamb of his own city. He aspired to rise from lowly origins, and saw involvement in community affairs as both a measure of his status and a means to greater fulfillment. He was an ambitious man who responded readily to the call for political activity of an extraordinary nature when, after 1763, imperial policies aroused the public's indignation. Although popular leaders everywhere were usually connected in some way with an established system of local loyalties and political interests, as McDougall was with the Livingston family faction, men such as McDougall were identified with the people more than other public figures of the time, opposing what they believed were unconstitutional encroachments upon colonial rights. Because of that identification with the interests and concerns of the people at large, the term "popular leader" is used to characterize the role of McDougall and others like him in colonial political life.[1]

McDougall's public career spanned two decades, during which time he rose from being a loyal worker and agitator among the political rank and file to the level of major general in the Continental Army. His rise from obscurity to national importance was spectacular, and it naturally raises the question of whether other popular leaders of the revolutionary era rose as far and as fast. Was McDougall typical of other ambitious men who found themselves contemplating rebellion? Was there, indeed, a revolutionary "type," and, if so, what were its defining characteristics? I have discovered no easy answer to this question; indeed, it remains essentially unresolved. The vast quantity of writing on the American Revolution in recent years has not, disappointingly, produced a clearly drawn model comparable to the discredited "radicals" of the Progressive historians.[2] Instead, much of the present scholarship, now termed neo-Whig, gathers together all revolutionary leaders into a single Whig category on the basis of, as one author has put it, "the political conclusions and strategy individuals shared in a common trajectory toward revolution and independence."[3] This approach is valuable in marking out the common ideological ground upon which the leaders of the Revolution stood. But it nevertheless provides a limited view of the politics of the period by ignoring the social and political differences by which political leaders judged each other and which influenced the actors in the events leading to independence.

Additional insight into the nature of revolutionary leadership is to be found in several new studies. First, as Patricia Bonomi has demonstrated in the case of New York, the popular leaders shared with many other men an intense interest in politics, that engrossing public activity by which men of talent and ambition contentiously competed for office and influence in colonial government. Whatever may have been the nature of a colony's political development (most frequently linked to the rise of the colonial assembly), by the middle of the eighteenth century politics had become the common expression of public life. Men entered politics because it proved to be a "satisfying outlet," to borrow Professor Bonomi's phrase, for able and energetic members of society. During the pre-revolutionary period, politics provided an opportunity of advancement for men of new wealth like McDougall whose upward movement in society would otherwise have been slower, if not checked, by the hierarchical structure of established wealth and position.[4]

I also found useful James Kirby Martin's analysis of colonial officeholding on the eve of independence. Involvement in public affairs, while potentially satisfying, was not always rewarding to men of ambition, even those who attained government office. Not all men were able to realize their political goals; elections were lost and royal appointments proved elusive. Men already in office frequently found their advancement blocked by the occupants of higher office. Failure to rise intensified political frustrations, increased tensions, and added to the instability of politics, an instability already arising from the social and economic conditions of each colony. Thus Professor Martin's statistical evidence on colonial officeholders gives weight to a characterization of colonial politics in the pre-revolutionary period as the "ins," versus "outs," a formula which provides insights into the political motivations of the popular leaders. As new men in politics in a period of public agitation, the popular leaders were either initially recruited by, or came to be identified with, an "out" faction bidding for the electorate's favor by means of a vigorous defense of constitutional rights. Invariably, the "outs" used rhetoric based upon the widely accepted ideas of radical English Whiggism.[5] That was a dominant feature of the association of Isaac Sears and John Lamb with the De Lancey faction in New York City before 1769, and of McDougall with the Livingstons after 1769. The rivalry between the political "outs" and "ins" provides insights into the tactics, rhetoric, and emotionalism of local politics before 1776. Such a pragmatic framework also helps to explain, in ways not possible through an intellectualist's view of men and events, why some men chose rebellion and others did not.

Perhaps it is not really possible to construct a model of those secondary political figures who were recognized in their own time as being different from the major leaders of the revolutionary generation. Certainly it cannot be done within the scope of a biography. Yet in my approach to McDougall's public life, I have attempted to establish his relationship to a larger constituency of popular leaders by confronting a number of questions. What enabled leaders like McDougall to rise so rapidly to prominence? Was McDougall's advancement the result of ambitious aims, consciously pursued and gratified in the turmoil of imperial issues, or was he pushed upward because of what his own success symbolized to the mass of ordinary men? As an aggressive political newcomer, what place did McDougall occupy in society's structure of rank and privilege as he passed through the stages of political success? What did the republican idealism of the Revolution mean to McDougall, and did that meaning remain constant throughout his life? I have tried to answer these questions about one popular leader of the Revolution, and thus to shed light on the entire group of men who led the successful rebellion against British rule.

# Chapter One
# The Early Years

Alexander McDougall was in his middle years when he first achieved notice among New Yorkers protesting Great Britains's imperial policies of the 1760's. A Scot whose heavy, stuttering brogue identified his ancestry, McDougall had broad shoulders, a muscular neck, and a well-proportioned head—all combining to give him a rugged appearance. A miniature painted by John Ramage sometime during the war shows a kindly face of near-handsome features and steady gaze.

McDougall's early life was a familiar American story. Born into a poor but hard-working and thrifty family, he advanced himself through personal ability and desire, seizing those opportunities and chances for success common in eighteenth century America. He was only a boy of six when his family arrived in New York in the early fall of 1738. The second of five children of Ronald and Elizabeth McDougall, Alexander was born in 1732 on the Isle of Islay of the Inner Hebrides, a chain of bleak islands along the western shore of Scotland.[1] Inhabited by livestock raisers and stout Presbyterians, Islay was an isolated area with limited economic opportunity. Its stubborn land yielded a poor living to farmers who worked the soil for absentee landlords. It is not known why Alexander's parents began thinking of emigrating to Great Britain's North American colonies. Perhaps they heard accounts of the "new world" and its vast expanse of fertile and wooded lands from land agents seeking settlers or from soldiers returning from the wars of King William and Queen Anne. In any case, the McDougalls joined a larger Highland Scot movement to the American colonies in the 1730's, hoping to find land and opportunity.

Ronald McDougall, his wife and three sons, including Alexander, came to New York as part of a speculative venture conceived by a Scottish army veteran, Captain Lachlin Campbell.[2] Encouraged by provincial authorities anxious to populate the frontier against French

incursions into the upper Hudson and Mohawk valleys, Captain
Campbell assembled over 170 Highlanders from Islay and elsewhere
who arrived in the colony sometime in August or September, 1738.[3]
Campbell's undertaking was bold. He planned to petition the governor for 30,000 acres on the upper Hudson and, with financial assistance from the provincial Assembly, to settle the immigrants on the
land as his tenants. But the enterprise did not turn out as Campbell
intended. Many of the Highlanders, Ronald McDougall apparently
among them, had paid their own passage to America, and they expressed disappointment when they learned upon arriving in New
York that they were to become mere tenants for Campbell rather than
free landowners.[4] The protests of the immigrants ultimately reached
the provincial Council, but not before Lieutenant Governor George
Clarke informed the Assembly of the Highlanders' plight and
requested money to settle them on the northern frontier. When the
Assembly refused, Campbell's scheme collapsed.[5]

The McDougalls and others among Campbell's group thus spent a
hard winter in New York City. Lieutenant Governor Clarke still
hoped to populate the frontier. Even though he had been unable to
raise funds, he promised free land to any who would go north at their
own expense. Subsequently a number of the Highlanders went to
look at the land in June, 1739.[6] It is not known whether Ronald Mc-
Dougall went along on the inspection tour, but in any case, he decided against settling in the wilderness. He chose instead the relative
security of dairy farming on Manhattan Island, eventually becoming a
prosperous farmer and one of the provincial capital's principal milk
dealers.[7] It was a twist of fortune, therefore, that young Alexander
McDougall's early years were conditioned by the urban-commercial
life of the New York City area rather than by the colony's isolated
frontier.

The New York City of Alexander McDougall's youth was far different from the city of the 1760's in which he eventually became a
successful merchant. It was only one-half its later size, hugging the
southern tip of Manhattan Island, and still as much Dutch as English
in architecture, custom, and religion. Still, it must have been a place
of wonder for a young Highlander born in the isolation of Scotland's
western isles. It was no doubt full of strange and exciting sights and
smells, a babble of languages as merchants and artisans went about
their work, a place inhabited by seafaring men who knew distant parts

of the world, with men and women dressed in splendid satins, silks, and linens, living in fine town houses on broad and shaded streets and moving about the city in elegant carriages. The city had a seamy side too—smelly tanning yards, garbage strewn streets and markets, boisterous waterfront taverns, and tenements over-crowded by the poor. The city also had slaves, who accounted for more than twenty percent of its total population; racial tensions had already erupted into violence in 1712 and would do so again in 1741.[8] By accompanying his father as he delivered milk and other farm products about the town, young Alexander came to know the city well. Indeed, in later years, McDougall was remembered as one of the city's milk boys and somehow managed to retain fond memories of the early drudgery.[9]

Although Alexander's family background and early life was of the soil, he never became a farmer. McDougall came to respect land as capital and later acquired modest holdings, but life as a landowner never attracted him. This was an unusual attitude for an aspiring eighteenth century man in a social and political system in which landed wealth was the essential attribute of importance and respectability, and the reasons for it are unclear. Nevertheless, young McDougall became convinced very early in life that the path to advancement for an ambitious boy was greater in the city than in the country. It was to New York City, then, with its trades and commerce, that Alexander was sent to seek a livelihood. Before McDougall reached early manhood, he served a short apprenticeship in tailoring.[10] Meanwhile, he imbibed his parent's habits of piety, which lasted throughout his life, and acquired the fundamentals of learning, upon which he was to build in later years.

It was the high adventure of the sea, and the still greater opportunities of trade, which attracted the young Scot. By his late teens he was at sea, probably sailing aboard coasting vessels operated by the Walton family, one of the city's leading mercantile firms. In 1751, when he was nineteen, he went on a long voyage to Great Britain.[11] A stop was made at his native island of Islay, and after a swift courtship, the young sailor married Nancy McDougall, a distant relative and the daughter of the island's land surveyor.[12] Upon his return to New York, he continued working in the coastwise trade, now as a master of small sloops carrying cargoes of grain and flour to the Carolinas, Florida, and the West Indies.[13] Thus, within a few years, the sea provided young McDougall—"a mean half starved Scotchman" as a later critic remembered him—with a means of upward advancement, from common seaman to boatswain, from master to part owner of small cargoes.[14] It was a rapid, though not untypical, advance.

The French and Indian War brought McDougall a modest fortune. Now in his middle twenties and already a deck-hardened ship captain, McDougall became a privateer, as did other captains sailing out of New York. In 1757 he commanded the *Tyger,* a vessel of six guns and a crew of fifty, and two years later, the nine ton sloop *Barrington* carrying twelve guns and eighty men.[15] Over the course of six years, McDougall touched at St. Christopher's, Antigua, and St. Croix, and he was so often at sea that in 1760 he contemplated sending his wife and three children on a long visit to Scotland.[16] The exact circumstances of McDougall's cruises into the Carribean are not known, except that he took a number of prizes, sometimes under suspicious circumstances. According to Thomas Jones, a New Yorker and loyalist historian of the Revolution, McDougall "made something considerable by levying contributions upon a number of Dutch ships which he seized in the West Indies under pretence of their being carriers for the French, the captains of which, rather than be carried to . . . English ports, prudently gave him sums of money for permission to proceed on their respective voyages." [17] Whether the charge was true or not, the extent of McDougall's good fortune during the war is suggested by an accounting of his assets in 1767. By that time he valued his estate at £7,640, of which over eighty percent represented credits with London business houses and debts owed him by relatives and friends. Although data is sketchy, it is improbable that he was worth that much before the war. The best indication that the privateering brought him wealth is the testimony of the admittedly biased Jones, who described McDougall as being poor at the beginning of the war.[18] Even allowing for an increase of wealth over the period from 1763 to 1767, which were bad business years, his profits from privateering must have been sizeable.

If the French and Indian War made McDougall a man of means, it was nonetheless also a time of personal loss. On February 21, 1763, his wife Nancy died, and within a year his father was also dead.[19] Under other circumstances McDougall might have continued a life at sea, but family responsibilities now made that difficult. As an executor of his father's small estate, McDougall looked after his mother's well-being. More importantly, he had to supervise the raising of his

three children. Elizabeth, the youngest, was sent to an aunt living on
Long Island, while McDougall kept with him his two sons, John
Henry and Ronald Stephen. He also looked after a nephew, whose
family, with whom McDougall had business dealings, lived on St.
Croix.[20]

At this time, in the middle 1760's, McDougall boarded out with
Mary Bostwich, widow of the minister of the Wall Street Presbyterian Church of which McDougall was an active member. The death
of his wife seems to have deepened McDougall's religious feelings.
For a time, possibly because of his piety and grief, he thought of urging his sons to become clergymen. But his father-in-law argued
against it: the ministry held out little future for ambitious young men.
McDougall was apparently convinced. Although he sent his sons to
the Presbyterian College of New Jersey (now Princeton), he did not
encourage them to become ministers.[21]

In the years following the war McDougall invested his new wealth
in trade and land, and his business activities were extensive and
varied. On the eve of the Revolution, he owned at least one vessel, the
*Schuyler,* and he may have owned a waterfront "slop-shop" or tavern.
He served as an agent for several planters on the island of St. Croix,
taking their sugar and molasses on consignment and sending merchan-
dize on their order. He may also have acted as provisioner, though the
records of his exporting activities are not clear. His sugar sales in New
York City were made in small lots; measured against the sales of
larger trading houses, they were of modest value, amounting to only
£250 in 1769. By then his sugar operations had grown to include Albany and Quebec, although his primary trading interest continued to
be in the Caribbean.

Of greater value were the fees he earned on commissions and the interest on money he loaned as a factor and an investor. He paid bills of
exchange drawn upon himself by St. Croix planters, made loans to
New York merchants, and invested nearly £1,000 in the West Indian
plantation of his brother-in-law. He also invested in three slaves—one
of whom was a seaman hired out for wages to another brother-in-law
in New York—and may well have imported other slaves. A smaller
portion of his estate was in lands located in Albany County, the very
area in which his parents had considered settling thirty years earlier.
He also had an interest in houses in Wilmington, North Carolina.[22]
By 1769 McDougall was negotiating an option to buy 3,000 acres on

the Delaware River, but there is no record that he completed the transaction.[23] Compared with the business operations of other merchants, McDougall's activities represented only a beginning toward a successful career in trade and finance, but his postwar assets nevertheless place him in an economic position far above his former shipmates; according to recent calculations, he was at least twenty times wealthier than the New York average.[24] He was in a very real sense a wealthy and successful merchant. He had come a long way in a short time since the days when he delivered milk to the city's wealthy families.

McDougall also adopted the social values of the merchant community. Greater wealth meant a higher standing among men (or so McDougall thought and expected), and among his old shipmates on the waterfront he probably was regarded as a man who had made it. He dressed in fine clothing, carried a snuff box, had a saddle horse, acquired books, supported the new Presbyterian Church, and sent his sons to college. When he married again in 1767, he purchased over £180 worth of furniture for his bride, Hannah Bostwick, daughter of his landlady, and had a slave girl to help with the housekeeping.[25] But money alone could not make a gentleman, and the wealthier and older families who dominated New York society regarded McDougall as an over-anxious newcomer. His clothes were garish, and according to one member of the established elite, his tastes and manners were those of a common seaman with a preference for rum over wine, and he talked too much. Among men of established social position, McDougall was still regarded as either the son of a rough sailor or a milkman. In 1770, when he had achieved notoriety in the emerging revolutionary movement, the city's printers, who knew well the subtle gradations of New York's social scale,[26] called him "Captain" rather than the more genteel "esquire". It was a reminder to him that many men continued to see him as properly belonging on the quarterdeck; it was also an indirect recognition that the city's elite were not ready in so brief a time to acknowledge that he had a higher place in the community. Some would never accept him as a social equal.

# Chapter Two
# Imperial Policies and Partisan Politics

The general colonial indignation aroused by England's postwar imperial policies following the French and Indian War established Alexander McDougall's importance in public affairs. At the same time, local politics, marked by two bitterly contested assembly elections, shaped his role in New York's political life. Local politics and imperial policies fused in a way that determined the form and direction of the revolutionary movement in the provincial capital. From the furious eruption over the stamp tax in the fall of 1765 to the controversy over non-importation in the early summer of 1770, few men among the city's 20,000 inhabitants escaped the tumult and strife which the conjunction of imperial policy and local politics produced. During those five years, hardly a week passed without some sort of public agitation against the mother country or contention between political rivals, whether in the form of newspaper polemics, protest meetings and marches, strategy caucuses, or legislative sessions. It was a period of prolonged public controversy; from the start McDougall showed an interest in the issues of the day, first as a spectator but soon as an active participant. Public affairs of this variety formed a set of new experiences for McDougall, as they unquestionably did for others of similar background and status. Men of McDougall's stamp were provided lessons on constitutional issues, partisan struggles, and mass appeals. The impact upon McDougall's political life was as decisive as his privateering experience had been on his economic well-being.

Although the imperial controversy provided unusual opportunities for McDougall, his entry into politics cannot be entirely explained in that context. Instead of enjoying a period of peaceful adjustment following the French war, New Yorkers were confronted by unprecedented economic, political, and constitutional problems, all of which

fueled the incipient imperial controversy. The interaction of local politics with imperial policies created an instability in New York society
which undermined the old social and political arrangements by which
community affairs had been directed.[1] Britain's efforts to rule and tax
her colonies more stringently found New York in a condition that already bordered on crisis. New Yorkers were beset by problems of political leadership, commercial stagnation, and social and economic
unrest in rural areas. Imperial taxes and currency regulations deepened the gloomy forecasts of merchants struggling to avoid the ruin
posed by a postwar recession; to the frustration and suffering of unemployment among artisans, seamen, and laborers was added outrage
over the Royal Navy's policy of impressment; the attitude of the home
government offered no assurances of support to the landed gentry in
their efforts to ward off the encroachments of landless settlers upon
their estates; and the challenges to the traditional constitutional relationship between England and her colonies heightened the competi-
tion for power among members of the patrician class as they competed
for public support in their opposition to parliamentary authority.[2]
The traditional political and social structure in New York seemed to
be dissolving, threatened by internal and external forces beyond the
control of leaders accustomed to directing provincial affairs without
interference. In this environment of tension, uncertainty, and flux,
Alexander McDougall entered into community affairs.

There were probably few imperial decisions that could have
aroused the people as thoroughly as did George Grenville's revenue
program for the American colonies. For McDougall, the Stamp Act
crisis of 1765–1766 marked the beginning of his active interest in New
York politics. He was one of a small group of middle class merchants
of similar age, background, and circumstances—men such as Isaac
Sears and John Lamb—who came to play important roles in the community resentment against the stamp tax. In the beginning, these
fledgling leaders were indistinguishable from the mass of outraged citizens. They called themselves Sons of Liberty, or Liberty Boys (as
did a large number of other men of various ranks), and at this stage,
the term lacked consistent meaning. Bound together by an emotion-
charged determination to resist what they regarded as unlawful parliamentary taxation, the broadly constituted Sons of Liberty had virtually nullified the Stamp Act in New York by the end of October,
1765. Stamp officials had resigned their commissions; merchants and

shopkeepers had agreed to boycott English goods until the tax law was repealed; and it was commonly agreed that no person would pay the tax.[3] McDougall was a street leader in the protest. Along the waterfront, his standing and reputation as a former ship master and privateer captain helped him muster the large body of sailors for demonstrations which fanned the flame of unrest in the city.[4] Although the record is not clear, he probably was involved in other protest activities as well. But considering the widespread unrest in the colony, he was no doubt interested in all phases of the effort to defeat the tax measure, from coffee house and street corner discussions of the constitutional issues to maintaining the seawatch for the ship carrying the stamps for New York.

Soon after it began, however, New York's opposition to the stamp tax threatened to dissolve into random violence, which frightened away many of the early critics of Grenville's imperial program. On November 1, 1765, the date the Stamp Act was to go into effect, a destructive riot followed a demonstration against Lieutenant Governor Cadwallader Colden. Colden was bound by royal oath and personal views to uphold the tax, and his obstinance triggered four days of disorder and terror in the city, which ended only when he surrendered the stamped papers to city officials.[5] Further violence was prevented, but the mob action of November 1 resulted in property damage of £1,500. Such widespread violence shocked the city. Some men who had earlier supported community action to defeat the stamp tax separated themselves from the proponents of extreme measures. The Sons of Liberty, once an all-encompassing term for colonial protesters generally, now became a well-defined, organized group of radicals under the leadership of Isaac Sears and John Lamb, who insisted upon a continued defiance of British power and the need for an intercolonial military defense of colonial rights.[6]

The available evidence does not show that McDougall was a member of the Sons of Liberty as that group was identified by the end of November, 1765. The traditional accounts of the Stamp Act crisis in New York place McDougall among the leading extremists of the time. But contemporary sources do not mention him as an active participant in the city's affairs. Considering his later political activities, his anti-British attitudes, and his claim that he had earlier been a Son of Liberty, it is fair to ask why he does not appear, along with Sears and Lamb, among the Liberty Boys of 1765–1766. Several explana-

tions may account for McDougall's absence from public view. In political matters he was influenced by William Smith, Jr., John Morin
Scott, and William Livingston, all eminent lawyers and established
Whigs, the "triumvirate" of New York politics. Also influential was
Robert R. Livingston, supreme court justice and assembly representative from Dutchess County. McDougall undoubtedly came to know
all four by way of a common interest in the affairs of the Wall Street
Presbyterian Church, to which they all belonged. According to a Livingston family tradition, McDougall was supposed to have revered
Justice Livingston and treasured his political writings.[7] Together the
four lawyers had fashioned the Assembly's constitutional arguments
against the Grenville taxes, and in October, 1765, they were instrumental in raising the public resentment against parliament and
stirring the people against Lieutenant Governor Colden. But they had
not intended to encourage rioting against private property. In the
week following the violence of November 1, all four were indefatigable in working to prevent further disturbances. Robert R. Livingston, judging that seamen were the principal element of the mob,
sought the assistance of ex-privateer captains in quieting the city.
"One came immediately into our measures," Livingston reported.
"With him we went round to every part of the town . . ."[8] It is
probable, though conjectural, that McDougall was the former captain
who responded to Livingston's appeal. By aiding community leaders
who were trying to control the violence, McDougall found himself in
opposition to Sears and Lamb. This would explain why he was not
counted among the popular leaders in 1765–1766.

McDougall apparently opposed Sears and Lamb in still another
way as a result of his association with the Livingstons. When the radical leaders proposed that the Assembly defy parliament by approving
a resumption of all business and government activities without
stamps, McDougall probably agreed with Livingston, Smith, and
Scott that the scheme was a challenge to Britain which would endan-
ger the Livingstons position in the Assembly and cost them their influence with the recently arrived governor, Sir Harry Moore. A mass
meeting on November 26 rejected the radical strategy in favor of
another legislative petition asking the mother country for relief.[9]

By siding with Smith, Scott, and Robert R. and William Livingston, in supporting a more restrained opposition, McDougall lost his
credibility with the main body of Sons of Liberty.[10] From the end of

November, 1765, to May, 1766, when news of the Stamp Act repeal reached the colony, he was not visibly involved in the activities of the Liberty Boys. He stood on the sidelines as Isaac Sears and John Lamb, who had perhaps more accurately measured public sentiment, attempted to revive the city's normal business routine while organizing the Sons of Liberty for military activity if Britain should use force to uphold imperial authority. McDougall's views had not changed— the new taxes were still unconstitutional—but because of his affiliation with the patrician leaders of the Livingston faction he was out of step with his more zealous friends. The political hostility between Sears and Lamb and McDougall was to last four years.

If McDougall was no longer associated with the Sons of Liberty during the Stamp Act period, his part in public affairs advanced considerably because of two provincial assembly elections which occurred within the space of one year. Coming at a time when the American colonies were again aroused by parliamentary taxation, this time the Townshend duties, the elections of 1768 and 1769 were bitter contests for power between the gentry of the Livingston faction and the heirs of the De Lancey coalition of the 1750's.[11] Lieutenant Governor James De Lancey, Sr., had been the dominant political figure of that decade, but his unexpected death in 1760 temporarily ended the faction's control of the colonial government. While complete power did not immediately pass to the coalition of upriver land barons identified with Robert R. Livingston and the capital-based lawyer triumvirate of William Livingston, William Smith, Jr., and John Morin Scott, it was clear after the assembly election of 1761 that the old De Lancey party could not prevent an erosion of its former popularity and power in government, especially its hold upon the legislature. The new leaders of the De Lancey group, Captain James De Lancey, Jr., and his uncle, Oliver, a member of the Council, breathed new life into the faction during the Stamp Act crisis by urging extreme opposition to Britain. The re-emergence of the De Lancey faction added a new element of discord. By the middle 1760's, New York's politics had become more unstable and volatile as aspiring politicians fought for ascendancy, carefully selecting their issues to win favor with the people and royal authorities.[12]

On the eve of the 1768 election, the first in seven years, the politics of the major figures were well known. The Livingstons momentarily enjoyed the friendship and patronage of Governor Harry Moore, while the De Lanceys, out of favor and attempting to restructure the tattered remnants of their old power, were popular with the capital's populace because of their support for the Sons of Liberty.[13] The De Lanceys aggressively and skillfully blended imperial and local issues. In 1768 a monetary crisis, precipitated by the Currency Act of 1764, gave them an opportunity to align themselves with the mass of the people, particularly lower class debtors and middling entrepreneurs suffering from the severe currency contraction. De Lancey candidates joined in the general resentment against the legal profession (identified with the Livingston party) which was associated in the public mind with the interests of creditors. The next year, in the election of 1769, when the Townshend measures raised once more the issue of parliamentary taxation, De Lancey men publicized themselves as the true defenders of the liberties and rights of Americans by vigorously attacking imperial authority, while charging that their opponents had only been lukewarm patriots in 1765.[14] Livingston politicians, on the other hand, who wanted to increase their strength in the Assembly, suffered disadvantages from their seven year tenure in office during times of grave crisis. The ill-feeling generated by the essential moderation of the Livingstons in the Stamp Act protest was matched by the discontent of tenant farmers who remembered how quickly certain Livingston landlords in 1766 resorted to royal troops to put down rural disturbances.[15]

The elections of 1768 and 1769 were thus hard-fought, producing quantities of unsavory campaign literature, political intimidation, and outright cheating at the polls. McDougall served as a campaign worker, especially for Philip Livingston and John Morin Scott, the faction's leading candidates in the capital city. He actively campaigned against his old patron, William Walton, a De Lancey candidate, whom he considered unqualified regardless of how strongly Walton denounced parliamentary taxation. As a Presbyterian, McDougall approved the attacks upon the established Anglican Church, which the De Lancey men defended. He portrayed himself as a Son of Liberty among his old friends on the waterfront to balance the De Lancey electioneering of Isaac Sears, an Anglican.[16] As an incident shortly after the 1769 election revealed, the hard campaigning intensified the ill-will between McDougall and Sears. It was customary by then for old Liberty Boys to celebrate the anniversary of the Stamp Act repeal, and dinners at different taverns were planned for the March 18, 1769, date. One was headed by McDougall, the other by Sears and Lamb. Both groups claimed to be the true Sons of Liberty. McDougall made a gesture toward peace by toasting the other group, but the other diners rejected the salutation as coming from a man unworthy to be called a Son of Liberty. After several more hours of drinking, McDougall sent a friend to talk with Sears and Lamb, who, equally flushed with rum, argued over whether to eject the visitor through a second-story window or merely to show him the door.[17] As McDougall discovered for himself in that incident, the public tide was strongly against his patrician friends. The De Lanceys, after gaining ground in 1768, won a complete victory over their rivals in 1769.[18]

At the opening of the Assembly in April, 1769, De Lancey followers from New York City immediately took charge of the legislative session, confident of their power and ability to deal with a set of legislative problems—the Quartering Act, a severe currency shortage, and an unbalanced budget—which had frustrated the Livingstons for several years.[19] Whether the De Lanceys recognized it or not, their power would stand or collapse on these issues; whether they expected it or not, the Livingstons would oppose them every step of the way. Ever watchful for opportunities to regain power, the Livingston faction searched for chances to attack the new majority, and eventually found an issue in the Quartering Act. Peter R. Livingston, heir to the Livingston manor lands, thought that something could be made of the Quartering Act in such a way as to "answer the end of another dissolution" and produce a new assembly election.[20]

These political developments marked a turning point in McDougall's public life. Convinced that the Quartering Act represented an assault upon colonial liberty, but equally convinced that the De Lanceys could not be relied upon to defend the public interest, McDougall threw himself into a variety of activities which challenged De Lancey leadership, made him a popular hero in the provincial capital, and publicized his name in neighboring colonies. He became a De Lancey-watcher, openly searching for evidence of self-aggrandizing behavior which he felt would surely appear. When he thought he found what he sought, he took up his pen to incite public opinion against them. In time, he even patched up his quarrel with Isaac Sears and John Lamb by emphasizing their common dislike of the king's soldiers. Before long, he again became a recognized leader of the Sons of Liberty.[21]

Even though the assembly in the spring of 1769 had carefully side-stepped the problem of the Quartering Act, the legislative session which began on November 22 could no longer dodge the issue. By the fall, provisions suppliers were owed nearly £700 and by the end of the year the debt was over £1,000, with Leonard Lispenard, David Johnson, and Oliver De Lancey the primary creditors. Money had to be found for past and future support of the royal troops, and McDougall was a frequent visitor in the public gallery in City Hall to observe how the majority under James De Lancey intended to deal with the Quartering Act.[22] The speculation over what might happen intensified with the death of Governor Moore and the passing of the administration to Cadwallader Colden, the octogenarian lieutenant governor in retirement on Long Island who was still remembered for upholding the hated stamp tax four years earlier. As McDougall followed the De Lancey moves in the Assembly, it appeared that an agreement had been reached with Colden involving a much needed paper currency bill, the Quartering Act, and Colden's salary. A currency bill had been passed the previous session, but Governor Moore, following his instructions, refused to sign the bill because it lacked a suspending clause.[23] Now in the fall, Colden agreed to accept a similar bill, in violation of a long standing royal order, and the Assembly majority in turn indicated that it would obey the Quartering Act and pay the lieutenant governor's salary.[24] It was a shrewd trade off, calculated to give Colden a quiet administration and to enable the De Lanceys, by means of a new money supply, to soften public criticism of the Assembly's compliance with the Quartering Act. Confident of their political strength among the people in the capital and eager to establish their control over the provincial government, the De Lancey leaders, James De Lancey, William Walton, James Jauncey, and Henry Cruger, saw no reason to act cautiously in the face of opposition from their defeated enemies.[25] They even went so far as to expel from the house Justice Robert R. Livingston, who represented the family manor, on the grounds that supreme court judges could not hold seats in the Assembly.[26]

As McDougall witnessed the unfolding of the De Lancey plan in the latter part of November and early December, it was clear that minority leaders in the Assembly—Philip Schuyler, scion of the wealthy Albany family, and George Clinton, a country lawyer from Ulster—were unable to break the majority hold. Friday, December 15, proved to be the crucial test for the De Lancey faction. Using a rule adopted nine days earlier which allowed the public gallery to be closed when the speaker was not in his chair, a long and heated debate was conducted behind closed doors. Two tactical questions were debated: Would Colden ignore his instructions and sign a currency bill without a suspending clause, and if so, how much of the new currency should be used to pay the army's expenses? Hoping that the king would take offense and dissolve the Assembly, Clinton and Schuyler wanted to fund the army bill entirely out of the new money, while James De Lancey proposed that half of the military costs be paid out of regular treasury funds and the remainder from the currency issue. When the committee of the whole approved the latter strategy by a margin of one vote, the public gallery was reopened. McDougall and others listened to the committee's report and saw how quickly the De Lancey lieutenant, Speaker Henry Cruger, appointed several members to draft a military supply bill, then abruptly adjourned the house.[27]

The De Lancey actions in the Assembly plunged New York into political turmoil again. Isaac Sears and John Lamb, apparently assured earlier that the Quartering Act would be ignored, were enraged by the Assembly action and deserted the De Lancey faction. In a dramatic reversal of their previous hostility toward McDougall, they joined him in denouncing the majority party for sacrificing colonial liberties.[28] McDougall, equally angered, took the issue to the people. He wrote and published anonymously a long broadside addressed "To the Betrayed Inhabitants of the City and Colony of New York," which appeared on the streets during the week-end of December 16.[29] McDougall heaped scathing criticism upon the De Lancey Assembly leaders and Lieutenant Governor Colden for surrendering American liberty at a time when people in other colonies were defying parliament and the city's own merchants were boycotting English goods to protest the unconstitutional Townshend duties. By its actions, McDougall charged, the Assembly had approved the arbitrary power of parliament and the ministry. Granting money to the troops in the province, "kept here, not to protect but to enslave us," was a desertion of the American cause and a betrayal of the "liberties of the people."

The Assembly's decision of December 15, McDougall warned, was the result of a bargain between Colden and the De Lanceys, which was "very manifest in the guilt and confusion that covered the faces of the perfidious abettors of this measure, when the house was in debate

on the subject." Colden's interest was to get a full salary out of the
legislature, while the De Lanceys wanted to preserve their seats in
order to attain a "sovereign lordship" over the colony; Colden agreed
to sign the paper currency bill against the king's order and the De
Lancey-controlled Assembly supported the British troops against public opinion. "Is this a state to be rested in, when our all is at stake?"
McDougall asked. "No, my countrymen, rouse! Imitate the noble example of the friends of liberty in England; who, rather than be enslaved, contend for their right with k--g, lords and commons. And will
you suffer your liberties to be torn from you, by your representatives?
Tell it not in Boston; publish it not in the streets of Charles-Town!"
McDougall urged the people to insist that the city's representatives
change their votes and to appoint a committee to publicize their betrayal
if they refused. He also summoned a mass meeting to consider the
appropriate response to the Quartering Act.[30]

McDougall's broadside was a product of his partisanship and political beliefs, both of which were rooted in his association with the Livingstons and the political turmoil of the times. From Robert R. and
William Livingston and William Smith, he had acquired his view of
the De Lanceys as self-serving politicians who, after the fashion of the
late James De Lancey, Sr., made use of government office to advance
their own interests at the public's expense. But it was more than a
jumble of partisan rhetoric. McDougall, though not a scholar, had
educated himself in eighteenth century political ideology. From the
same Livingston leaders, he undoubtedly learned his first lessons in
radical Whig ideology. Livingston, Smith, and John Morin Scott had
established themselves as New York's foremost Whigs when, a decade
earlier, they had patterned their political writings in the *Independent
Reflector* after the style of the English radicals John Trenchard and
Thomas Gordon. Whatever political tutoring McDougall received from
the Livingstons was strengthened by the pamphleteering, newspaper
writings, and tavern discussions which, from the Stamp Act onward,
educated the public generally in radical Whig political ideas and values.
McDougall also went to the sources of eighteenth century political
thought. He read the works of Plutarch and Seneca, Locke and
Montesquieu, *Cato's Letters*, and Francis Hutcheson's *System of Moral
Philosophy;* he also read Somers and Blackstone on the common law, a
number of histories, and a score of nonconformist religious tracts. From
these sources, McDougall fashioned political ideals which caused him to

conclude that the De Lancey-controlled Assembly and Lieutenant Governor Cadwallader Colden should be censured.[31]

At the heart of McDougall's concern over the manner of De Lancey compliance with the Quartering Act was his view of the role of elected representatives in government. The election of representatives was a "priceless privilege" which the people derived from the contractual foundations of society and government. Elected representatives were agents of the people whose essential function was to defend and protect the "liberties" of the people from the encroachments of governmental power. Having accepted the "trust reposed in them and their duty to their constituents," representatives were not their own masters; they were "answerable to the people" for the way in which they fulfilled their obligation to defend liberty. And in order to assist their representatives, the people had an "undoubted right" to instruct them on questions of the moment and to insist that those directions be followed. If elected representatives failed to follow the wishes of the people or were otherwise remiss in their defense of liberty, they were guilty of betraying the trust committed to them.[32] McDougall's broadside to the people, therefore, was a warning that public vigilance was necessary if liberty was to be maintained in the face of an elected assembly unmindful of popular sentiment.

The political values expressed by McDougall were soundly based in radical Whig ideology. So too was his explanation of the cause of what he considered to be the "betrayal" of the people's liberties. Constitutional checks and balances were under constant pressure from the designs of corrupt officeholders and politicians who used governmental power to satisfy their personal desires for power and gain. That belief explained the mother country's incessant attacks, by means of parliamentary taxation, upon the constitutional rights of colonials; it also explained why the New York Assembly complied with the Quartering Act and why Lieutenant Governor Colden disobeyed his instructions from the crown. Despite past differences and hostility, the De Lancey family and Coden had formed a "party" to realize their own selfish goals. That "coalition" destroyed the "checks resulting from the form of our happy constitution" when Colden failed to guard the royal prerogative by signing a bill excluding judges from seats in the Assembly. By voting money for the royal troops, the Assembly members "sunk themselves into the abject state of being a mere executive body to the parliament of Great Britain" and thereby surrendered "that check on an undue exercise of prerogative which our happy constitution intended to be given to the people or their representatives." The De Lancey family, "like true politicians," formed the party with Colden "in order to secure them the sovereign lordship of this colony." The liberties of the people were thus sacrificed to the "private purposes of the Lieutenant Governor, council and general assembly." Royal soldiers would remain in the colony to "awe us to a submission to the arbitrary and unconstitutional claims of the commons of Great Britain which if carried into execution will enslave us." Only the "virtuous jealousy of the times for the liberties of the continent," McDougall believed, would prevent the "minions of power and the tools of government" from realizing their "arbitrary designs" and "diabolical purposes" of destroying colonial freedom.[33]

To arouse the people to a sense of their danger was McDougall's intention in addressing his broadside "To the Betrayed Inhabitants." But his profession of faith in the rights and power of the people should not obscure the fact that he was also a committed follower of the Livingstons, a partisan whose political vision tended to be narrowly focused. He saw the De Lanceys as entirely self-serving, while failing to recognize, at least in 1769, that his own political friends were also engaged in the politics of self-interest, the principal difference being that they were out of power.[34] The political squabbles over the Quartering Act were nonetheless the real beginning of Mc-Dougall's attachment to popular power that would in time lead to independence and republican government.

The mass meeting called by McDougall for December 18 went just as he planned. The crowd was large and friendly, with only a few De Lancey men in sight. McDougall's speech impediment barred him from outdoor speaking, but John Lamb took firm command of the proceedings, posing questions to the people which produced a strong condemnation of the Assembly's support of the army. A committee of ten, including McDougall, Lamb, and Sears, was instructed to inform the city's representatives of the popular sentiment against the Quartering Act.[35] But if McDougall truly expected the city's assembly representatives to change their votes on the military bill because of public pressure, he discovered instead the reality of De Lancey power. When the committee went to City Hall the next morning, they were brusquely told by James Jauncey, James De Lancey, Henry Cruger, and William Walton that it was too late for anyone to change their votes. In fact, the Assembly's first order of business that morning, at the request of James De Lancey, was a review of "To the Betrayed Inhabitants" which was condemned by a vote of twenty to one as a "false seditious, and infamous libel" upon the Assembly and Lieutenant Governor Colden. A £100 reward was offered for the discovery of the author.[36] If the De Lanceys had known that McDougall had written the broadside, he would surely have been arrested immediately.

Meanwhile, McDougall tried yet another way to wake the city against the self-interest of the De Lancey leaders on a measure he knew they opposed, a bill requiring the use of ballots in future elections. He and the Sons of Liberty supported the balloting bill and called the public to the Liberty Pole to demonstrate in its favor. But everything went wrong. Only a handful of people were there on December 29, and when the meeting was postponed for a day, the weather made an outdoor gathering impossible.[37] The Liberty Boys went ahead anyway. They passed a few resolutions and sent a committee to the city's assemblymen, only to discover that the De Lanceys had called a meeting of their own to be held indoors at the Coffee House on January 5. McDougall and one or two others attended that meeting, interrupting and arguing with every speaker, but anti-ballot instructions were approved and signed by a thousand people in the next ten days.[38] Once again the De Lanceys showed that, whether in the Assembly or in the open meetings of the capital, they were confident of their ground and leadership.

By the first month of 1770, tension was clearly rising in New York City, and McDougall had contributed to the stress by attempting to swing public sentiment against the Assembly's majority party. Although he failed to change the decision to support the royal troops, he was making headway, along with Sears and Lamb, in winning over the rank-and-file Sons of Liberty who had previously favored the De Lancey leaders. An additional element in the city's troubled state was the friction between townspeople and soldiers of the royal garrison of Fort George. Civilian-military relations had been poor since the impressment riots of the French war. Relations had deteriorated further during the Stamp Act troubles, and now the ill will was intensified by the public criticism of the army supply bill.[39] For ordinary people the situation was aggravated by the poor condition of the city's economy and by unemployment among mechanics, laborers, and seamen. Even as the colony was compelled by parliamentary law to supply necessaries to soldiers, the troops during their free hours entered the local labor market at less than current wages, thus depriving the poor of job opportunities.[40]

A clash between the city's poor and the soldiers seemed inevitable under the circumstances. On January 13, 1770, when a squad of troops made an unsuccessful attempt to blow up the Liberty Pole, sacred to the Sons of Liberty, the long expected clash occurred. Spectators outside a nearby tavern jeered the soldiers as they attempted to destroy the pole, and the infuriated regulars charged the public house, breaking windows, smashing glassware, and wounding a barman before they ran off to their nearby barracks. Even the subsequent arrest of three soldiers did not stop the outcry over what had happened.[41] McDougall and his friends were outraged by the incident and called a public meeting for Wednesday, January 17, to discuss the presence of the troops in the city. "Is it not enough," it was asked in a broadside which may well have been written by McDougall, "that you pay taxes for billeting money to support the soldiers, and a poor tax, to maintain many of their whores and bastards in the work-house, without giving them the employment of the poor . . . ?"[42] It was a challenge to the 16th Regiment. During the evening of January 16, the troops made a more elaborate assault upon the Liberty Pole, using explosives to break the iron band protecting the lower part of the mast. Awakened by the noise, McDougall joined a small group of Liberty Boys to guard the pine mast, but when nothing more happened, everyone returned home. The next day they awoke to find the Liberty Pole sawed into pieces and piled in the doorway of Montagne's tavern. Expressions of anger were common among the several thousand people attending the meeting that morning and they readily adopted two resolutions, one against the employment of soldiers and the other forbidding ordinary military persons to carry weapons and walk the streets at night.[43]

The destruction of the Liberty Pole and the public meeting rallied a great number of people to McDougall's campaign against the Quartering Act. Tension in the city further increased, erupting into open fighting two days later. Isaac Sears and a friend apprehended several soldiers posting a broadside of their own denouncing the Sons of Liberty as the real enemies to the country, phony heroes who "thought their freedom depended upon a piece of wood."[44] The short-tempered Sears hauled two soldiers off to the mayor's office, where he demanded that they be arrested for libelling the city. People quickly gathered in the street, but before Mayor Whitehead Hicks could decide what to do, a squad of twenty soldiers appeared with drawn swords and bayonets, demanding the release of their friends. Angry townspeople, most of them seamen and artisans, cursed the redcoats, who then moved away on Mayor Hicks' orders. But instead of returning the way they came, the soldiers made their way through the older part of town along the East River, where the narrow side streets and alleyways were lined with workshops and tenements. More people joined the trailing mob. When the surrounded troops tried to push their way through the crowd, fighting broke out, with stones, clubs, and bayonets as weapons. Soon the clash was a full-scale riot. As the hard pressed soldiers climbed Golden Hill, they were joined by another squad, but the soldiers were still outnumbered as more and more townspeople were drawn into the fist-swinging brawl. Not until army officers, city magistrates, and constables arrived to separate the combatants did it end.[45]

The Golden Hill fighting was over, but the city was in an uproar and the tension was kept alive by isolated incidents in the evening. Fighting between merchant seamen and soldiers resumed the next day on the other side of the town near the North River, at the head of Chapel Street, on which McDougall lived. Several blocks away another fight started on the grounds of the Presbyterian Church, drawing soldiers from the barracks on the far side of the Commons; Mayor Hicks and the City Council happened to be meeting in the new jail nearby to discuss the previous day's riot. The city magistrates rushed out, but they were helpless as the throng of townspeople and troops grew larger with the arrival of more rioters from the lower part of the city. Only the quick appearance of army officers prevented bloodshed.[46] The city government and the military command quickly reached an agreement which brought a truce. Soldiers were to remain in quarters at all times unless under command of an officer. When McDougall and four others requested the city's permission to put up another Liberty Pole on the Commons near the barracks, the request was denied as a provocation to the royal garrison.[47] Still, tension in the city remained high, prompting some men to carry weapons for self-protection.[48]

McDougall and the other Sons of Liberty had no intention of quitting. A new Liberty Pole was both a point of honor and now an even greater symbol of resistance to the tyranny of a standing army. His friend Isaac Sears purchased a small plot of land near the old site, and a new mast was erected on February 6 as a "monument to perpetuate the remembrance of great events." [49] It was an awesome piece of timber, measuring 68 feet above ground with two-thirds of its length encased in iron bands to protect the pole against vandals. At the top was a gilt vane inscribed with the word LIBERTY. Six horses were needed to draw the mast from the North River shipyards, and several thousand people watched the procession of flag-bearers, a band, and marching Liberty Boys. As the pole was dropped into a twelve-foot hole and raised to its full glory, french horns played "God Save the King." [50] Two days later McDougall was arrested and jailed as the author of the broadside, "To the Betrayed Inhabitants." Overnight he became a martyr in the cause of American Liberty.

# Chapter Three
# "The Wilkes of America"

The importance of McDougall's imprisonment to his emerging reputation as a popular leader cannot be exaggerated. Before he went to jail, he had been only one of several local leaders voicing criticism of the provincial assembly's action on the Quartering Act. Although he unquestionably opposed on principle the presence of a standing army in the city and sympathized with the economic grievances of the lower class against moonlighting soldiers, there was always a partisan tone to his words and activities. Through the fall and early winter months of 1769 he acted as a Livingston party worker, and was seen as little more than a Livingston loyalist. Imprisonment changed everything. Overnight he became a local popular hero, a man who sacrificed his personal freedom to further the libertarian cause. The Sons of Liberty hailed him as a martyr and rallied behind him; in the rush to defend him against the vengeance of the De Lancey-controlled Assembly, whatever enmity remained from earlier days was forgotten. Outside of New York, McDougall was also seen as a martyr to the cause of freedom, a fellow sufferer with John Wilkes of London, jailed in 1763 on orders of George III for publishing a scathing criticism of the king's speech to parliament. It mattered little that McDougall's arguments against the Quartering Act were unoriginal and unlikely to rouse the colonies as John Dickinson's writings had done two years earlier. What really counted to leaders in other colonies was that he appeared to be a victim of arbitrary power, living proof of the malignant conspiracy against colonial liberty.[1]

A young Irish journeyman printer named Cummins was the initial informant against McDougall. Angered because James Parker, a local printer, had discharged him, Cummins reported to Lieutenant Governor Colden that the broadside had been printed in Parker's shop. Chief Justice Daniel Horsmanden issued a warrant on February 7 to

bring Parker in, and while Colden and several Council members questioned him, the sheriff returned to the print shop and brought in the
three apprentices. The young boys admitted under threats of imprisonment that the broadside had been printed in Parker's shop and that
McDougall corrected proof and left with some of the printed sheets.
Confronted with the story told by his workers and assured immunity
from prosecution, Parker identified McDougall. Early the next morning Sheriff John Roberts took McDougall into custody. Chief Justice
Horsmanden tried to get McDougall to admit his guilt, but the former
ship captain insisted upon a jury trial. Bail was set at £2,000—an excessive amount for the day—which McDougall refused to post, and he
was hurried off to jail. He remained there for 80 days.[2]

The city was shocked by the news of McDougall's imprisonment
and the threat of political retribution it implied. His friends in the
Sons of Liberty and among the followers of the Livingstons immediately rose to his defense, drawing a parallel between McDougall's arrest and that of John Wilkes. As Wilkes' offense against the king appeared in "Number 45" of the *North Briton*, the number forty-five was
used to symbolize the political nature of McDougall's arrest. A stream
of newspaper articles, prominently displaying "Number 45," appeared
as part of the effort to make McDougall "the Wilkes of America." [3]
Two days after he was jailed, he was presented with a side of venison
stamped with 45, a reference to page 45 on which his broadside appeared in the Assembly's journal. On February 14, the 45th day of
the year, 45 men dined with McDougall in his quarters at the New
Jail, disposing of 45 pounds of steak from a steer 45 months old. A
month later, "45 virgins of this city, went in procession to pay their
respects," and McDougall "entertained them with tea, cakes, chocolate and conversation adopted to the company." The visit was closed
by the singing of the 45th Psalm. In early April Hannah McDougall
led a parade of ladies from Chapel Street to the jail, entertaining them
later at her home.[4]

While the Sons of Liberty sought to instill in the public mind that
McDougall was suffering a political martyrdom, De Lancey supporters immediately printed replies to discredit McDougall's performance and to disrupt the harmony among the Sons of Liberty.
McDougall was referred to as "Milkman" by one writer, and by another as "an empty, insignificant, self-conceited im-p--t body, utterly
incapable of writing the scandalous paper laid to his charge, altho' he

may have been the publisher of it." [5] The public was reminded that McDougall was only a recent defender of American rights, and that he and Sears and Lamb had been enemies only a few months before. Indeed, according to these charges, McDougall's earlier reputation among the Sons of Liberty was that of a government informer, not a patriot, a man whom Isaac Sears had many times publicly called a "rotten hearted villain." [6]

James Duane, related to the Livingstons by marriage but a political friend of the De Lanceys, was responsible for the most sustained newspaper attack on McDougall. Entitling his twelve part attack on the former privateer captain "The Dougliad," he never really questioned that McDougall was the publisher of the offending broadside, but he could not believe that the former privateer captain-turned-politician was its author. The broadside, Duane strongly implied, was the work of leaders of the discredited Livingston faction, who lacked the courage to openly attack the Assembly. In addition, therefore, to ridiculing the efforts of the Sons of Liberty to transform McDougall into a great public hero, Duane raked the Livingstons for their failure when in office to stand against parliamentary authority. Although McDougall was merely a "vessel" for Livingston leaders who preferred anonymity, Duane insisted that McDougall was still culpable and should be prosecuted to the full extent of the law, which the "honor, interest, and safety of the community" demanded. [7]

The questions of authorship raised by Duane have never been fully answered. Did McDougall actually write "To the Betrayed Inhabitants," or was it the work of someone else, as his critics alleged? There is a striking similarity between the broadside and the political views of William Smith; perhaps James Duane had Smith or William Livingston or John Morin Scott—the old "Triumvirate"—in mind as the real authors. While a draft copy of the broadside in McDougall's handwriting has not survived to settle the question, the available evidence nonetheless points to his authorship. In addition to what he learned of Whig principles and politics under Livingston tutelage, he certainly had access to printed materials from which to draw Whig ideas. He could, for example, turn to *Cato's Letters* for arguments against the presence of a standing army in time of peace. Moreover, during his imprisonment he wrote a lengthy elaboration of the charges made in the broadside which demonstrated his writing ability and his strong familiarity with Whig political ideals and rhetoric. One visitor to McDougall's jail cell was quite impressed with the abilities of the former ship captain: "Whatever may be reported of him as an insignificant and obscure man, I assure [you] that from the Little Conversation that passed while we visited him he appeared to be as well read in History as any Person I ever conversed with, an extream distinct manner of conveying his ideas, and his language of as well Chosen Words as you would expect from an accomplished Speaker. . . ." [8] All things considered, there is no reason to doubt McDougall's authorship of "To the Betrayed Inhabitants."

The anniversary celebrations of the repeal of the stamp tax provided still another opportunity for the De Lanceys to attack McDougall and other popular leaders. Without fanfare the De Lanceys rented Montagne's tavern, favorite haunt of Sears and Lamb and their friends, the scene of the Liberty Pole troubles. They were, the De Lanceys advised the public, the "true" Sons of Liberty, and they intended to claim a large share of credit for the 1765–1766 defense of American rights. Not to be outdone, Sears and Lamb, along with the imprisoned McDougall, signed a long-term lease on a near-by tavern, symbolically renaming it Hampden Hall in honor of the seventeenth century English revolutionary.[9] Each group claimed to be the Sons of Liberty, but the well-attended celebrations of March 19 were strikingly different in tone. The De Lancey group at Montagne's referred to their meeting as a "friend to liberty and trade." And in a pregnant toast to future developments, they praised "trade and navigation, and a speedy removal of their embarrassments." The Hampden Hall crowd ignored trade. Calling themselves the "real friends to Liberty," they sent a delegation to the jail to dine with McDougall. Forty-five toasts were offered at Hampden Hall, centering on a theme of freedom of the press and resistance to arbitrary authority, while the diners at Montagne's praised the governor, Council, and De Lancey-controlled Assembly and condemned the "authors of discord, and promoters of intestine feuds." At sunset Sears and Lamb closed their festivities by marching with their friends across the Commons to give McDougall three cheers and then parading with flags and music about the town. The more than 500 persons attending the two dinners on March 19 all undoubtedly thought of themselves as Liberty Boys.[10] The fact that rival groups could each claim to be Sons of Liberty revealed how generalized New York's earlier response to British policies had been before the weeks of violence and tension gripped the city in the fall of 1765. The two celebrations also emphasized the political value which public leaders, whether Livingstons or De Lanceys, expected to gain from appearing as Sons of Liberty and defenders of American liberty.

The politics of McDougall's imprisonment were important to the political fortunes of the De Lanceys and the Livingstons, but since McDougall still faced a serious criminal charge he could not afford to think only in terms of political advantage. Between visits of family and friends, McDougall and his lawyer, John Morin Scott, prepared a defense. According to English law of libel, New York's Attorney General, John Tabor Kempe, had only to establish the fact that McDougall was the broadside's publisher, without concern for the truth or falsity of the statements made in it. Since he could not deny being the publisher, McDougall's only line of defense was to draw upon the famous Peter Zenger libel trial of 1735 in which it was argued successfully that a jury had the right to determine both the facts of publication and the truthfulness of alleged libelous statements. It was a risky strategy. The Zenger case was an isolated precedent, and Chief Justice Horsmanden could, if he chose, follow the traditional practice of disallowing a defense based on truth.[11] But unless he was willing to stand silent in court, McDougall had no choice except to enter a plea of innocence and attempt to convince the jury that his charges against the De Lanceys and Colden were true.

As his day in court neared, McDougall and his friend prepared for the legal battle. He spent hours researching the published journals of the Assembly on New York's response to the Quartering Act. His purpose was to show that the Livingstons had protected and the De Lanceys had surrendered American rights. He carefully dissected the broadside, amplifying each major assertion, indicating those points on which certain witnesses could furnish corroborating evidence to prove that an alliance of interest existed between Lieutenant Governor Colden and the De Lanceys.[12] Friends contributed to his defense by informing the public on the law of libel, emphasizing that McDougall's case would be a "Star Chamber persecution" unless a jury decided the truth of the broadside. James Parker's *New York Gazette* and John Holt's *New York Journal* printed essays on the importance of jury trials to the cause of freedom, published extracts from legal authorities, and revived James Alexander's account of the Peter Zenger case. Isaac Sears and other Liberty Boys hinted to the sheriff, who was to name

D.r Sir

It is with the utmost chagrin I am obliged to inform you that I am not able to return you all your pamphlets; and what is still worse the most valuable of them is missing. — I beg you will not impute it to carelessness; for I assure you upon my honor the true state of the case is this — I put your pamphlets in the case with my other books; and some person about the College got into my room through the window, broke open my case, & took out The friendly address, Bankroft's treatise, two volumes of natural philosophy and a Latin author — I have procured another Friendly address to replace the one lost; and have taken all possible pains to recover Bankroft's treatise or to get another in its stead; but my endeavors have hitherto been fruitless. — M.r Abram Livingston thinks he can get one for me, and has promised, if possible, to do it —

I beg Sir you will not take amiss an accident, which has been unavoidable; for be assured, I have had no small uneasiness on account of it — I am Sir

Your most respectful servant

A Hamilton

Be pleased to let me know the proper title of Bankroft's pamphlet (which I have forgotten) and I will publish it with the offer of a reward to any person that will restore it —

I have delayed the discovery of the true state of the matter hitherto; because I was still in hopes to have regained the pamphlet; and was unwilling, in the mean time to let you know it was missing —

*Alexander Hamilton to Alexander McDougall, apologizing for the loss of borrowed pamphlets stolen from Hamilton's room at King's College, c. 1773–75.*

—W. WRIGHT HAWKES COLLECTION, SCHAFFER LIBRARY, UNION COLLEGE

the jury panel, that since they had free time, they would be happy to accept jury duty.[13] But these activities meant little. Although the defense made careful legal and political preparations, McDougall did not have much chance of success. Attorney General Kempe, an able lawyer, was assisted by Mayor Whitehead Hicks, Thomas Jones, and James Duane, augmented at times by assemblymen Henry Cruger and James De Lancey.[14] Sheriff John Roberts had carefully chosen for jury duty a panel of freeholders made up entirely of De Lancey men. When the jury was called on April 17, Leonard Lispenard, a military creditor who stood to gain a great deal from the Quartering Act, was named foreman. Among the jurors were Assemblyman William Walton's brother, Gerard, his son-in-law, David Johnson, and a former employee and distant relative, Jonathan Lawrence; Lispenard's son-in-law, Thomas Marston; and George Harrison, known as a close friend to Lieutenant Governor Colden, and Harrison's son-in-law, George Folliot. According to published voter lists, a majority of the other jurors had voted for De Lancey candidates in the 1769 assembly election. Only three jurors out of the eighteen could be expected to side with McDougall.[15]

The grand jury sat eight days before reaching a decision on April 25. McDougall's planned defense was destroyed when Chief Justice Horsmander ordered the jury only to determine the facts of publication, which Attorney General Kempe quickly presented. Three witnesses, apprentices to printer James Parker, were examined; and all agreed that McDougall and a friend came to Parker's shop on the night of December 16 and corrected galley proof, dried and cut paper, and left with copies of the broadside. McDougall's friend, Captain Berrian, was also called by the prosecution, and he was forced to admit that McDougall had indeed been in Parker's shop. The crown's final evidence was James Parker's admission that McDougall had paid £3 to have "To the Betrayed Inhabitants" printed. McDougall was helpless. He could not deny the weighty evidence on the question of publication, the only issue to be decided; consequently, the strategy of appealing directly to the truth of the statements in the broadside had no impact on the carefully chosen jury. John Morin Scott called a number of men who offered old pamphlets, including one written by Colden himself, to show that McDougall's broadside was no more critical of government than earlier writings, and arguments were made on the politics of the last Assembly session. But the jury was not moved.[16] On April 25, by a 15 to 3 vote, McDougall was indicted for seditious libel and bound over to the Supreme Court for trial. The grand jury's charges against McDougall, who was branded as a person of "turbulent and unquiet mind," were sweeping in scope, and held him responsible for publishing a "wicked, false, seditious, scandalous, malicious, and infamous libel" to the "great disturbance of the public peace and tranquility" of the colony.[17]

Three days later McDougall was allowed to plead to the charges in person, and his friends made a spectacle of his appearance in court. Hundreds of people walked along with the sheriff and McDougall from the jail, and over the protest of the sheriff, the imprisoned agitator made a short speech before entering the City Hall. His friends, McDougall said, had convinced him to give up his imprisonment, already eleven weeks long, and post bail; but he wanted the people to know that he would stay in jail for eleven years for the cause of liberty.[18] As the admiring William Smith put it, McDougall "made a grand show yesterday when he was brought down to plead—an immense multitude— He spoke with such propriety and awed and astonished many who wish him ill and added I believe to the number of his friends." [19] During the formalities of pleading to the indictment, McDougall had another chance to speak out. He told Chief Justice Horsmanden and others sitting at the Attorney General's table that he thought his prosecution was an arbitrary affair and that he intended to let the people judge his innocence or guilt. The Court ignored this admonition and bail was set at £1,000. McDougall posted £500 in New York currency and provided two sureties of £250 each, furnished by Philip Livingston and Nicholas Bayard. After 80 days in prison, McDougall was now free, at least until the Supreme Court tried his case. Six hundred people escorted him from City Hall to his house on Chapel Street. He assured them, in a parting speech, that he could be counted on to defend the people's just rights and liberties, "even at the expense of his life and fortune." [20]

When Alexander McDougall went to jail in early February the public's attention was on the Quartering Act and the troops garrisoned in the city. But when he gained his release in late April, a different issue—the economic boycott against England—was before the people. The rivalry between the De Lanceys and the Livingstons and the friction between the Liberty Boys and the De Lanceys grew in intensity and heat. Each side distrusted the other; each suspected the motives and intentions of the other; and each covered the city with propaganda questioning the patriotism of the other. Although Mc-Dougall's imprisonment and trial were no longer the center of public attention, he was now more than a mere Livingston supporter, as he had been a year earlier. He was now a figure of political notoriety, admired by some but still ridiculed by others. Yet even his new popularity did not immediately alter political realities. As the ensuing battle over non-importation was to prove, New York's capital was still De Lancey-controlled. It was a simple political fact that McDougall, Sears, Lamb, the Liberty Boys, and the Livingstons still possessed a smaller popular following than did De Lancey partisans such as James De Lancey, Henry Cruger, William Walton, and James Jauncey. Despite this, McDougall's experiences in jail seemed to have a profound psychological impact, expanding his perception of himself as a public leader and intensifying his interest in politics and city affairs. Three days after he returned home from jail, he began a rough journal ("political memorandum" he called it) in which he carefully recorded each day's political development. Though his notations were brief, they revealed his enthusiastic concern with public affairs.[21] It was an interest that would grow ever larger until his death sixteen years later.

In the spring of 1770 public attention concentrated on the issue of the city's economic boycott of English merchandise. Non-importation, as the boycott was called, had been initiated in November 1768, as a constitutional protest against the Townshend duties levied to produce a revenue from colonial trade. The boycott received broad support in New York, where its effectiveness in shutting off British imports quickly surpassed that of any other American commercial center. Firmly enforced by a merchants' committee of inspection and the Sons of Liberty, non-importation substantially reduced the volume of British goods entering the colony. By the beginning of 1770, however, merchant enthusiasm for non-importation began to wane when reports were received that the British government intended to repeal all the Townshend duties except that on tea.[22]

It was not until the middle of May, 1770, that merchant discontent with non-importation became a serious matter to Alexander McDougall and other Liberty Boys. There always had been some grumbling, but now there was common talk about ending the boycott. Leaders of the merchant community insisted that they alone should determine whether or not to continue non-importation.[23] McDougall disagreed. Since the Townshend duties involved the rights and liberties of every person, he wrote, non-importation was a city-wide matter. "Brutus," who very likely was McDougall, reappeared in print and urged the people to stand firm on the city's non-importation agreement. "Brutus" warned that those merchants who suggested a resumption of trade with England despite the remaining tax on tea were actually aiding the ministry's efforts to destroy American liberty. The appeal was made to the whole community, for it was evident that only the weight of public opinion might conceivably hold the merchants in line.[24]

But the desire of those who wanted to be free of all economic restraint proved to be the stronger force, and McDougall and other leaders of the Sons of Liberty could only fight a delaying action. Each side appealed to the public, and after several indecisive public meetings, the city committee of inspection, reflecting the anti-boycott attitude of the merchant community, finally proposed to neighboring trading towns on June 2 that a Congress be called to decide upon a common plan of action. McDougall commented acidly in his journal that it was the work of "inartificial tools of a party." But the fact remained that he and the Sons of Liberty were unable to arouse public opinion sufficiently to force a continuation of the boycott of English goods.[25] Unconcerned with the efforts of "Brutus" to arouse public opinion the merchant committee wanted an end to non-importation, in concert with the other colonies if possible but alone if necessary.

Knowing that their proposed congress was unacceptable to Boston and Philadelphia, the New York City merchant committee decided upon a lone course. The first move came on June 11 from a small group of merchants who demanded that the city committee make a house-to-house canvass of the city to determine the public's view on non-importation. That evening the committee met in a tavern and ordered that each of the city's six wards be polled by two men who would ask the householders whether they preferred a continuation of the old agreement or a boycott of only the dutied tea.[26] Though McDougall later described the group not as a representative body of merchants but as "selfish, mercenary importers, and a few mechanics, the tools of a party," the canvass proceeded. Early the next morning the poll takers began their rounds, catching McDougall and his friends off guard. Hurriedly those advocating a continuation of the total boycott called a noon meeting on the Commons, warning the populace not to sign anything until after a more "general determination upon this matter." But it was too late. By the end of the week the merchant committee had 1,200 signatures against non-importation. Although McDougall joined others in roaming the city and even canvassing the rural areas of Manhattan Island with a counter-proposal, only 350 persons signed in favor of the general boycott. On June 16 the merchant committee informed Boston and Philadelphia that the people of New York wanted to end non-importation.[27]

McDougall and the Sons of Liberty were unable to prevent the breakdown of the economic boycott, now almost complete, but they were nevertheless an irritant to the merchant committee and the leaders of the De Lancey faction. McDougall, Sears, and John Morin Scott, as leaders of the opposition, represented a challenge to De Lancey influence in the city and province. The challenge had to be met. Newspaper writers, now thoroughly sympathetic to ending the boycott, criticized and ridiculed the Liberty Boys in June and early July. Hugh Gaine's *Mercury* continued the "Dougliad" series, which heaped contempt on McDougall as a "ignoble wretch" who strained every nerve to delude the people into thinking "that he who they well know to be a busy idle forward and insignificant tool, was suddenly metamorphized into an illustrious patriot." [28] Several writers even questioned whether Isaac Sears, McDougall's new political ally, had ever been a Son of Liberty, one claiming that Sears had abandoned the De Lanceys only because his political payoff after the last election was not great enough. Isaac Low, chairman of the merchant committee and a staunch De Lanceyite, openly brawled with John Morin Scott in the newspapers, reminding the public that it was Scott who in 1765 had damned as treasonous the resolutions of the Virginia House of Burgesses against the stamp tax.[29] Flustered and angry, McDougall, Sears, and Scott printed replies but failed to win the city over to their side.[30]

By the beginning of July, news had arrived that Boston and Philadelphia had rejected New York's proposal to boycott only tea. The merchant committee was neither surprised nor dismayed; its leaders were now determined to end non-importation with or without approval of other colonies. When McDougall and the Liberty Boys heard that a small group of merchants were to meet at Bolton's tavern on July 4 to decide the next move, they attended in force to defend the non-importation association, shouting down a suggestion that a second poll of the city be taken. Bedlam followed when McDougall and Sears demanded that the Boston and Philadelphia letters be published so that the people could judge for themselves the arguments of their neighbors. The meeting ended in confusion.[31] Two nights later twenty-three men met secretly at Bolton's tavern again and agreed to send for British goods by the mail ship scheduled to leave in a few days. They also agreed to poll the city the next day, a Saturday, confident that the people would approve a resumption of trade with England.[32] Non-importation was clearly over in New York City.

New York was tense on July 7. The break between the Sons of Liberty and the merchant committee was total, and it was evident that the committee was seeking a showdown. Both sides had scheduled meetings at nearly the same hour in different parts of the city, the Sons of Liberty at City Hall and the merchant committee at the Coffee House. The latter group was grimly determined to proceed with the city poll while secretly preparing their merchandise orders. By early afternoon the house-to-house canvass was under way. McDougall and Sears, presiding at their own meeting four blocks away, were equally determined to prevent the canvass, recognizing that the result would be a merchant committee victory. Sears even rashly threatened physical violence against any merchant who imported contrary to the existing boycott agreement.[33] As the poll-takers went about the city, McDougall joined other Liberty Boys in trailing after them, jeering and arguing with those who agreed to importation and obstructing the work of the merchant committee. But violence finally occurred later in the day. After following the canvass for a while, the Liberty Boys congregated in the tavern of Jasper Drake, Sears' father-in-law, and "heating themselves with liquor, in the glorious cause of liberty," they planned a parade for the evening. Headed again by McDougall and Sears, the Sons of Liberty left Drake's tavern at six o'clock with music playing and a flag inscribed "no importation, but in union with the other colonies." Hearing that a demonstration in support of non-importation was in progress, a number of gentlemen in the Merchants Coffee House went outside and requested Alderman Elias Desbrosses to stop the Liberty Boys from disturbing the peace. Desbrosses, followed by those from the Coffee House armed with canes, confronted McDougall, Sears, and the parade at the narrow end of Wall Street. The Liberty Boys refused to surrender their flag or disperse. Scuffling began, with canes and fence slats slashing the air. Fortunately the street was so narrow that the fighting never became serious, and Mayor Whitehead Hicks's hurried arrival restored order.[34] As a measure of the emotions involved in the non-importation controversy, the merchant committee demonstrated that it was not afraid to meet the Liberty Boys on the street with fists and clubs, as they had the previous Saturday evening.

Thoroughly defeated in nearly every way, McDougall and his friends had few worthwhile options open to them after the fight on Wall Street. They did lodge a complaint with city officials that Alderman Desbrosses had exceeded his authority, and they even started assault and battery suits against several individuals.[35] But on the vital matter of non-importation, there was little they could do. The city was losing interest in the squabble over the boycott, and efforts to foment public indignation against the merchant committee produced disappointing results. The second city poll, closed on Monday evening, showed only eight hundred people interested in the question, and the city remained quiet the next day when the mail ship sailed with merchants' orders of English goods. Almost as an acknowledgement of his failure, McDougall made only four entries in his journal after the street fighting, stopping altogether on July 17. The Liberty Boys did publish the names of the importers, and as a last gesture of opposition, McDougall and Sears drafted a "Protest" on July 25 against the merchants. Only a few people at Jasper Drake's tavern signed.[36]

Non-importation was an important test of strength for McDougall and his friends among the Sons of Liberty. For the merchants and De Lancey faction leaders it was one of a series of challenges to their leadership in dealing with sensitive public issues. Since the De Lanceys' election victory in early 1769, the political initiative throughout the colony had belonged to them. The public response to the way they dealt with the major issues—the Quartering Act, currency emission, balloting bill, McDougall's arrest and trial, and finally the economic boycott—showed that they still had a wide following among all classes in the capital, that they were more nearly the colony's "popular party." [37]

McDougall learned valuable lessons from his losing battles with the De Lanceys. From the politics of the period he gained a practical experience in the tactics of political organization, public meetings, and newspaper polemics—vital elements in establishing and directing support of the populace. The De Lanceys had shown a mastery of those techniques in winning elections and defending their actions, but Mc-Dougall would demonstrate in a few short years that he had comparable skill. But the most important thing that McDougall derived from the political turmoil of the closing years of the decade was confirmation of his fear that his opponents were power-hungry politicians, unmindful of the public's true interest. His political experiences with the De Lanceys appeared to give proof to the radical Whig belief that liberty suffers when the private interest of officeholders is elevated above that of the people's general well-being. In the lexicon of radical Whiggery, self-interest meant corruption. In the eyes of many colonists, the corruption of British politics had seemingly crossed the ocean and taken root in America, posing as much a threat to the rights and liberties of Englishmen as the unconstitutional expansion of parliamentary and ministerial power. As a popular leader of growing stature, now joined with Isaac Sears and John Lamb in the common cause of defending American rights, Alexander McDougall would never again fully trust the traditional leadership of New York's aristocracy of wealth and birth.

# Chapter Four

# The Tea Act

New York City had become relatively peaceful by the fall of 1770. The city's three newspapers still carried columns on non-importation, primarily reporting the reaction in other colonies to events in New York, but such reports caused hardly a ripple on the colony's apparently placid political surface. It was a deceptive peace, however, for New York society still swirled with the currents of factional politics. At best a truce had settled over the province, mainly because politicians lacked domestic issues comparable in volatility to those furnished previously by the British parliament. But this is not to say that the major participants, including McDougall, wanted peace; no one forgot the past and each sought fresh opportunities to attack the other. Since the De Lanceys controlled the provincial Assembly and Council as well as the city government, they enjoyed all of the advantages of power, and they used it to further undermine their opponents.[1] Once more McDougall fell victim to De Lancey vengeance.

McDougall's political stock dropped rapidly during the summer months of 1770, as did that of the Sons of Liberty generally. As one public writer remarked, McDougall was now forgotten instead of honored:

The relation of your deeds, like a bad tale often told, fatigues the ear; the very air, seems unwilling to bear the burthen of your name; your glory is setting in an ocean of oblivion, never to rise again, and your memory, after being a little longer the sport of singing school boys, will flee away like a shadow.[2]

"Swaney" lampooned other popular leaders with equal force: "How many nights at Hampton Hall, have these lids been unclosed? How often with the sagacious Captain [Sears], and intricate John [Lamb], have I stood armed with sword and musket, and suffered not a dog to p-ss against our sacred pole of freedom, with impunity. Can none remember?"[3]

James De Lancey, Jr., remembered McDougall and did not intend to let him fade completely away before the ex-prisoner answered for "To the Betrayed Inhabitants." Initially, events seemed to favor acquittal. Although McDougall was out of jail, he was still under indictment before the Supreme Court. John Morin Scott, McDougall's lawyer, urged Attorney General Kempe to prosecute the case or drop the charges, and after repeated delays Kempe decided not to prosecute because of the summer death of James Parker, upon whose testimony the crown's case depended.[4] But James De Lancey refused to quit. He initiated a legislative inquiry to determine the authorship of the broadside.

Assembly action began on the morning of December 13, 1770, when McDougall was ordered to appear for questioning. McDougall had no legal alternative, and he faced a hostile group of questioners who demanded to know whether he wrote "To the Betrayed Inhabitants." Through many interruptions and rising tempers, McDougall informed the house that he could not answer the question because the Assembly had already condemned the broadside as a seditious libel and that he was still under a grand jury indictment as its author and publisher, a clear case of double jeopardy. His predicament, he concluded, was like no other he knew and was against both common law and justice.[5]

McDougall's speech angered the house; one member even hinted that torture could be used to force a confession from him. But if McDougall was in danger of any physical harm, Speaker Henry Cruger momentarily calmed the atmosphere by ordering McDougall to write out his reasons for refusing to either admit or deny authorship of the broadside. It was only a short respite. His written statement proved to be stronger than his initial oral comments, emphasizing once more the principle of double jeopardy. Although he tried to explain his meaning to an increasingly angry Assembly, he was cut short by James De Lancey, Jr., and James Jauncey, who declared that he was attacking the Assembly's honor and therefore was guilty of a breach of privilege. George Clinton, McDougall's only real ally in the house, was helpless to defend him against the contempt charge and could not prevent a demand that McDougall ask the Assembly's pardon. With a raised fist, McDougall replied that he would sooner have his right hand cut off than "resign the rights and privileges of a British subject." [6]

Bedlam followed. Some members, believing that McDougall had defiantly shaken his fist at them, shouted that he should be hauled away to jail. Speaker Cruger dashed off a warrant to the city gaol-keeper to hold McDougall prisoner pending further orders of the Assembly. Now standing defiant, McDougall refused to leave the chamber with the sergeant-at-arms until the Assembly formally ordered his arrest. The Assembly quickly granted his wish; McDougall was taken off to jail where he remained for nearly twelve weeks.[7]

His second confinement was significantly different from his first. Then he had been the center of public interest, accepting the attention of admirers and performing perfectly his role as the "Wilkes of America"; now he sat alone, without the satisfaction of public acclaim. Only half-hearted efforts were made to transform McDougall's personal tribulation into everyman's cause. After two long letters to the public early in his jail term, McDougall stopped writing, and other polemical pieces on the sacredness of jury trials were too occasional to be effective.[8] It was as though his friends knew the futility of trying to arouse an indifferent public. John Morin Scott did seek McDougall's quick release by a writ of habeas corpus from the Supreme Court, but the Assembly informed gaolkeeper James Mills that McDougall was its prisoner and therefore not subject to ordinary judicial procedures. If the Assembly refused to recognize an order issued by the Supreme Court, McDougall had no other source of relief. Unless the Assembly made some other disposition, which seemed unlikely, he would remain in prison until the end of the legislative session when, by English tradition, legislative prisoners were released. On March 4, 1771, Lord Dunmore, the new governor, prorogued the Assembly and McDougall was then freed after 82 days, bringing his total days of confinement in a twelve-month period to 162.[9]

Although the circumstances which put McDougall into prison a second time made him a political prisoner of the De Lanceys, his predicament was not unique. According to the principal historian of free speech in early America, colonial history furnishes numerous examples of similar action. Indeed, "Any verbal attack on government officials or policies which might be deemed an affront to the authority or honor of the legislature was subject to a power of repression from which not all the writs precious to the liberty of the subject could effect a rescue."[10] It seems unlikely, therefore, that the Assembly's order to appear caught him unprepared, for New York's legislative history was marked by a number of instances where the Assembly had punished offenders for far less.[11] If he was unaware of that fact, John Morin Scott or William Smith would have warned him of a possible legislative inquest and armed him with a defense.

Knowing that the judicial proceeding might become a legislative vendetta from which there would be no appeal, did McDougall then purposely seek political martyrdom? His second arrest certainly suggests such a conclusion, for the alternative to confronting the De Lanceys, even on their ground in the Assembly, was to leave the colony, certainly a high price to pay under the circumstances. Moreover, there was a certain stiff-necked, self-righteousness about McDougall that compelled him to stand his ground. He believed that he was right and that the De Lanceys were wrong. He regarded himself as a soldier in the higher cause of freedom, armed with the might of the English Constitution, against the mere self-interest of his enemies. What had begun as a common protest against unconstitutional taxation and the presence of a standing army in peacetime had now become a matter of basic English liberty, including the rights of free speech and press, jury trials, and freedom from arbitrary arrest. McDougall may have been only blustering when he said that he would rather give his right hand than desert the rights of Englishmen, but he was nevertheless unwilling to retreat before De Lancey power, displaying an unyielding attitude that conditioned his response to the exercise of British power in the future. Thus his confinement was an affirmation of his principles and contributed to the eventual establishment of free speech and press in America. His confinement was also a step in the making of a revolutionary.

As long as Anglo-American relations remained reasonably amicable, McDougall's political life was at low tide. His interest in public affairs was high, but he was a spectator rather than a participant after April, 1771. The Council chamber and the drawing-room became the new political forums as men sought the favor of the colony's new governors, Lord Dunmore in 1770 and William Tryon in 1771. This was patrician politics, conducted by and for men who were already established social and political leaders, and it held no place for a former privateer captain. In general, the months between McDougall's release from jail in March, 1771, and the fall of 1773, constituted a period of relative political calm. Popular leadership in New York City had reached its nadir.

The Tea Act of 1773 brought McDougall flying back into politics. The now-familiar alarm of "no taxation without representation" was once more taken up by McDougall and the reinvigorated Sons of Liberty.[12] In one way the Tea Act was easily defeated in New York. Only three merchants agreed to act as East India Company wholesalers, and if McDougall and Sears and Lamb had learned nothing else about political tactics, they knew that the mere possibility of violence could effectively intimidate so small a group. It was first necessary to isolate the tea agents from public sentiment. Through October and November, McDougall and his friends busied themselves in various ways to arouse opinion against the agents. The *New York Journal* compared the tea agents, Henry White, Abraham Lott, and Benjamin Booth, to the hated stamp officials of 1765, warning them to protect themselves from the coming storm that was sure to overwhelm and destroy them.[13] A coffee house meeting on October 15, which McDougall no doubt attended, expressed gratitude to the city's ship captains who had earlier refused to carry company tea to America; when it was learned by the end of the month that tea ship was on its way, harbor pilots were warned not to help her when she arrived. McDougall was probably the "Brutus" who informed the "Friends of Liberty and Commerce" (the name of the De Lancey-dominated, splinter group of "Sons of Liberty") that they were honor bound to enforce the boycott of duted tea agreed upon in 1770.[14] Finally, a public meeting, on November 24, appointed McDougall and several others to visit the tea agents to obtain their promise not to receive or sell East India tea. The company agents readily agreed the next day that if company tea was liable to a duty in America, they would resign their commissions.[15]

Throughout this early activity against the Tea Act, McDougall discovered that the De Lancey hold upon the city was weakening because of quarrels among the leaders of the faction over government patronage. For example, Isaac Low, John Watts, and even James Jauncey were noticeably cool toward James and Oliver De Lancey. The problems among De Lancey leaders allowed the popular leaders to seize the political initiative, but it could easily slip away unless a means was found for transforming adverse public opinion into political action. On November 29, McDougall and the Sons of Liberty covered the city with 1,500 copies of an "Association" which branded anyone dealing with company tea an enemy to the country. Two days earlier the "Mohawks" (the name adopted by the anonymous participants in the protest) had warned that anyone who aided the landing and storing of tea could expect an "unwelcome visit, in which they shall be treated as they deserve." McDougall thought that if thousands of signers could be found for the "Association," violence would be avoided by bringing the full weight of public opinion against the Tea Act. Force would be used only as a last resort.[16] But the fact that so much advance publicity seemed necessary was an indication that McDougall and other leaders of the new Association—Philip Livingston, Isaac Low, Isaac Sears, John Lamb, and Samuel and John Broome— were unsure of public sentiment.

When the tea agents received their commissions on December 1 and learned that their consignments would be taxed in America, they made good their earlier promise by announcing they would not accept the tea. Instead, they asked Governor Tryon to take the tea into custody when it arrived and Tryon agreed to store the tea in the army barracks under the protection of the royal garrison.[17] At first McDougall thought this would be a satisfactory arrangement, but a week later he shifted ground. The tea was not to be landed under any circumstances. Several reasons accounted for the stronger policy. McDougall and Sears had received a letter from Boston on December 7 outlining that city's opposition to the East India Company, including a decision to send the tea back to England.[18] Stimulated by Boston's example, the Sons of Liberty had decided to face the fact that their Association had been greeted by a dangerous indifference, complicated by a severe tea shortage in the city. If the tea ship arrived as soon as expected, and if its cargo was stored in the military barracks as Governor Tryon planned, an apathetic, tea-drinking populace might demand that it be made available to them. The opposition to the Tea Act would then collapse. The only protection against this possible break in ranks was to keep company tea out of the city altogether. But just as public apathy might defeat the cause of self-taxation through neglect, a stringently enforced order against landing the tea might force the Sons of Liberty into the position of appearing to sanction violence if Governor Tryon used troops to land and protect the tea. Violence was to be avoided if at all possible. On Friday, December 10, and again on Monday, therefore, McDougall joined Philip Livingston, Isaac Low, Isaac Sears, and the Broome brothers in visits to William Smith, a Council member, and discussed their desire to keep the city peaceful. They urged him to convince Governor Tryon that, unless he ignored the tea, the city might explode with violence.[19] The prospect of bloodshed in New York was like an exposed nerve to Tryon, who wanted no repetition of the disorders that had marred his administration in North Carolina. The cautious governor agreed to a compromise. If public opinion was against the sale of company tea, he would store it. Moreover, he would not use force to land it; in return, Livingston and others of the Association agreed not to oppose the landing.[20]

McDougall was not entirely happy with the patient, often cautious, approaches of Philip Livingston and Isaac Low. Though he disliked open fighting as much as they, he insisted on blocking a tea landing no matter what Governor Tryon decided. He showed his impatience in a meeting with William Smith by suggesting that the problem could be resolved by killing the governor and his Council. He probably only intended to shock his more temperate friends, but McDougall's remark did reveal that he wanted more action and less talk.[21] The aroused agitator also helped plan a mass meeting for Friday, December 17, when the Sons of Liberty hoped to obtain a public declaration that the tea ship must return to England. It was a large meeting, attended by 1,000 people according to the mayor's estimate. Through the skill of John Lamb, who acted as moderator, the Association of the Sons of Liberty was approved and McDougall was appointed to a city committee of correspondence. Seeking to calm the city, the governor sent a message assuring the meeting that he would not release any tea taken into his safe-keeping until he was ordered to, and then only in full public view. This was not enough, and Tryon's proposal was overwhelmingly rejected. The meeting then endorsed a decision already reached in Boston and Philadelphia to send the tea back to England.[22] The meeting was a victory for the Sons of Liberty. When he saw his old enemies Isaac Low, Leonard Lispenard, and James Jauncey in the crowd, along with other principal merchants, McDougall anticipated that they would demand a head count on the question of storing or returning the tea. To his surprise, they stood quiet, and with good reason. The earlier public apathy that McDougall had reported to the Boston committee of correspondence had begun to disappear, and the people were swinging behind the Sons of Liberty. As McDougall later told William Smith, he was now confident that if the governor tried to land the tea, three-fourths of the city would oppose it.[23]

William Smith and Governor Tryon both might have argued with McDougall that popular support for the Sons of Liberty was not as great as he claimed, except that by Tuesday evening the point became immaterial. An express from Samuel Adams arrived in New York City with an account of the Boston tea party. Indecision in New York vanished. McDougall found that even the most timorous men (and some who supported the governor) now demanded that as the only way to preserve peace and protect property in the city, New York's tea ship be kept out of the harbor. Support for landing the tea virtually disappeared. Governor Tryon was still an obstacle because of his insistence that company tea be landed and stored, but finally the tea agents persuaded him that, unless he reversed himself, a "tea party" would happen in New York. Although Governor Tryon never publicly announced his change of mind, McDougall learned privately Tuesday evening of the governor's retreat, and the next day the news was leaked to printer James Rivington.[24]

Unquestionably the tea agents and the city's wealthy citizens were motivated by fear, and the issue remains whether the city really was in danger of violence. It seems clear that McDougall and Sears were the chief promoters of the tough policy against the East India Company, and if violence were to occur, they certainly would be at the center of any trouble. McDougall and Sears were stimulated to more direct action by events elsewhere, particularly in Boston and Philadelphia. An early correspondence was formed with Boston's popular leaders, from whom the New York City Sons of Liberty derived encouragement to continue their agitation despite the early indications of apathy and opposition. It was a letter from Boston, rather than popular approval, which largely prompted McDougall and Sears to insist that company tea not be landed; McDougall probably had Boston's success and New York's hesitancy in mind when he made the bizarre suggestion to kill the governor and council. His attitude was more accurately reflected, however, in a letter to Samuel Adams at about the same time. He assured Adams that the "zealous friends" of the cause in New York would adopt Boston's measures, "but I cannot yet assure you that we shall succeed." [25] A week after that letter, news arrived that Boston had dumped company tea into the harbor without, as Adams said, "the least injury to private property." Boston had again set an example, and McDougall, Sears, and others made the rounds of the city's taverns "to concert measures for the day of the Shipp's arrival." [26] The possibility of violence in New York, therefore, was real, and McDougall was certainly in a position to incite it if he wished. Increasingly he was moving away from the moderation he had adopted after the Stamp Act. The frustrations of continued British efforts to tax, added to his experiences over publication of "To the Betrayed Inhabitants," was turning him into a revolutionary.

If McDougall anticipated trouble in December when the tea ship was expected, the failure of the tea-carrying ship, the *Nancy*, to arrive was a disappointment. Without that stimulus, the provincial capital returned to its normal, sedate winter tempo as quickly as it had reached an explosion point. There was little that McDougall could do until the tea ship arrived. He continued to meet with his friends, and they agreed that week after week of inaction was a drain upon the vitality of the Sons of Liberty. Beginning in mid-March, 1774, therefore, the Liberty Boys were summoned each Thursday evening to the tavern operated by Sears' father-in-law where they were probably as intemperate in drink as they were in speech. [27]

But while they waited for the *Nancy*, McDougall and his friends realized that the problem of the Tea Act for America was more complex than resisting a ship carrying company tea. Beneath the emotion of the moment was the fundamental issue of parliamentary taxation, joined now to the new problem of the East India Company's monopoly power. If one monopoly could be fastened upon the colonial economy, it could mean the establishment of others in America. McDougall, along with Sears, Samuel Broome, John Aspinwall, and Jacob Ludlow, as the committee of correspondence of the Sons of Liberty, informed the Boston leaders of their conviction that the Tea Act would provide revenue to parliament through profit-sharing from monopolistic trade as surely as if American taxes were collected. An American-wide non-importation of items traded by English companies might protect the American market-place, and McDougall urged that English tea should start off the boycott. If Boston would sound out New England, New York would write to Philadelphia and the southern colonies. [28]

When a reply was received a month later, McDougall was more interested to learn that the *Nancy* could be daily expected in New York than to hear that Boston had approved the non-importation scheme.

Battered and damaged by a storm in early April, the tea ship finally appeared off Sandy Hook in the early evening of April 18. The agreement of the previous December between the tea agents and Mc-Dougall and Sears still held, and Captain Lockyer made no effort to bring his ship to port, even promising not to come ashore himself without the permission of McDougall and the other members of the committee of correspondence.[29] But a complication shortly developed that was to cause trouble. According to reliable reports from Philadelphia, New York could also expect tea in another vessel, the *London*, due any day from England. When this report was confirmed and while Captain Lockyer's ship was being hurriedly provisioned and repaired outside the harbor, the Sons of Liberty manned a small craft off Sandy Hook to watch for the second ship. Preparations for Saturday's departure of the *Nancy* were also made, and the populace was invited to Murray's wharf so that Captain Lockyer could see "with his own eyes, their detestation of the measures pursued by the ministry and the India Company, to enslave this country." [30]

Before the city could celebrate its triumph over the East India Company, the *London* under Captain Chambers entered port and set the scene for New York's own tea party. At first the luckless captain tried to bluff his way past McDougall and other experienced sea captains. But when a large dockside crowd became ugly and threatening, he admitted that he had tea on board. The fact that Captain Chambers himself, and not the company, owned the cargo was not enough to save the tea, since Chambers had earlier duped the public into believing that he opposed the Tea Act.[31] While McDougall's friends stayed between the ship and the mob that evening, tally clerks below deck carefully checked the tea chests against Captain Chambers's manifest, and as quickly as the chests were brought on deck, a group of "Mohawks" emptied them into the East River. It was reported that Captain Chambers barely escaped with his life that night.[32]

Early the next morning church bells summoned to Murray's wharf the largest crowd ever seen in the city. Shipping in the harbor blazed with the colors of flags and ensigns, and a band assembled in front of the Coffee House on Wall Street where McDougall and other Sons of Liberty waited with Captain Lockyer. The band struck up "God Save the King" when they appeared, but the music was lost in the crowd's noise when it was seen that Captain Chambers was not with the committee. A tense moment followed, but assurances were quickly given

that Chambers would sail as a passenger aboard the *Nancy;* and Captain Lockyer, accompanied by music and a guard of Liberty Boys,
boarded the pilot boat waiting to take him out to his ship. As the
small craft pushed away from the dock, loud cheering broke out and
guns were fired, marking the final triumph over East India tea.[33]

The events of that week brought an end to nearly eight weeks of
community interest in the Tea Act, and in comparison to former
times, the public proceedings had been firm but orderly. It was Mc-
Dougall's first opportunity to act in an independent role as a popular
leader. Along with Sears and Lamb, he could justly claim credit for
alerting the people to the danger of the Tea Act and sustaining that
alarm over a long period. At no time did the popular leaders lose control of the situation; at no time did they allow the rougher elements
among the Liberty Boys to run wild in the city. Still, their reap-
pearance was an unwelcome sight to men of greater political and social
standing, who saw their control of the city challenged and then taken
away by men of inferior rank, those "cobblers and tailors" whose love
of popularity and power was allegedly greater than their respect for
lawful authority.[34] Perhaps it was McDougall again as "Brutus" who
answered the criticism. Far from being the work of a few men, "Brutus" insisted, it was a spirit of liberty, founded on a just constitutional
basis, that had aroused people of all ranks against England's design to
enslave them. Whatever else had happened, Britain was forced to
come to terms with the sustained defense of American rights. "Can
any one in his sense imagine," it was asked, "that the American Lion,
which has once roared so loudly, as to have been heard with astonish-
ment across the Atlantic, is now fallen asleep?" [35] But there was little
comfort for anyone in such high-blown sentiments. Several days later
news reached New York that parliament had closed the port of Boston, and the imperial crisis deepened.

# Chapter Five
# The Committee of Fifty-one

A fortnight after Captain Lockyer sailed for England, Captain Lawson passed the Hook in the *Concord*, six weeks out of Liverpool, bringing to New York the astonishing news that parliament had closed the port of Boston. Until complete restitution was made to the East India Company of £9,659 for the tea dumped into Boston's harbor, all traffic in and out of that port was prohibited. Other ships carried the same alarm to other ports, and soon everywhere in America there arose cries of outrage and protest against the latest instance of British tyranny.[1] News of the Boston Port Act and the other bills against Boston (dubbed the "Intolerable Acts,") changed McDougall's life as dramatically as did the Quartering Act and his imprisonment four years earlier. He was determined to raise the cause of American freedom above local partisan politics which had been typical in New York in the past. He seized the initiative in advocating a course of action and appealed to the people for approval to accomplish his goal. McDougall saw himself as the true representative of the public good, which demanded a firm defense of liberty, and he relied upon the public to assure that opposition to the Intolerable Acts was not manipulated for the benefit of factional rivals. His actions and the events of 1774 marked the beginning of his reliance upon the power of the people as a basis for revolutionary decision-making. This was a first step toward implementing the notion of popular sovereignty in American government, which would eventually reach full expression in the republican state constitutions.

News of the Boston Port Act spread quickly through the city as did the additional information received on May 12 that General Thomas Gage, formerly stationed in New York, had been named governor of Massachusetts.[2] Some men openly insisted that Boston could save herself by simply paying for the tea her own inhabitants destroyed and that, at any rate, the Act did not concern New Yorkers. But the general feeling was one of shock and dismay. McDougall thought at once of reviving non-importation as a measure of retaliation. He had wanted to do it several months earlier against the Tea Act, but he had held back then because public opinion in February would not support it. Now the situation was better. Even prominent civic leaders such as James Duane and Oliver De Lancey were boldly expressing concern, the latter claiming that "he would rather spend every shilling of his fortune than that the Boston Port Bill should be complied with." [3] Though McDougall distrusted the sincerity of De Lancey and his friends, believing that they wanted only to gain public favor by being on the right side, he hoped to exploit their efforts in the same way the De Lancey followers hoped to exploit the Sons of Liberty.

During the first days after the news arrived of the closing of Boston, McDougall proved to be as devious as he accused his opponents of being. Convinced that the De Lanceys only intended to talk against unconstitutional parliamentary authority without taking action to defend American rights, he and Sears took steps to guard against inaction. First, they "stimulated" the dry goods merchants to approve a call for a general meeting on Monday, May 16, to appoint a city committee which would decide upon a proper means of supporting Boston.[4] Next, they hastily and secretly wrote on May 15 to their Boston friends, purposely misrepresenting the situation in New York. "As no time was to be lost," McDougall recorded in his private journal, "we judged it unnecessary to detain the express till the other members of our committee signed it." The people of New York, Sears and McDougall claimed in the letter to Boston, agreed that broad commercial sanctions must be established to bring the home government to its senses. The merchants, who would meet the next evening, supported a "general non-importation, and non-exportation of goods . . . until the American grievances are redressed, under such regulations as may be agreed upon by . . . a general congress to be held here for that purpose." They urged that Boston leaders make that proposal to the towns of eastern Connecticut and the remainder of New England; New York would be responsible for New Haven south to Philadelphia, while, hopefully, a Charleston committee would see to southern towns. McDougall and Sears closed their letter to Boston with a promise to send a letter to Philadelphia the next day to advise the committee there of the plan.[5]

It was a bold proposal amounting to a colonial declaration of economic war on the mother country, to be executed by a political union forged under conditions verging on rebellion. It revealed the strength of McDougall's anti-British attitude and his firm intention, short of rebellion, to defend colonial rights. But the letter written by McDougall and Sears was clearly deceptive, inasmuch as New York, though disturbed by the Port Act, was hardly ready to accept a complete commercial boycott. Why did he and Sears mislead Boston? It seems unlikely that they had completely misread public opinion in their own city, or that they believed the merchants, shopkeepers, and tradesmen would readily adopt a program of economic sanctions against England. More likely, McDougall and Sears recognized that New York, because of internal divisions, would not accept a boycott unless similar action was taken elsewhere. By suggesting that measure to Boston, they intended to provide an external stimulus to New Yorkers to make a firm defense of colonial liberties. If major trading towns in other colonies quickly fell into non-importation to protest the Boston Port Act, then New York would most likely follow along. That strategy accounts for the haste and secrecy of writing to Boston; it also accounts for the outright lie which McDougall and Sears later told when asked if they knew who had written the published version of the letter. As McDougall and Sears well knew but dared not admit to the Boston Committee, there was no consensus for a boycott. The people in New York City were as divided as ever.

The weeks following demonstrated the full range of New York's divisions. The basic one, to which McDougall was so sensitive, pitted the De Lanceys against the Livingstons for the distinction of being the staunchest defender of American rights. As the most astute politician of them all, Lieutenant Governor Cadwallader Colden, cynically remarked, "The people in this place have been in continual ferment of division among themselves upon their political measures, which at bottom arises solely from the local party views—they have all an eye to the next election, more than anything else." [6] Economic differences were also present, cutting across factional lines. Merchants disagreed over the issue of a strong economic boycott, which some feared would spell an end to their revived prosperity, while the mechanics insisted that they should be consulted on any decisions effecting their interests. Finally, McDougall's leadership disturbed those men who disliked having social inferiors dictating public policy; to many, he was still a busy-body who did not know the difference between a "pole and a poll," a seeker of that popularity which was a "perpetual itching, without the benefit of scratching." [7]

Careful preparations were made to assure a good attendance at the first public meeting called for May 16 to consider Boston's plight. In the morning McDougall posted several notices in the coffee house as a reminder to merchants, and in private conversations, emphasized that the Sons of Liberty did not intend to push radical measures, but only to insist that Boston be supported. He did not, of course, mention the letter sent to Boston the day before. Three hundred people turned out, forcing an adjournment to the nearby Merchants' Exchange, and those present proved how deeply the controversy had penetrated into all social ranks. In addition to the city's wealthiest merchants—among them the Crugers, Waltons, Beekmans, Ludlows, and Livingston—there were five members of the governor's Council and several assemblymen, leading lawyers, and a throng of merchants' clerks and mechanics. Despite a few differences of views, all agreed that the city required a new committee to correspond with other American towns. Only the committee's size was at issue. McDougall insisted that a small number would be more able to act, particularly to enforce an economic boycott, but it was evident that others wanted to curb the popular leaders by a large committee under merchant control. After considerable wrangling, during which tempers flared, a fifty-man committee, including McDougall and Sears, was nominated. In McDougall's opinion, a committee of this size was unlikely to make a spirited stand behind Boston. It would be, he predicted, more of a handle for De Lancey politicians seeking favor with the people than a means to defend constitutional rights. [8]

Although McDougall was unsuccessful on Monday evening, the proposed committee of fifty had to be approved at a public meeting, and he seized the opportunity to let the public choose between a large or a small city committee. He was encouraged by what he heard as he made the rounds of the city's taverns. The Tuesday-night crowd at the coffee house became excited when he read several Boston letters brought to town an hour earlier by Paul Revere, and in talking the next night with clergymen attending an Episcopalian conference, he learned that some favored non-importation. When McDougall met the Liberty Boys, now styling themselves "mechanics" to offset the merchant tactic of claiming to speak for the laboring class, twenty-five out of the fifty men named two days earlier were proposed as the city's committee of correspondence.[9]

McDougall could not attend the afternoon meeting of May 19 because of illness, but it was just as well, for it proved to be a disappointment. The crowd was smaller than expected, and more artisans and laborers were on the De Lancey side than with the Liberty Boys. Isaac Low, wealthy merchant, became the temporary chairman, which meant, according to McDougall, that Low boldly thrust himself into that job. Isaac Sears, chief spokesman for the Sons of Liberty, was barely heard over the noise when he tried to speak in favor of a smaller committee. His only accomplishment was the addition of Francis Lewis to the larger committee slate, making it fifty-one, and the passing of an agreement that the city be polled about the committee. But when Sears met later with Low and other leaders to arrange the canvass, they argued over who would take the poll and the plan was dropped.[10] As far as the leading men were concerned, the Committee of Fifty-One would now direct the city's opposition to the Intolerable Acts. McDougall, Sears, and the others had no choice but to agree, if a semblance of unity was to prevail in the city. When McDougall met his friends at Hampden Hall on Friday, they agreed to give the committee a chance. But "if they misbehaved they would be removed." [11]

It hardly seems possible that McDougall did not know New York City was still basically controlled by wealthy merchants, lawyers, and officeholders who, if they exerted themselves, could decide public policy. No amount of bravado in letters to fellow extremists in other places could cover the fact that, when it came to a showdown, patrician leadership would prevail with the people. The appointment of the city committee proved this. Perhaps it was because he understood the city's political condition that he did not immediately write to Philadelphia, outlining his scheme of an economic boycott and intercolonial congress, as he promised Samuel Adams he would. The creation of the Committee of Fifty-One had been a slap at McDougall's independent action in writing to Adams in the first place. He then had to wait to see what would really happen in New York. Only when it was evident that a large city committee would be named did he write to Charles Thomson urging upon him the same program he proposed to Boston leaders, thus trying to get other cities to take the lead in a continental movement.[12] But even this delay appears to have been part of his strategy, for if New York would not take the initiative, perhaps she would follow her neighboring sister cities into a firm defense of Boston. New York was heading in the right direction, even if the city was not leading the pack.

But it was not an easy thing to keep moving. When the Fifty-One held its first meeting on May 23, McDougall turned over letters he had received from Boston and Philadelphia and the wrangling started all over again. Was Boston's trouble New York's concern? Was the time right to propose an intercolonial congress? McDougall's views were known and of little interest to most members, but those of James Duane and John Jay, both of whom agreed with McDougall about the need for intercolonial unity, were persuasive. The people were indeed suffering in the cause of American liberty and a congress was needed to decide upon a proper defense of that liberty. Thus, McDougall's desire for a continental movement was winning even though not in the way he planned. A cautiously worded letter was sent off to Boston the next day, and McDougall asked Paul Revere to give Samuel Adams a message that Boston would have to set the time and place for the intercolonial meeting since New York would not do it. On May 25 he wrote much the same thing to Charles Thomson in Philadelphia.[13] All that was practical had been done, and McDougall knew it. When it was suggested that a "constitutional" postal system was needed to protect American letters, McDougall recognized that even so innocent a proposal as that would divide New York. Everything had to await developments in Boston and Philadelphia.[14]

For nearly a month it appeared that Boston would fail McDougall. There appeared in the *Boston Gazette* an altered version of the May 15 letter from McDougall and Sears to the Boston committee, without mentioning their names, implying that New York had already formed a committee that favored both a congress and economic sanctions. Fortunately the phrase that McDougall had "stimulated" the merchants was dropped from the newspaper version. But the members of the Fifty-One were astounded by what they knew was completely untrue. Questions were asked around town and, since the Fifty-One suspected that the old committee of the Sons of Liberty was responsible, McDougall was asked directly if he knew the authors. Considering the circumstances prevailing in the city, he had little choice: he simply lied, disclaiming any knowledge of the letter.[15] In still another way the Boston committee seemed intent upon hurting the cause in New

York. Replying to the Fifty-One's letter of May 23, Boston agreed that a congress was necessary but strongly recommended that each colony fashion its own trade boycott of British goods. A local boycott was exactly what New York's merchants opposed and the Fifty-One, rather belligerently, reminded Boston that a "suspension of trade" would be the primary issue to be resolved by the proposed congress.[16] Philadelphia, too, seemed to be working against McDougall. During the last week of May, a report circulated in New York City that at a Philadelphia meeting John Dickinson, the famed "Pennsylvania Farmer," had pronounced the Boston Port Act constitutional. Mc-Dougall immediately asked Charles Thomson for clarification, preferably a denial. If the rumor was true, McDougall wrote, it would undoubtedly give encouragement to those New Yorkers who thought Boston should take full responsibility for its actions.[17]

Time proved to be McDougall's best ally. Each week brought news of the spreading reaction to the Intolerable Acts, and he carefully rode the mounting wave of public opinion in New York, cautioning Samuel Adams to be "firm and prudent and a little time will effect your salvation and a glorious deliverence to America."[18] He was merely looking for the right moment. It came over the weekend of June 25–26 when the Fifty-One received a report of Philadelphia's mass meeting of June 18 at which a congress was approved and the legislature urged to appoint delegates. "Since the advice received from Philadelphia of passing their resolutions," McDougall informed Samuel Adams, "stocks have risen in favor of liberty. Those few who wished nothing would be done here as an excuse for our passivity are crestfallen." It was time to push the Committee of Fifty-One, he added, and it would be done the next morning.[19]

When the Fifty-One convened on Monday, June 27, it was clear that leaders like Isaac Low and John Thurman were loosing their grip on the situation in New York City. Reports were coming in that county meetings in the colony were taking a stronger stand than the provincial capital; Philadelphia and Boston were behind a congress and were taking steps to name deputies; and John Holt's *Journal* told the public that newspapers received from other colonies were full of accounts of meetings proposing a congress and a cessation of trade with England.[20] McDougall's timing was right and debate within the Fifty-One started on his motion to consider the appointment of a delegation to an intercolonial meeting. The whole evening was spent on a proposal to ask the Assembly, as the only representative body in the province, to name the delegates. But to McDougall, it seemed improbable that Colden, momentarily taking Tryon's place as governor, would convene the Assembly for that purpose. The city radical leader favored instead a convention of county deputies to name a provincial delegation, and when the Fifty-One met again on Wednesday, he offered a specific plan. The capital should nominate five men as representatives to either a provincial convention or the general congress, subject to the concurrence of a "committee of mechanics" and the city's voters. If a convention did not meet, the five delegates chosen in the capital would need the final approval of county meetings. Only then could it be said that New York was represented in the general congress.[21]

Several assumptions in McDougall's proposal alarmed most of the committee members. First, he took other men at their word that congressional deputies should be representative of the colony. As the city committee was named by and spoke for the trading community, it was only right that the mechanics—the artisans, shopkeepers, and common laborers unrepresented on the Fifty-One—should have a voice in the nominating process. Thus McDougall argued that the Mechanics Committee had a different constituency and was coequal to the merchant Fifty-One in city policy-making. Another and greater cause for alarm was the implication in McDougall's proposal that the De Lancey-merchant majority lacked political credibility among the city's skilled and unskilled workers, a charge that ignored the developments of the recent past. According to the committee's reasoning, the Fifty-One's membership was as representative of the city as the Assembly was of the colony and therefore concurrence of a competing group in the capital was unthinkable. Furthermore, a "mechanics committee" was a bold assertion that the common people were capable of exercising leadership and wisdom on a level equal to that of gentlemen of proven responsibility, a direct challenge to aristocratic stewardship that could not be allowed.[22] It probably mattered little to McDougall that his plan would be unacceptable, for he had succeeded on the larger strategy. He had "pushed" the committee, and the majority now had to either reject the general congress or propose an alternative to his specific plan.[23]

Committee leaders were not ready to deal with McDougall's motion at the meeting on Wednesday, June 29, but they were on the following

Monday, July 4. The part of his plan requiring the concurrence of the Mechanics Committee was rejected 24 to 13 and an alternative was passed. Five delegates would be nominated by the Fifty-One and approved by the freeholders and freemen of the city; the counties could, if they wished, select their own delegates. The way was now cleared for nominations and both McDougall and committee leaders were ready with rival slates of candidates. Three men, Philip Livingston, Isaac Low, and James Duane, were common to both lists. But McDougall's slate included himself and John Morin Scott, while the other had John Alsop and John Jay. Despite three common candidates, there was a fundamental difference between the two slates. McDougall's candidates stood for a hard line toward the British, while John Alsop and John Jay were at best cautious men who could be relied on to seek out an accommodation with the mother country. A majority of the Fifty-One preferred Alsop and Jay, along with Livingston, Low and Duane, and asked the people to assemble at the City Hall on July 7 to approve those five or choose other delegates.[24]

The Fifty-One's nominees were a victory for the members to the extent that they had striven from the beginning to save New York from rash and violent measures, especially locally imposed economic sanctions. They assumed, as one of their writers put it the next day, that the voice of the committee was the voice of the people, while Mc-Dougall wanted only to plunge the city into confusion and ruin.[25] But as far as McDougall was concerned the voice of the people had not been heard and therefore the choice of delegates was far from over. As the Fifty-One had decided on a public meeting on Thursday, he invited the public to meet in the fields on Wednesday evening to push further the committee by exposing the misrepresentations of those who claimed that the Fifty-One reflected public sentiment. He presided himself, although his speech impediment required a double reading of everything so the people could fully understand his propositions. A total stoppage of trade with Great Britain was the only way that "right, justice, and social happiness, and freedom" could triumph over "fraud, power, and the most odious oppression," and New York's delegates to congress must work for that policy. A provincial convention should be convened to select delegates to represent the colony and whatever measures the congress agreed upon must be binding on the city. The mass meeting readily approved McDougall's propositions, and as the people had made known their sentiments, the meeting insisted that the Committee of Fifty-One regard them as binding instructions.[26]

The city committee was not entirely bowled over by McDougall's successful effort to circumvent the committee through mass pressure, though it did have to give ground. When the Fifty-One's public meeting assembled the next day, July 7, McDougall, other popular leaders, and their followers appeared with a mandate from the previous night's meeting, and forced two concessions from the city committee. The candidates of the Mechanics Committee—Livingston, Low, Duane, McDougall, and now Leonard Lispenard in place of John Morin Scott—were to be presented along with the Fifty-One's nominees—Livingston, Low, Duane, Jay, and Alsop—to the city's taxpayers, representing a broader electorate, who would choose one of the lists.[27] It was hardly a ringing endorsement of McDougall's program, but a number of committeemen were nevertheless furious over what Mc-Dougall had done to their plans and angered that his resolutions of July 6 had been published as though they expressed the city's position.

At the Fifty-One's regular evening meeting on July 7, John Thurman challenged McDougall to his face. Questioning the right of any committee member to call a public meeting, adopt resolutions, and publish them without prior approval of the Fifty-One, Thurman moved that the committee disavow completely the whole proceedings of July 6 which were designed "to create groundless jealousies and suspicions" and to divide the city. The committee's vote of 21 to 9 in favor of Thurman's motion of censure was only one sign of an obvious desire to put McDougall in his place. The Fifty-One repudiated the resolutions of the mass meeting by appointing a committee, including McDougall and Sears, to draft proper resolutions which could be presented and approved by the city as expressing its true opinion of the Boston Port Act and what might be done to relieve American grievances. The only concession to public pressure was the decision to conduct a poll of the city jointly with the Mechanics Committee. Finally, it was agreed to suspend the committee's rule of secrecy and publish the evening's proceedings to inform the public of its disapproval of McDougall's unwarranted and divisive activities.[28]

Presumably committee leaders thought they had effectively put Mc-Dougall down and had established the Fifty-One's claim to exclusive leadership in the city. Events of the next two days were to prove them

wrong on both counts. In the first place, the committee ended the evening in a fashion that could only confuse the public as to what really
happened. McDougall and Sears reported to the populace their side of
the affair. Near the end of the meeting, they claimed, a motion to
publish the evening's work had been "judged inexpedient" and was
rejected, but after the committee adjourned and some members had
left for home, Thurman once more offered his motion to publish.
Contrary to parliamentary procedures, Chairman Isaac Low then permitted the remaining members to vote, the motion passed, and Low
ordered publication. It was, McDougall and Sears concluded, a high-
handed and arbitrary affair. But defenders of the Fifty-One told a different story. When it was proposed to publish the resolution of censure, McDougall, Sears, and several others "quitted the chamber in a
rage, ordering their names to be struck off, and afterwards bawling
along the streets, 'the committee is dissolved; the committee is dissolved'." [29]

It was impossible for the people to sort out the contradictions in the
two accounts and instead merely provided additional arguments to
those already disposed in favor of or against the Committee of Fifty-
One. McDougall, Sears, and nine other members, on July 8, further
confounded the Fifty-One's claim to exclusive leadership by resigning
from the committee. Rather self-righteously, they said their resignations were necessary because the committee's actions "tended to hold
up a disunion amongst us, which must impede the public business,
and retard a redress of our grievances. . . ." [30] McDougall went still
further. The day after his resignation, on July 9, he withdrew his
name from the Mechanics Committee's list of candidates for congress
on the grounds that the people would not be allowed to select five
names out of the total of seven different candidates, as was the custom
in regular elections. Instead, they could only vote for one slate of candidates or the other. McDougall showed his disapproval of that policy
both by his resignation from the city committee and by withdrawing
his name from the election. No longer could the Committee of Fifty-
One contend that it was representative of the whole city. [31]

To interested observers in other colonies, developments in New
York were probably viewed as incomprehensible or, at the very
worst, appeared to indicate that New Yorkers might be the only people unwilling or unable to send delegates to a congress which they had
themselves proposed. The situation was even difficult for some New

Yorkers to understand. "Strange that the colony who had the first intelligence of the Parliamentary measures," William Smith wrote to
Philip Schuyler, "is behind all the rest." [32] Actually, throughout the
sequence of events from July 5, when the Fifty-One approved five
candidates for congress, to July 9, when McDougall withdrew as an
opposition candidate, McDougall was playing a slick game of cat-and-
mouse with committee leaders like Isaac Low and John Thurman.
While they sought to prevent precipitate and rash measures, especially
an economic boycott, and were cautiously guiding the city committee
toward an intercolonial meeting, McDougall sought to hurry the committee along by exploiting the growing public indignation over the Intolerable Acts. The mass meeting of July 6 was held for that purpose.
When it produced among committee members a stiffened attitude
toward his activities instead of a firmer resolve to oppose the Intolerable Acts, his resignation along with the others was intended to bring
the work of the committee to a full stop. He admitted as much to
Samuel Adams. If enough members resigned, the Committee of Fifty-
One would be dissolved and a new one, more sympathetic to Boston,
named. Even if the committee continued, McDougall thought that the
resignations would create a "jealousy of the people to watch it." [33]
McDougall was gambling that he would be able to accomplish outside
the committee what he could not do as a member. Initially, it looked
as though he might have overplayed his hand. The Committee of
Fifty-One, reduced in numbers, simply continued its work, drafting
resolutions on July 13 and renominating their candidates to congress.
But then it called a public meeting for July 19 to approve these actions.[34] The odds that McDougall's gamble would pay off instantly
improved.

The call for a public meeting was either a lapse of political good
sense on the part of the committee members or an indication that they
were unable to read accurately the signs of the times. The turnout
was so small that the Fifty-One was seriously embarrassed. John
Morin Scott ridiculed the city committee's statement of policy, term-
ing it "destitute of vigour, sense, and integrity." When it was suggested that the Fifty-One make amendments or draft a new set of resolutions, McDougall and Sears insisted that a special committee of
fifteen be appointed, themselves included, to make the necessary alter-
ations. The public meeting also refused to approve the committee's
candidates, ordering that the selection should be done by a city poll

and that McDougall and Leonard Lispenard be added to the list from which five would be chosen.[35] Dismissing the results of the morning as indecisive (a ludicrous act in light of the public meeting's actions), the Fifty-One that evening made a few changes in its resolutions, recommended again its five candidates, and approved a city poll, "leaving those who may dissent from us to declare their opinions in such other phrases or modes of expression as they shall think proper." The Fifty-One adjourned, apparently confident that it was still in charge of New York's opposition to the Intolerable Acts.[36]

New York's affairs were clearly in a muddled condition after the two meetings of July 19. Even John Alsop, John Jay, and Isaac Low, three of the Fifty-One's candidates for congress, were uncertain of the situation and informed the city that they could not possibly go to the congress until the public's sentiments were known with "greater precision." [37] The fact that the city's stand remained unclear was the result of the unyielding attitudes of both the Fifty-One and its critics such as McDougall. But the edge of the controversy was turning in McDougall's favor as he had gambled that it would. The occasion was the July 20 meeting of the special committee of fifteen. It agreed upon twelve resolutions which repeated that a congress was the best means to formulate a united policy on the Boston Port Act, that the best policy was a comprehensive stoppage of trade, and that a provincial convention was necessary to elect delegates to congress. The public was invited to meet on Monday, July 25, to hear the special committee's report and approve the resolutions.[38]

A compromise was the obvious solution. It is not known who arranged it, nor the arguments used in its favor, but it had to come. In any case, McDougall participated in meetings on July 25 and 27 which approved the most important part of his objective, economic sanctions against England. He relinquished any hope he may have had to become a delegate, by agreeing to support Low, Livingston, Duane, Alsop, and Jay in a city poll. In return he received a pledge from the five that they would work in congress to establish a boycott of English goods. Although the Fifty-One continued to act as though anything done outside its membership was inconclusive, even conducting a city poll on July 28, everything of importance had been arranged the day before. Perhaps it was out of boredom over a contest lasting five weeks that the newspapers failed to announce the results of the city canvass; the Committee of Fifty-One merely noted that the delegates were unanimously elected.[39]

New York never recovered from those summer months of 1774. Men on both sides of the Atlantic drove the wedge deeper between America and Britain, making it impossible to heal the breach. It would be easy to give McDougall greater credit than he deserves for widening the gap. Still, from the Tea Act to the First Continental Congress, he seemed to become more anti-British as the months passed, insisting upon an increasingly firmer assertion of American rights, and drawing upon a wider constituency to defend the public interest. With each small success he became bolder, and perhaps haughtier, in pushing community leaders who were accustomed to presiding over public business. Men of rank and stature had always been dismayed by the failure of men like McDougall to remember their place in society, and they were more disturbed in 1774 because of the seriousness of the crisis facing America. As "Mercator" wrote in *Rivington's Gazetteer*, "It has given great pain to many of the most respectable inhabitants of this city, as well as to myself, to see a number of persons who have not a shilling to lose in the contest, taking advantage of the present dispute, and forcing themselves into public notice." [40] Out of patriotic conviction, some patricians made whatever emotional adjustments were necessary and acknowledged that McDougall and other leaders were there to stay; others, of deeper social and political conservatism, were never able to accept the intrusion of self-made men into their orderly world. Their inbred response was to cast ridicule upon popular leaders lacking the social graces of polite society. To be lampooned and mocked in print was not a new experience to McDougall—he could hardly forget the "Dougliad" series of 1770—but it had become venomous in 1774, intending to kill off with the pen what could not be removed by political means.[41]

The worst of these published attacks was "Debates of the Robin-Hood Society," a copy of the London original reprinted in New York's newspapers. The scene was an imagined meeting of the Sons of Liberty, the debate involving the Boston Port Act, and the cast of characters the popular leaders "labouring to raise themselves out of obscurity." McDougall was "Make-Do-All"; Isaac Sears, "Mr. King"; John Lamb, "Matt-of-the-Mint"; John Morin Scott, "Mr. Silver-Tongue"; and Peter R. Livingston, "Fight-the-good-Fight-of-Faith, Peter, Moderator." Their purpose was to consider resolutions drafted by Silver-Tongue and they were depicted as sitting around a tavern table, tankards in hand, giggling with excitement over their sense of importance, yet trying to be serious. They turn the meeting into a shambles instead, demonstrating their fundamental incapacity to do anything right. When one character chides Mr. King that he might need to brush up on his reading, Mr. King as Sears loses his temper: " 'Sblood! Mr. Smart Cock, this is no time for joking; by heavens! I'll—lifting up his hand in a passion." Silver-Tongue corrects their grammar, pointing out that "unite and die" is wrong; they must use the particle "or." Make-Do-All, with rolling r's, stutters when he speaks, continually dipping into his snuffbox, in child-like imitation of his betters, as he vainly tries to appear profound and wise. One resolution containing the phrase "an assembly of the continent" brings Make-Do-All to his feet: "Continent -Continent!" he exclaims, "Is not his expression rather e-qui-vo-cal, Mr. Moderator! If I misapprehend not, Mr. Johnson, in his dictionary, defines continent to be chaste, moderate, temperate: An assembly of the continent may, I humbly conceive, be taken for an assembly of such kind of people. . . ." Silver-Tongue gently quiets him and then extols the glories of American geography. Only the patience of crafty Silver-Tongue and Mr. Moderator save the meeting from complete chaos.[42]

As in all parody the "Debates of the Robin-Hood Society" contained truth for some men, mirroring their view of what went on in meetings of the popular leaders: emotional outbursts, pretentious behavior, bungling endeavors to keep order, everything a gentleman of wealth and learning expected from society's lower orders. Gouverneur Morris, the cynical and brilliant twenty-two-year-old scion of the manor Morrises, thought of the future: "The mob begin to think and to reason. Poor reptiles! it is with them a vernal morning, they are struggling to cast off their winter's slough, they bask in the sunshine, and ere noon they will bite, depend upon it. The gentry begin to fear this." [43] But fulminate though their betters might, a formidable alliance was being constructed between the stuttering Scotch privateer and the discontented mass in New York. Patrician leaders, long accustomed to ruling, were unable to prevent their orderly world of status and gentility from crumbling.

# Chapter Six
# The Continental Association

Neither the Committee of Fifty-One nor McDougall and his friends emerged victorious from the summer contest over leadership in New York City. Each side had been forced to concede something to the other, but in terms of the established values and practices of provincial society, McDougall was able to gain more from compromise than did his opponents. With each concession made by the Fifty-One to leaders such as McDougall, the customary leadership exercised by the city's elite was weakened. McDougall's status as a popular leader grew in importance in the months ahead as the opposition to Britain took on a recognizable structure in the formation of local committees, a provincial convention, and an intercolonial congress. All of these incipient revolutionary bodies owed their legitimacy to the proclaimed right of the people to defend themselves against tyranny, even a tyranny in which their own local leaders were implicated. As the center of power shifted to the populace at large, McDougall became a major figure in the growing revolutionary movement in New York.

In August, 1774, McDougall served as an unofficial host to the Massachusetts, New Hampshire, and Connecticut delegates passing through on their way to the first Continental Congress at Philadelphia. He conducted tours of the city, and arranged introductions and dinner meetings with local patriots. He even saw to it that John Sullivan's servant, ill with smallpox, was nursed to health.[1] John Adams found McDougall to be a "very sensible man, and an open one. He has none of the mean cunning which disgraces so many of my countrymen." He also found McDougall a talkative person, but not really different from other New Yorkers he met: "At their entertainments there is no conversation that is agreeable. There is no modesty—no attention to one another. They talk very loud, very fast, and altogether." Whether at McDougall's home, the Exchange, the coffee house, or in small dinner groups, Adams met the right people: Sears and Lamb and Hugh Hughes, old Sons of Liberty; Philip Livingston, Philip Van Brugh Livingston, and William Smith of the Livingston faction. The talk was of politics. From McDougall, Adams learned of the De Lancey-Livingston struggle for power and how each group had acted during the summer months. He added the caution that many men were still sensitive about the outcome and that it would be better not to discuss the topic openly.[2]

The experience of meeting and exchanging views with men from other colonies was valuable training for McDougall. He obviously liked the attention paid him by Adams and New Hampshire's John Sullivan; they reinforced his belief that the imperial crisis was truly continental in scope and that the assembling of the colonies in a congress held the key to the future of freedom in America. The week spent with the Massachusetts leaders was an important step in the conversion of McDougall from a local political partisan to a man of continental influence and concern. Consequently, after the delegates left New York at the end of August, McDougall followed them to Philadelphia within a few weeks.[3] Why he went is not entirely clear. Perhaps he was encouraged by the Massachusetts delegates, who saw in him a true ally. Perhaps he wanted to observe at first hand how New York's deputies performed, to see whether they would keep their promise on non-importation and non-exportation. Or perhaps he wanted to be at the center of activity as he had been in New York and to be near the Congress even if he could not be an active member of it. In any event, McDougall was not a stranger in Philadelphia. He could visit Jonathan Smith, merchant, correspondent, and a friend for years; Joseph Reed, who had earlier managed a few business matters for him; George Clymer, whose wife, Elizabeth, John Adams had met in McDougall's home; or Daniel Roberdeau, married to Mary Bostwick, sister of Hannah McDougall. Interestingly, all of his Philadelphia friends had a common bond with him; they too were noted for their extremism on the Boston Port Act.

How long he remained in Philadelphia, and whether he made one or two trips, is not known. John Adams noted in his diary that McDougall spent the evening of September 18 with him, but his next visit was not until October 2, and in between, it is probable that McDougall returned home for a short time. In any event, he was back in New York no later than October 12 and was the bearer of the news that the Continental Congress had approved a stoppage of trade with Britain. While in Philadelphia he spent a number of evenings with John Adams, in the company of Charles Lee of Virginia, Roger Sherman of Connecticut, William Floyd, a country delegate from New York, and Joseph Reed, his old friend. Their conversation concerned Congress. During McDougall's first visit with Adams, the Suffolk Resolves supplied the topic; in the first week of October, it was the non-importation resolution of September 27; and Joseph Galloway's plan of union was discussed on September 28. He found that New York's delegates, especially Jay and Duane, supported economic sanctions but insisted that Congress had a responsibility to establish a basis for reconciling America's difficulties with the mother country. To accomplish that end, they favored the creation of an American parliament, proposed by Joseph Galloway of Pennsylvania, to deal with issues of common concern to the colonies and England.[4] McDougall's reactions to Galloway's plan and to the position of Jay and Duane are unknown, although none of those with whom he associated at Philadelphia thought the plan would work. For the moment, he was probably satisfied that the Congress had supported a cessation of trade with England.

McDougall left Philadelphia before Congress formally adopted the Continental Association, and it must have been satisfying to him that he should be one of the first to announce in New York that a boycott was almost certain.[5] By the end of October New York's delegates returned and the Association's provisions were generally known. It was everything the supporters of the crown feared, and, even worse, it came from a congress they had hoped would be prudent and moderate in action. Far from moderation, the First Continental Congress appeared to be leaning toward extremism. As Colden wrote to Lord Dartmouth, the Association surprised the people because they did not think "such a measure would probably be resolved on by the Congress." Now the city would have to be protected from the ravages of the mob and of dangerous men like McDougall who, as Colden put it, "Under the pretense of executing the dictates of the congress would immediately throw the city into the most perilous situation." [6]

At first the Committee of Fifty-One discussed the details of establishing a committee of inspection as directed by Congress, and James Duane, still allied to the De Lanceys, proposed that each of the city's wards elect eight men who would become a new city committee responsible for enforcing the Association. Duane's suggestion of a city election, or a poll, was a clever plan designed to capitalize on merchant unhappiness over non-importation. In 1770 a poll had been effective in ending the city's boycott of England goods, and such a method was seen again as the merchants' best chance to control the direction of community affairs. McDougall was not anxious for a popular contest at the ballot box, for he was uncertain whether the patriot cause could win an election that would surely see the De Lancey-merchant group use every tactic to get voters on their side. He preferred a negotiated committee list upon which all could agree, thereby giving up seats to his opponents while assuring that the basic strategy of the Association remained intact. Responding to pressure from the Mechanics Committee, the Fifty-One on November 4 abandoned its polling scheme and approved a manageable procedure by which 60 men were jointly selected as the Committee of Inspection, to be approved at a public meeting. Only thirty or forty people assembled at City Hall on November 22 for the formality of approving the new city committee, evidence of at least a momentary agreement among the city's leaders.[7]

The manner by which the Committee of Sixty was established demonstrated that the question of predominance among the various groups contending for public support remained unresolved. Neither of the older patrician factions, De Lanceys or Livingstons, nor the new men like McDougall could claim to dominate city affairs. As the sequence of events of the summer and fall revealed, no single political figure or group had emerged to command the support of the populace. The reason for this was the imperial crisis created by the Intolerable Acts, and the political nature of New York's response to them. No matter what was proposed by one group as the most appropriate and effective method of upholding colonial rights, it was bound to prompt criticism and opposition from the others as being either too excessive or too timid. If New York was to do anything, compromise was the only practical solution, as had been shown in July and now again with the selection of the Committee of Sixty. The De Lanceys, whose victories in 1769–1770 had previously given them control in the capital, were the principal losers because of their cautious and guarded reactions to parliament's treatment of Boston. McDougall and the Livingstons, on the other hand, gained the most.

As one of a number of leaders actively involved in city affairs, Mc-

Dougall possessed several advantages in his bouts with the De Lanceys. His involvement with the Sons of Liberty and the Mechanics Committee, along with Isaac Sears and John Lamb; his appeals to the people at large; and his use of mass meetings and demonstrations to further his political ends—all carried implied threats of intimidation and violence. He was showing that he and his friends could plunge the city into turmoil if they wished, as they had in 1770 over the Quartering Act, and more recently over the Tea Act. However ridiculed and detested he might be by his opponents, McDougall could not be ignored. But McDougall was not intransigent; his political behavior during 1774 shows that he was a political realist who recognized that he could not totally displace the established leadership. If he was to achieve anything, it was necessary for him to meet his political opponents on some common ground, contenting himself with influencing rather than controlling developments in New York. Yet above all McDougall had the advantage of being associated with a growing intercolonial protest movement. In the broader context of American reaction to the Intolerable Acts, his advocacy of nothing more than an economic boycott and an intercolonial meeting made him seem far less extreme than some of the real firebrands in other colonies. As the city's newspapers reported to the public, what was taking place in New York was no more, and was perhaps even less, than was transpiring in other colonies. From events and protest leaders elsewhere, especially in New England, McDougall derived encouragement as he grappled with the problems of revolutionary leadership in New York.

New York's unity under the Committee of Sixty, however, was an illusion, quickly dispelled by a patchwork of fears and suspicions. McDougall distrusted the motives of some committee members, and many among the provincial elite saw in the Continental Association and its committees of inspection a threat and danger to the very foundations of society. Thus, practical problems of politics quickly raised more fundamental questions of the rightful exercise of power.

Ever since the "Mohawks" dumped Captain Chambers's tea into the East River, public writers had demonstrated an increasing uneasiness and agitation over developments in New York. At first the leaders of the Sons of Liberty were the targets of their scorn and ridicule, but by the fall months of 1774 the patriot victory which the Continental Association seemed to herald became the primary concern of men who disliked McDougall and others like him. The activism of socially inferior men disturbed those accustomed to ruling society.[8] Basic to this concern was the constant appeal of McDougall and others to the ultimate power of "the people." Few disagreed with the proposition that society and government rested upon the consent of the governed; the idea was ingrained in English Whig thought. But once the structure of government was determined, the elite insisted that an essential distinction existed between those who ruled and those who were ruled. In the mind of the elite, both reason and experience provided sufficient proofs that the generality of men were dominated by their emotions and were incapable of making those decisions necessary to preserve order and peace in society. The ends of society and thus of government—order, peace, and safety of property—could be entrusted only to men of ability and learning, who had by means of reason conquered the baser instincts of human nature, and who had demonstrated the ownership of property a sufficient "interest" in the well-being of society to be charged with ruling it. Rulers were privileged men, exercising a paternal stewardship over and in the name of all men.[9]

Public mass meetings and committees which attempted to circumvent society's rulers and institutions were expressions of anarchy. Moreover, allowing men from society's lower orders into places of authority blurred the prized distinction between the governors and the governed and endangered the concept of stewardship. When McDougall insisted that the populace at large should fully participate in decision-making, discussing and weighing the soundness of measures and judging the fitness of men, he seemed to be advocating nothing less than social and political revolution. It was no comfort that the appeal to the people was made in the name of liberty and that the disorders resulting from protests were justified by the cause of freedom. The seizure or destruction of property, the disrespect shown to lawful authority and its officers, the establishment of committees and congresses outside the regular system of government—all were more fearful than British taxation because they struck at those very restraining forces which had originally raised men out of the jungle into civil society. Under such circumstances, McDougall's adversaries reasoned, liberty became license and freedom became chaos, creating a state in which neither property nor life were safe. The only alternative to McDougall's leadership and its excesses, the frightened leaders of New York argued, was to take refuge in the arms of British power. "No," the Reverend Samuel Seabury exclaimed, "if I must be enslaved, let it be by a King at least, and not by a parcel of upstart lawless committeemen. If I must be devoured, let me be devoured by the jaws of a lion, and not gnawed to death by rats and vermin." [10]

McDougall was not the irresponsible demogogue that some men thought him to be, satisfying his ambition for popularity and power by unleashing the passions of the lower orders. But he was indeed becoming a revolutionary. The radical variant of English Whiggism provided him with an explanation for the mother country's repeated efforts to impose unconstitutional taxes and regulatory practices upon the colonies. Only the abuse of governmental power, the design of corrupt ministers and politicians to subvert the constitution in order to satisfy their lust for power, could possibly account for the incessant attacks upon the rights of Englishmen over colonial protests and pleas for relief. Once convinced he was right, McDougall never again doubted that parliament and the ministry had for a decade conspired to destroy colonial rights of self-government; nor did he believe that Britain would alter her course except when compelled to do so by a countervailing force.

Implicit in McDougall's activities since 1769 was a belief that the public interest took precedence over any single element in society and that the people at large were capable of protecting themselves. If the political system went sour, if leaders could not be trusted because of greed and corruption, only the people could be relied upon to purge government of its venality and decay. Thus, appeals to the people for support were more than tactical maneuvers of local politics; by 1774, popular appeals were acknowledgment that the people were the best and final judges in all public matters involving the general happiness of society. In the litany of radical Whiggery, virtue and commonsense wisdom existed in the mass of men, and if freedom was to be saved, that virtue had to be harnessed and directed against those who pursued only their own narrow interests at the expense of the public good. As McDougall's opposition to Britain stiffened after the closing of the port of Boston, his dependence upon the general populace to defend American liberty became a paramount feature of his popular leadership and took explicit form in the extralegal structure of committees and congresses elected by the people. In promoting that particular structure to organize America's defense, he committed himself to the revolutionary tenent that the people possessed an inherent right to assure their own happiness and could exercise that right even against their rulers. That order and tranquility were disrupted, that the values of place and deference were challenged and then brushed aside, that committees and congresses were the seeds of separation from Britain—all were of only passing concern compared to the imperative need and right of the people to defend their own liberty. In the autumn of 1774 the cause of liberty, to McDougall's way of thinking, demanded that the Continental Association become a reality in New York.[11]

From the first meeting of the Committee of Inspection on November 28, 1774, to the following April, McDougall had to surmount a number of obstacles as he sought to bring New York to a level of organization comparable to that reached in other colonies. The Association, primary object of attack from crown supporters, or Loyalists as they were now being called, passed through a series of tests, each of which raised doubts whether New Yorkers would follow the Continental Congress or devise a policy of their own. "As this is their last game," Hugh Hughes commented, "we may be assured that they will play the severities." [12] Colonists outside New York also doubted whether New York would stand by Congress. As Thomas Young of Boston wrote to John Lamb, "I understand by all hands that you have an over-proportion of tories with you to any place on the continent." And William Hooper in Philadelphia reported that when he told his friends that New York was behind the Association, they viewed it "as a kind of change which required the immediate and almighty interposition to effect." [13]

The first crisis came almost at once when James Duane, never a warm friend of economic sanction, surprisingly urged the adoption of a boycott greater than the Association's non-importation provisions. "I thoroughly suspected," McDougall informed Samuel Adams, "that his end in contending for this severe construction of the association was to first destroy it." To adopt sanctions greater than those approved by Congress "would be construed a wanton exercise of power, void of wisdom or justice, and the restless miscreants who are eagerly waiting to improve the least misconduct would not fail to lead the sufferers to charge the committees impolitic measures on the congress, and brand them all with folly and injustice." McDougall was convinced that the Association would not last a week under those circumstances; ironically, Lieutenant Governor Colden agreed.[14]

Although the Committee of Inspection rejected Duane's arguments and agreed to follow Congress, the Association and its supporters faced a second test in January, 1775, when the Assembly began its regular session. According to Colden, "Many people hope the assembly will take a rational and conciliatory method of settling the unhappy differences. Under a persuasion that they may do a great deal of good, and cannot make matters much worse than they are, I have called them to meet the 10th of January." [15] Men on both sides of the Association now looked upon the Assembly as the new battleground. Anti-Congress men hoped that the Assembly would condemn the intercolonial meeting and thereby deal a fatal blow to the economic boycott. Pro-Congress men saw in the session an opportunity to bring to the Association the stature and sanction it needed to succeed. And the fact that Congressional supporters looked to the Assembly for assistance (knowing full well that it was controlled by their opponents) was a measure of the seriousness of New York's divided response to the First Continental Congress.

Unlike former sessions at which McDougall had been an attentive observer of roll-call voting, he was now concerned with higher matters than the politics of the Livingston and De Lancey factions. If the Assembly approved the Association and also elected delegates to attend the second congress scheduled to meet in May, the cause of liberty would be strengthened. It was actually a vain hope. The pro-Congress faction made its move early in the session while ten members were still absent. On the morning of January 26, before a packed gallery intended to intimidate one or two country members into deserting the De Lanceys, a motion was offered to consider the proceedings of the Congress. It was defeated by an eleven to ten vote, the first in a series of De Lancey victories. As the session wore on through February, late arriving members added strength to the majority, which easily beat back every effort to bring the Assembly over to the side of Congress.[16] McDougall had to assure Sam Adams that the "friends of liberty in and out of the house will leave no stone unturned to make the union of assemblies as complete as that of the Congress." [17]

Anti-Congress men were encouraged by the Assembly's early refusal to take up the Association, and McDougall thus noticed an immediate change in the temper of the Committee of Inspection. At a regular evening meeting at the Exchange on January 30, the Assembly's action four days earlier hung as a pall over the members. As McDougall could have predicted, Isaac Low and James Duane rose to the Assembly's defense. They argued that the Congress and the Association were private matters and that the Assembly lacked a legal basis for recognizing them. When McDougall's friend, William Goforth, later to bury one of McDougall's sons in the Canadian wilderness, proposed that the other colonies be assured that New York would adhere to the Association, the Committee of Inspection could not agree.[18] It was increasingly evident that the Association was barely alive in New York, and it had yet to face its severest test. Probably to lift his own spirits, as well as to maintain face with other popular leaders, McDougall wrote to Samuel Adams that New York was firmly behind Congress. But in response to the suggestion that New York follow Massachusett's example and form independent militia companies, he warned that his colony would be the last to take up the sword. "From the knowledge I have of the state of this colony," he informed Boston, "I am morally certain, they will not fly to arms as a colony; but by the influence of one of these contingencies vizt. The attack of the troops on your people; fear of the other colonies, or stimulated by their example, in taking up arms." He gave a final caution to his Boston friends: "Tis incumbent on me to inform you, what you are to expect from us, least your ignorance of this, might lead you into measures, which might be fatal to yourselves and to all America." [19] Thus he knew that greater unity of purpose was first necessary before any further steps could be taken, that if he could not instill life into the Association little else was possible in New York.

Until February 1, 1775, the economic sanctions of the Association were not difficult to implement and enforce, but after that date a full boycott of imports was required. McDougall knew that the Association now faced its greatest challenge. Would the trading community obey the non-importation regulations? McDougall was uncertain, for he recognized that some merchants from the beginning had wanted no part of a boycott, and others were doubtful at best. The shrill protests of Loyalist writers added to the uncertainty in the city. Four days before the deadline for complying with the Association, the Assembly had refused even to discuss the actions of Congress. Then, with only two days remaining, leading members of the city committee charged with enforcing the Association could not announce with certainty that

New York would adopt non-importation. The expected arrival of two vessels sometime in early February would be the test. With surprising calmness, McDougall assured Samuel Adams that when the first ship arrived, "I have no doubt of our giving you a good account of her." [20]

McDougall had an alternative to legislative sanction. If merchants would not submit to non-importation, intimidation was the only answer. It would be necessary to stimulate their fear of violence, a strategy at once evident upon the arrival of the first ship. The *James* out of Glasgow, carrying coal and drygoods, docked on February 2 and became the first test. The city committee warned the captain not to break cargo and to leave quickly. A throng of men milled about the docks; it was certain that they would not hesitate to attack the vessel if unloading began. Captain Watson caught the meaning and moved the *James* four miles out into the Bay, where he was watched by a sloop carrying armed men commanded by Isaac Sears. But when he brought his ship back on Thursday, February 9, under the navy's protection, he was promptly seized by the Sons of Liberty and paraded through town. Two days later the *James* sailed for Jamaica under the vigilant watch of Sears' armed men. [21]

A London vessel, *Beulah*, expected any day, offered another opportunity for the Loyalists to attempt to break the Association. Mc-Dougall recognized the challenge, and when the vessel appeared in the sea approaches to the city in the early evening of February 17, the patriots were ready. Harbor pilots were warned to stay away from her, while Sears and his armed sloop blocked the *Beulah's* course into the harbor. She would not even be allowed near the docks. [22] The next day Robert and John Murray, consignees of part of the cargo, petitioned the Committee of Inspection for an exemption. Even though the petition was supported by six members who argued that the cargo had been ordered before the Association's adoption, the committee rejected the plea and ordered Captain McBussell back to London or to another port. But McBussell was of the same Scottish mettle as Mc-Dougall; he intended to land his cargo in defiance of the committee's decision. [23] He remained at anchor in the Narrows for three weeks, through storms and high seas and under the guard of the Liberty Boys. On March 5 under threatening skies Captain McBussell raised sail as if he intended to go out to sea. Sears followed him as far as Sandy Hook when a sudden storm forced the Liberty Boys to find calmer waters. With Sears out of sight, another vessel carried off part of the *Beulah's* cargo to Staten Island from whence the Murrays planned to bring it into the city. When the *Beulah* finally left under fair winds the next day, McDougall suspected something had gone wrong; inquiries along the docks of New York and Elizabethtown, New Jersey, where Robert Murray operated a store, revealed that the goods had entered the city.[24] McDougall took a hard attitude toward the Murrays, insisting that the whole story be published and the public urged to boycott their store. The Committee of Inspection agreed. It was an important victory for the Association.[25] "The success which the violent party have had in preventing these vessels from landing their cargoes here," Lieutenant Governor Colden informed Lord Dartmouth, "has given them great spirits, and is a strong counterpoise, to the conduct of the Assembly. Your Lordships will believe it has chagrined me a good deal." [26]

It was indeed a victory for McDougall and the Association, but anti-Congress men were hardly in full flight. The problem of electing a delegation to the second Continental Congress would be the severest test of all, for the first Congress had broadened and deepened the opposition of those who opposed further activities against the mother country. Added to those who wanted nothing at all to do with Congress were those who sought to confine its membership to men of stature who would guide it toward more temperate measures. At first it was hoped that the Assembly would simplify matters by making a selection of its own, thereby eliminating the need for an election that would surely be divisive and unpredictable. Although McDougall was pessimistic about favorable Assembly action, he had no choice but to let matters run their course, hoping that the cause would be advanced whatever happened. Writing to Boston two weeks before the Assembly session, he reported that "We have not chosen delegates to meet the next Congress, waiting till we know whether the assembly will do it or not. If they don't, we shall be able with more ease to bring about a provincial congress." [27] When the Assembly on February 23 refused to appoint delegates, McDougall's plan of calling a provincial convention came much closer to implementation.[28]

McDougall never explained why he advocated creating a provincial convention in 1774 or early 1775, but he probably saw the need to broaden New York's revolutionary base by including rural and upstate areas. His own position in New York City was still uncertain, and possibly he hoped that by bringing in the outlying areas, he would find more support. This was a variation of the tactics he used in allying himself with the New England radicals. A provincial convention would also bring greater credibility and weight to the Association and any other policies of Congress, a status not attainable by patriot activity in the capital alone. There was, perhaps, another reason for McDougall's advocacy of a convention. He was constantly apologetic to his friends outside the colony that New York was trailing developments already under way in other colonies. He continually assured them that his colony would not desert the cause.[29] It almost seems as though he feared a loss of stature in the informal network of revolutionary leaders if he could not accomplish what they had already achieved. In the acceleration of revolutionary activity, from local committees to an inter-colonial congress, from the Association to committees to enforce the anti-British sanctions, a provincial convention was a step to a higher level of leadership in New York. Perhaps McDougall saw that his own star was attached to the success or failure of the continental revolutionary movement. A provincial convention might bring New York more strongly into that unified movement.

The Committee of Inspection moved as quickly as possible. The people were invited to meet to decide whether deputies should be named to a provincial convention for selecting Congressional delegates, or, in lieu of that, to devise an alternate method. McDougall wanted a short public discussion, for the longer the "enemies of liberty" had to work among the people, the more difficult it would be to put the convention over.[30] He was nearly right. Two days after the public announcement of March 1, Loyalists gathered at the widow Montagne's tavern and condemned the Committee of Inspection's action. Under the leadership of John Thurman, they wanted everything delayed until the arrival of the spring ships, which would unquestionably bring news of an imperial settlement, making unnecessary more congresses and conventions. The meeting also urged the people to assemble on Monday morning to march in a body to the public meeting at the Exchange and prevent a "hasty" decision.[31] It was as much as McDougall expected from Thurman, who earlier in the day said that he had had enough of deputies. McDougall was ready for Thurman and his supporters. He met his friends Saturday night at widow Van De Water's tavern to plan a march for Monday morning, and sometime Sunday evening clubs and staves were collected in a cellar near the Exchange in case of an emergency.[32]

There are no estimates of the crowd's size that Monday noon. It was later described as very large, but whatever the number it was an impressive gathering of government officials, military officers, merchants, and Sons of Liberty. McDougall did not march that morning, for the Committee of Inspection gathered as a group at the Exchange to wait for the people to appear. The Liberty Boys arrived with their usual flourish. They met at the Liberty Pole near Van De Water's house and hoisted a "Union" flag, and with Isaac Sears, back from his seawatch, in the lead and accompanied by trumpets, fifes, drums and two standard bearers, they marched down Nassau Street, past City Hall to Broad Street, gathering people along the way. Meanwhile, the group which intended to oppose the proceedings started from Widow Montagne's, led by Mayor Whitehead Hicks, seven members of the Governor's Council, General Robertson and his aides, in the city to procure supplies for the British troops in Boston, and Captain Jacobs and other naval officers from a visiting warship. As they neared the exchange at Dock and Broad Streets, they found the Liberty Boys ahead of them, and the scene became a melee of pushing and shoving men as the two groups fought for the best position at the front of the meeting.[33] But what began with so much display dissolved into a dull affair, tightly controlled by the Committee of Inspection. The crowd approved the idea of calling a convention and authorized the committee to nominate eleven men for endorsement at a future time. The Liberty Boys paraded back to the Liberty Pole to celebrate their victory, and that evening the committee selected the five old congressional delegates and six others, including McDougall, to serve in the provincial convention.

Anti-convention men raged over the way the March 6 public meeting was conducted. They accused the patriots of purposely avoiding a city poll because they knew a convention would be defeated and the old delegation re-elected. Even though he had chaired the March 6 meeting, Isaac Low announced that he was opposed to a convention and would therefore not serve either as a convention deputy or as a congressional delegate. Now committed to the election of convention deputies, the Committee of Inspection ordered the city's freeholders and freemen to vote at City Hall on March 15.[34] Ironically, Lieutenant Governer Colden gave the Committee unexpected assistance two days before the city voted. Colden had received an order from Lord Dartmouth to prevent the election of delegates to any more congresses, so the lieutenant governor asked his Council whether he should issue a formal proclamation forbidding the people to participate in extralegal elections. Although it was decided that a proclamation would only drive people into the arms of the extremists, the Council urged Colden to show Dartmouth's letter to the Assembly, still in session, as an approval of the De Lanceys' anti-Congress stand. The decision was a blunder. Within two hours after the Council adjourned, the contents of Dartmouth's letter were known throughout the city and "animated many for a congress, who were before luke warm." [35] When the city voted on March 15, convention deputies were approved 826 to 163. [36]

The city quieted after the patriot victory. McDougall became involved in a quarrel over the exportation of boards, straw, and nails to the British army in Boston, but it was only a minor disturbance while the city waited for the convention to meet. [37] When the deputies from seven of the colony's twelve counties finally assembled on April 20, the work of naming delegates to the Second Continental Congress was quickly completed. [38] Although it had been earlier hinted in the newspaper that McDougall wanted to go to Philadelphia, there is no evidence that he pushed himself as a candidate. Highest leadership even among Whigs still went to those of established wealth and social position, and McDougall had to content himself with the more practical matters of safeguarding the cause at home. He could always, of course, go it alone, as he had done before.

# Chapter Seven
# The Provincial Congress

Israel Bissel reached New York around two o'clock Sunday afternoon, April 23, the day after the provincial convention finished its work. His account of bloody fighting between Minute Men and British regulars in Massachusetts shocked and excited the city, reverberating throughout the colony.[1] The armed clash at Lexington and Concord dramatically transformed the political climate in New York. To some men the British raid was the final proof of Britain's intention to impose a military despotism upon America; to others the dream of peace dissolved into a nightmare of rebellion and civil war. McDougall's reaction was instinctive: New York must prepare immediately to defend herself. He quickly discovered, however, that forming a military defense was far different from organizing opposition to Britain and enforcing the Association's restraints upon trade. Military preparations demanded more direct action. Men had to shoulder arms and march and perhaps die; they had to be armed, fed, and quartered; war supplies had to be purchased; and the people, somehow, had to pay for it all. In the months ahead, McDougall attacked the problems of defense with energy; he never had a second thought about the fact that New York's military activities amounted to rebellion. The fighting in Massachusetts seemed to mean that the mother country was determined to destroy American freedom. Thus, force would be met with force. But McDougall was not opposed to reconciliation with Britain. Influenced by Livingston Whigs, whom he generally admired, he would save the empire if New York's and America's self-determination could be preserved. Until such an accommodation was reached, however, he would stand fast against British military tyranny.

News of Lexington and Concord opened the floodgates of popular activity in New York's provincial capital. There was no restraining Isaac Sears, John Lamb, and Marinus Willett that Sunday as they led a mob first to the docks where two ships were emptied of provisions intended for the British army in Boston, and later that evening to the City Hall, where five hundred and fifty muskets were taken and hauled five blocks away to John Street and Abraham Van Wyck's backyard.[2] Squads of men shouldering muskets awkwardly learned military drill and constantly marched about the city; postriders were stopped and letters inspected for anti-American sentiments. James Rivington, Loyalist printer, fled to the safety of a warship, and Myles Cooper, president of King's College, was saved from a mob by Alexander Hamilton. Cooper quickly joined other Anglican clergymen in hiding.[3] On Friday, customs collector Andrew Elliot was confronted by three hundred and fifty men armed with muskets and was forced to surrender his keys to Isaac Sears, who then declared the port of New York closed. Loyalists were terror-stricken and so "humbled as only to sigh or complain in whispers." In the afternoon, shock waves hit the city again when a Philadelphia newspaper accused Oliver De Lancey and several others of writing to England for troops to be used for crushing New York's patriots. Only the influence of prominent Whigs prevented an angry mob from holding a lynching party.[4]

Little is known of McDougall's activities during that critical week. There is no doubt that he felt as outraged as other men over Lexington and Concord or that he approved the city's martial spirit as a necessary precaution against a similar attack in New York. His prediction in March proved correct that it would take a dramatic bloodletting before New Yorkers would take up arms, and before the week-end, he joined Isaac Sears, John Lamb, and one hundred other men in forming a military association "to defend liberty, property, and country, against any power whatsoever, that may attempt to invade the same." [5] But he also insisted that the city affairs required greater order and regularity and that the old Committee of Inspection lacked the power to direct the people's military ardor. When the Committee of Sixty met, McDougall urged the creation of a larger general city committee and a new Provincial Congress to adopt measures for the common safety. By the end of the week a provincial congress had been proposed to the counties, and on April 29 a new general committee of one hundred members (soon to be called the Committee of One Hundred) and twenty deputies to the proposed congress, were elected with hardly a ripple of opposition.[6] McDougall was chosen for both bodies, and he signed willingly a new association by which the people pledged to follow the orders of the city committee and the provincial and continental congresses.[7]

Order and quiet returned by Monday, May 1, or at least the danger of random violence passed. But the city had undergone a profound change from which it would not soon recover. Partisan strife, so dominant in the past, went underground, and only the hardiest Loyalists failed to pay lipservice to the new city committee and association. "People here," Robert R. Livingston informed his wife, "are perfectly fearless I mean the whigs and the tories turn whig so fast that they will soon be as much united as they are in the Massachusetts Bay." [8] The Whigs were triumphant, free of the necessity of making compromises to achieve even limited goals. But Loyalism was not dead; it was only temporarily silenced. Soon it would re-emerge as the implacable enemy of the patriots, waiting for the right moment to settle old political scores and to strike down those who would raise the standard of rebellion.

Of greater importance than loyalist activity was the prospect of British troops coming to New York to uphold imperial authority. The helplessness of Whigs to resist such a landing was uppermost in Mc-Dougall's mind in the weeks following Lexington and Concord. Until the Provincial Congress met on May 22, he attended the daily sessions of the new city committee and became one of its dominant figures, sponsoring more resolutions and serving on more subcommittees than any other member. Isaac Sears and John Lamb might storm the streets and Isaac Low and Henry Remsen might become committee chairmen, but McDougall found his place managing the military details of the local revolutionary organization.

To McDougall defense preparations took priority over everything else. Little immediate danger existed, since the one hundred British troops quartered in the city had more to fear from the populace than vice versa. But rumors swept the city that troops were on their way, and all knew that the next sail off Sandy Hook could well be a troop transport from Boston or England.[9] McDougall threw himself into the job of making New York ready. Actively involved in nearly every military measure adopted between May 1 and May 22, he found little or no opposition from the more cautious members as the Committee of One Hundred virtually became a council of war.[10] Many things had to be done. Muskets, powder, and shot in the city were inventoried; cannon in private hands were removed to places of safekeeping;

the seven newly-formed volunteer militia companies, organized in the frantic days after April 23, were brought under committee control; and military drills were started among the city's male population. The committee also upheld law and order in the city. McDougall supported James Duane's resolution, by which assistance was pledged to the regular magistrates trying to keep the city peaceful, and he assisted in drafting regulations for a military night watch drawn from the volunteer companies.[11] Like other men of property, McDougall did not intend to turn armed thugs loose on the city; nor was he interested in using the committee's powers to conduct a political purge. While he wanted to know who in the city refused to sign the April 29 association and thought that some sort of policy toward them was needed, he was opposed to mobs singling out individuals for special punishment. Only the Committee of One Hundred and the Continental Congress had power to declare persons dangerous. One category of men did disturb McDougall: those who refused to sell arms and ammunition to the city committee and those who sold weapons to Loyalists. The One Hundred agreed with McDougall that such persons were the country's enemies.[12] In addition to all of this, McDougall was a member of a sub-committee created to handle the voluminous correspondence from other revolutionary groups, and to deal with special problems of harbor traffic. The latter was an easy assignment; by the end of May, New York's harbor was empty except for the ominous presence of the *Asia*, a warship of sixty-four guns.[13]

The city committee's defense preparations were an emotional response to Lexington and Concord. Stimulated both by anger and fear, Whigs anxiously sought to arm themselves for a battle in their own streets, but after three weeks of activity, it was evident that the city lacked the physical resources to cope with British troops. Everything was lacking, but gunpowder was the article most needed.[14] When a startling request for aid came from Albany, the shortage of supplies everywhere in the colony assumed greater importance and raised vexing political questions.[15]

The call for help from Albany was prompted by the successful expedition of Connecticut and Massachusetts men against the British posts at Ticonderoga and Crown Point on Lake George, necessitating a request for supplies and additional men to go north.[16] The New York City committee faced a dilemma. Whigs asked themselves whether they should give indirect approval to an offensive operation against crown property by sending supplies northward. The military activity so far had been predicated on New York's need to defend herself from attack, but what had happened at the northern forts was quite different. If those forays were condoned, New York would be making war upon Great Britain.

McDougall found himself in the minority when he argued that New York should immediately confer with Albany on sending a reinforcement to Lake George. He thus met his first defeat in the city committee. A majority favored handing over the problem to the Provincial Congress, and the majority's mixed motives for doing so traced the outlines of future problems.[17] Hopeful that Anglo-American differences could be reconciled, some Whigs resisted any action that would render an accommodation impossible to achieve, and they looked to the forthcoming Provincial Congress to take the lead in reconciliation. Still other Whigs felt that Crown Point and Ticonderoga posed military problems far too important and involved for local committees to deal with; the Lake George situation and other military matters were opportunities to elevate the Provincial Congress into a position of superiority over county and city organizations. McDougall neither rejected the hope of reconciliation nor favored local autonomy over provincial unity, but he saw in postponement a danger that nothing would be done. After the defeat of his motion in the city committee, he too looked toward the Provincial Congress.

If McDougall found himself busy as a member of the Committee of One Hundred, the Provincial Congress was even more demanding of his time. From the opening meeting on May 22, 1775, to the session's adjournment on July 8, Congress met twice daily Monday through Saturday, with an occasional Sunday meeting. A day's work was long enough, but McDougall took on more than most members. Only Gouverneur Morris served on as many committees as did McDougall, and his assignments concerned basic questions of supply, military organization, ways and means, and reconciliation.[18] Later, when he assumed command of New York's First Regiment, he had the added burden of supervising the many details of establishing an army unit.

Although many problems confronted the sixty-eight men at the Provincial Congress's first meeting on May 22, the first issue before the deputies was a move to free the colony from outside interference. Isaac Low from the capital and youthful Gouverneur Morris from Westchester County offered a motion that recognized the Continental

Congress but affirmed New York's right to control its own "internal policies." It tested the determination of everyone on whether New York would organize its own military resistance to Great Britain or follow some other line of conduct. McDougall was with the majority in rejecting an independent role for New York.[19]

An important factor in the defeat of the Low-Morris resolution was the Lake George situation, which involved New Englanders, New Yorkers, and the Continental Congress. Ticonderoga and Crown Point were of immediate military importance because they were strategically located to sever the Montreal-Albany-New York City link. But the forts were also in the vicinity of territory long a matter of dispute between New York and the New England colonies, the scene of rival land claimants and occasional clashes. A number of New York Whigs were heavy speculators in the "Hampshire Grants" region (now Vermont), and even McDougall had invested in several Argyle farms, near the Hudson less than 100 miles south of Ticonderoga.[20] Now Crown Point and Ticonderoga were held by the very men who had given New York authorities so much trouble in the past, Ethan Allen and Seth Warner and their Green Mountain Boys. Their appeal to Albany, the New England governments, and the Continental Congress for aid had to be answered.[21] The national Congress on May 18 asked New York's Provincial Congress to send assistance, drawing upon Massachusetts and Connecticut for troops if needed. The meaning of this request was clear: Congress wanted the artillery from the forts, and if New York refused to act, other colonies would be asked to step in.[22] If this happened, the New England troops might resolve the land dispute once and for all. New York could thus no longer afford to pretend that the situation was only an "internal" matter to be dealt with by herself alone. The preeminent role of the Continental Congress had to be acknowledged, even if it meant a level of political and military activity which some Whigs wished to avoid.

McDougall and his fellow provincial delegates thus followed the lead of the Continental Congress. Committees were formed to succor Lake George and remove the artillery, deal with the Northern Indians, fortify the Highlands and New York City, collect supplies, and enlist a 3,000-man army.[23] From the beginning, the Provincial Congress was aware that every military act carried profound financial implications, and at its fifth meeting, McDougall was named to a committee to consider the possibility of a currency emission. The committee's report of May 30 emphasized that only paper money, issued under the authority of the Continental Congress, would enable New York to pay for its defense measures. In addition to meeting an urgent financial need, a continental currency had the advantage of creating a "new bond of union to the Associated Colonies," binding people together to redeem the currency. The Provincial Congress approved the scheme and sent it off to the colony's delegates in Philadelphia for presentation to the Continental Congress.[24] Until Congress acted, however, expenses were paid from the regular colonial treasury, loans from merchants, and money advanced by the capital's city committee. Another common method of financing was to assign a member the responsibility of purchasing certain articles from his own resources, to be reimbursed later by the Provincial Congress. McDougall did this several times.[25] Whatever the means employed, New York was engaged in activity that would have been impossible a few weeks earlier.

A tax levy was an obvious solution to New York's financial problem, and it is significant that the committee on currency failed to mention taxation as an alternative. To have imposed taxes, whether to support a currency or to otherwise obtain funds, would have required that the Provincial Congress function as a legislature, to convert itself into a revolutionary government whose goal was independence. This New York Whigs had no intention of doing at the moment. It was clear at the outset that a majority in New York viewed the Provincial Congress's purpose as restricted to defending American liberty from British military power. Beyond the objective of defense the Congress could not go without directly challenging the very structure and authority of the colony's established government. New York Whigs in mid-1775 were not yet ready for that step, and the Provincial Congress, therefore, carefully avoided measures which implied a complete rejection of royal authority. The people were told to exercise restraint. When the king's military stores at Turtle Bay were seized by a city gang, the Provincial Congress ordered their return and paid for the transportation. Fort George in the capital was not to be touched. Even putting the troops into uniforms was of questionable legality.[26] Thus the Provincial Congress was caught in the dilemma of how to create an army to resist British arms while avoiding the appearance of rebelling for independence. It was an impossible policy. Livingston, an active Whig since 1764, expressed the sentiments of other New

York Whigs, including McDougall, when he wrote, "Every good man wishes that America may remain free: In this I join heartily; at the same time I do not desire, she should be wholly independent of the mother country. How to reconcile these jarring principles, I profess I am altogether at a loss." [27]

One answer to the dilemma was to heal the breach between America and Britain by reconciling imperial differences. This subject was taken up eight days after the Provincial Congress opened. Encouragement was drawn from Lord North's offer made in the House of Commons in February to exempt any colony from taxation if it would provide funds for the common defense and support civil government, an offer New Yorkers never had an opportunity to act upon because of the turmoil of Lexington and Concord.[28] Motions were offered on May 30 and June 2 calling for a plan of accommodation, and the report on reconciliation—most of it written by Gouverneur Morris—was approved on June 24 with only minimal opposition. Restating constitutional principles proclaimed in New York since 1764, the report suggested a modified version of Joseph Galloway's "American Congress" as a means to settle future difficulties. The Provincial Congress ordered that the plan be sent to its Philadelphia delegates for their information and guidance.[29]

McDougall's response to reconciliation was a mixture of apprehension and approval. When it was first proposed, he opposed efforts to divert attention from the urgent business of preparing the colony's defenses. At that time, in late May and early June, 1775, much had already been done for which he could take some credit. But one measure essential to the colony's defense—creation of an army—dragged on. Without a military establishment, organized, equipped, and ready to fight, the Provincial Congress had little reason to exist. When McDougall urged that New York request discretionary power from the Continental Congress to deal with Fort George in the capital, the soft attitude of the majority prevailed and the suggestion was ignored. When the capital's Liberty Boys, under Marinus Willett, raided the baggage train belonging to British troops evacuating the city, that same timid majority ordered the return of the arms taken, even though there was a critical shortage of military supplies in the colony.[30]

In these as in other matters, McDougall favored action promoting the colony's military readiness, but he was not opposed to peace. He worked on the committee preparing a plan of accommodation, and joined a large majority in declining to subsidize the manufacture of saltpeter because the subsidy implied that military activities might last two years.[31] By the third week of June when New York's army finally began to take shape—on paper at least—McDougall saw no reason why New York should not outline those conditions upon which an Anglo-American reconciliation depended. He was thus among the supporters of the reconciliation report of June 24, while John Morin Scott and Isaac Sears, along with four others, were the only avowed opponents of an accommodation. McDougall's support of reconciliation might appear as an abandonment of his old allies at the very moment when he had achieved a measure of power and respectability. Probably a more accurate view is that he recognized as in the past that concessions to political reality were sometimes required. New Yorkers, or at least those in the Provincial Congress, were not prepared to blindly accept an aggressive military defense; like Robert R. Livingston, they clung to the hope of an accommodation with England at the same time that they reluctantly prepared to make war upon her. McDougall it seems, unlike Sears, Scott and a few others, accepted renewed efforts at reconciliation as the price for the creation of a badly needed army in New York. On June 27, McDougall got his army, which moved him closer, despite his support of reconciliation, toward war and independence.[32]

Fear of British troops landing in New York stimulated the Provincial Congress's military activity. Despite the seven volunteer companies under the authority of the capital's city committee and the isolated units in the Albany area, the colony was virtually defenseless and at the mercy of any invading force.[33] A small Connecticut force under Colonel Daniel Wooster was nearby, but the colony's main reliance had to be on its own efforts. Even if the Provincial Congress had been of one mind on military policy, which it was not, the task of preparing the colony was enormous. A main concern was still the shortage of powder and weapons. McDougall and Sears started an inventory of saltpeter stocks among New York's apothecaries. When gunpowder was received, McDougall was given charge of the precious supply, most of which he forwarded to the Continental army camp at Cambridge, Massachusetts, where the need for it was even greater. He also made arrangements to import a large quantity of powder from the West Indies. Artillery was needed as badly as powder, and under

McDougall's supervision attempts were made to cast a few experimental pieces. When New York's army came into being, gunsmiths were needed to repair the firing locks on the odd collection of civilian muskets. Even the supply of such items as steel ramrods and bayonets caused concern.[34]

New York's army finally came to life on June 30, 1775, with the appointment of four regimental colonels, one of whom was Alexander McDougall. The army had been created to protect the inhabitants from British soldiers and to assist the Continental army, a course of action urged on New Yorkers by the Continental Congress and Whigs in other colonies. McDougall's acceptance of command of the First Regiment, under the authority of New York, was in keeping with his conviction that Britain's latest policy of coercion was a fatal blow to American liberties and had to be resisted at all costs. His appointment was certainly political, a recognition of his importance to the revolutionary movement, but it was also an expression of confidence that his essential restraint could be relied upon. There was little fear that he might act impetuously, as, for instance Isaac Sears might.[35]

Within days, companies began filling. Enlistments were to last until December 31. McDougall's two sons, commissioned as junior officers, assisted the recruiting efforts. Supplying the companies was a scrounging operation. The men were armed with muskets taken from the royal armory on April 23 and were living in the upper barracks near the commons. From the colony's barrack-master, an office created years earlier during the French wars, McDougall obtained other necessities; he also borrowed £1,000 in cash on his own credit from merchant John Broome to pay his troops. The Provincial Congress had authorized him to purchase raw materials to make muskets, but he discovered that the city's gunsmiths were reluctant to work for the new army because it lacked money.[36] That he was without military experience, other than his privateering of fifteen years ago, was not crucial; basic organization, discipline, and drill maneuvers were taken from Thomas Symes' *Military Guide for Young Officers*. And what he and his citizen-soldiers lacked in training was compensated for by enthusiasm. Yet within a short time, McDougall discovered that the first rush of enthusiasm quickly wore off among the recruits, most of whom were homesick and unaccustomed to the discipline of army life. Many simply went home. It was the start of a practice that was to plague the American army to the end of the war.[37] The war had hardly begun, and already McDougall was learning the hard realities of command.

Within a month, the colony's four regiments became part of an invading army sent by the Continental Congress into Canada. At the time of their creation, New York's army and McDougall's regiment came under the command of General George Washington and Philip Schuyler, now a major-general in the new Continental army. Along with other members of the Provincial Congress, McDougall welcomed General Washington and his party to New York on June 25, 1775. The Virginian dined at Leonard Lispenard's country home and reviewed the city's militia units.[38] General Washington went on to the main army at Cambridge, Massachusetts, and Schuyler remained to assume command of the Northern Department and the Canadian expedition. As early as July 3, Schuyler had urged the Provincial Congress to send troops northward as soon as companies were formed, but it was not until the end of the month that McDougall's recruiting and supply efforts produced four companies sufficiently armed and equipped to assume active duty. Writing to Schuyler on August 9, he complained that the shortage of muskets was the principal reason for his failure to fill his regiment, and he insisted that there was little that could be done until arms were procured from outside the colony. Even with those handicaps McDougall's troops, led by Lieutenant Colonel Rudolphus Ritzema and including McDougall's sons, were the first of New York's regular establishment to reach Ticonderoga. McDougall remained in New York City while his regiment went north, company by company, to take part in the attack upon Canada. At first he stayed behind to complete his regiment, assuring Schuyler in early August that he would head north as soon as possible.[39] But by the end of August, when only two companies remained unfilled, he found that New York's initial military zeal was gone and that interest in reconciliation was growing. McDougall thus stayed out of the Canadian expedition to deal with pressing matters at home, and to guard against the possibility of allowing the protest momentum to wane. As he later described the situation to Philip Schuyler, "the temper of the colony was such, in and out of doors, that [it] induced many of the members of the congress, best affected to the cause of the country, to insist on my staying, to assist them; and Mr. Jay also advised me not to quit the city in that state of public affairs." Schuyler later gave his approval.[40]

A number of things made McDougall uneasy about New York's affairs: The expected attack on New York never materialized, and even
though the danger appeared greater by August, attendance in the second session of the New York Congress fell off so that some counties
lacked a quorum. Even the city's clergymen failed to appear to open
the day's proceedings with prayer, a bad omen indeed.[41] In addition,
those who opposed New York's military measures grew bolder and
seemed to pose a greater immediate threat to the capital than did the
British army, which was expected soon to sail from Boston. Rallying
around Governor William Tryon (who had returned from England on
the same day that Washington entered the capital), Loyalists in the
city, Weschester County to the north, and Queen's County across the
East River, sufficiently intimidated Whigs to cause them to adopt a
more cautious attitude. When a barge belonging to the sixty-four-gun
*Asia* was burned on the Commons and its replacement similarly
destroyed a short time later, Isaac Low even found sufficient support in
the Provincial Congress to secure passage of resolutions condemning the
outrage, although McDougall was able to soften the original intention of
declaring the persons responsible "enemies to the Country. . . ." [42]
When a suspicious newcomer, Patrick Sinclair, was found to be the new
governor of Michilimackinack, McDougall supported Isaac Sears'
demand that Sinclair be confined to Connecticut rather than on Long
Island; but the cautious majority overruled them. John De Lancey and
John Morin Scott shouted obscenities and exchanged blows with each
other over that incident, while Sears, disgusted with New York's
temporizing, left for New Haven and more profitable interests in
privateering ventures.[43]

McDougall gave no thought to quitting his political and military responsibilities, which seemed to become larger as the spirit of moderation spread wider. For three weeks in August, he served on a military
committee which had the power to direct the colony's defense, and as
a fitting climax before the New York Congress recessed on September
2, McDougall witnessed the panic of Whig leaders when the *Asia*
opened fire on the capital to drive off a party of men removing royal
artillery from the battery at the southern tip of Manhattan Island.[44]
Alarmed townspeople, fearing that the dreaded day had come, took
flight. Philip Livingston and James Duane ordered their personal and
household goods shipped up the Hudson River, and Peter Van Brugh
Livingston, President of the Provincial Congress, took his family

upriver and never returned. Meanwhile, a frantic Provincial Congress agreed with Governor Tryon that the battery should remain untouched, and the *Asia* continued to receive necessary water and food supplies.[45] When the Committee of Safety, left in charge during Congress's recess, sought to disarm Queen's County Tories by authorizing McDougall to send in two militia companies, the expedition was stopped at the last moment when it was learned how strong the Tories were. Instead, deputies went to Long Island to persuade the people to surrender their weapons peaceably. In the name of peace, the Provincial Congress later voted a disapproval of even this restrained policy.[46]

In many respects it appeared by the fall that the revolutionary movement was not going well in New York, and leaders in other colonies were becoming suspicious. McDougall wrote to Charles Thomson, secretary to the Continental Congress, in an effort to remove the suspicions against New York, and Hugh Hughes went to Philadelphia to see Thomson and other men in order to explain the colony's situation.[47] Criticism even began to fall on McDougall at home and elsewhere for failing to lead his regiment into Canada. James Duane reported from Philadelphia that McDougall's continued presence in New York was being questioned and suggested that he ask General Schuyler to give an explanation to the Continental Congress to clear the air.[48] The letter was upsetting to McDougall, especially as members of the New York Congress and other leaders such as John Jay had persuaded him to stay behind rather than take the field. As he told Schuyler, "Whether I have been of more service to the country here, in the present state of her affairs than I should have been at the posts above is not for me to determine. Certain it is I should never have taken the charge of the regiment if I had apprehended I should be detained here." Schuyler's reply was frank: "if I had thought you could have been of more service here, than at New York, I should not have hesitated one moment to have requested your attendance." This gave McDougall only momentary assurance, for a month later he learned that his oldest son, John Alexander, was dead from a fever and buried in a Canadian church yard, honored by the regiment his father was unable to lead into battle.[49] The loss of his son as well as criticism of his conduct blunted McDougall's enthusiasm for revolutionary politics, and by the early spring of the next year, military developments in New York gave him an opportunity to enter active service. He remained there until the end of the war.

# Chapter Eight
# Whigs versus Tories

McDougall rarely mentioned the death of his son, but it became a factor in his decision to take an active role in the army at the earliest possible moment. First, however, the revolutionary movement in New York had to be invigorated, stimulated to greater activity, aroused from its do-nothing timidity. As he surveyed New York's political condition, McDougall had much to complain of as fall turned into winter. When a new Provincial Congress was elected in early November, the people were unenthusiastic in most counties and were actually hostile in Richmond and Queen's. It took weeks for enough deputies to straggle in to make a quorum on December 6, 1775.[1] There was also a shortage of leaders. Some were in Philadelphia attending the Continental Congress, others were on military duty, while still others were simply absent. As McDougall reported to Schuyler, "Mr. V. B. Livingston has not attended Congress since the firing of [the] Asia; Mr. Scott has been very ill for six weeks, Mr. Thomas Smith often out of town; many of warm whigs removed to Connecticut; others of them make long faces, and the Tories impudent." [2] Even the tempestuous Isaac Sears, disgusted with conditions in New York, had moved to Connecticut in early November, prompting one Loyalist to observe that if he meant to punish the colony by his absence, "all people seem to wish he may persevere in such a punishment." [3]

At the heart of New York's troubles was a hesitancy or unwillingness on the part of New York Whigs to deal harshly with men determined to hold the colony to its old loyalty. Earlier, McDougall had tried to act against the armed Tories of Queen's County, but at the last moment he "was restrained by authority." Isaac Sears, without authority, simply took matters into his own hands. Returning from Connecticut on November 23 at the head of ninety-six mounted men,

Sears paraded down Broadway to the print shop of the Loyalist publisher James Rivington, and destroyed it. Within an hour Sears was gone, stopping on his way back to New Haven long enough to seize Reverend Samuel Seabury, arch-Loyalist writer.[4] Sears' raid did more harm than good. Many New Yorkers were outraged by the brazen foray, and it contributed to a desire "to prevent the violences of such madmen as Capt Sears which must infallibly introduce utter anarchy and confusion." [5] But as McDougall assessed the situation, the Provincial Congress was simply marking time and allowing Loyalism to spread, making outside assistance to the revolutionary movement in New York necessary. Writing to John Jay in November and again in December, 1775, McDougall urged that Pennsylvania and New Jersey troops be stationed in New York to maintain order, to root out Tories, and "to make the principle of fear, which now causes many to look back, operate in our favor. . . ." He warned Jay that two counties were already seriously infected and the contagion was spreading, endangering a third county.[6] Alarmed by these reports, the Continental Congress directed Nathaniel Hurd of New Jersey and David Waterbury of Connecticut to disarm the disaffected of Queen's County and to arrest the Tory ringleaders and send them to Philadelphia. McDougall also wrote to his friends in Stamford, Connecticut, describing the weakness of southern New York and the vulnerability of the capital to attack by either British troops or Tories. He asked that the Connecticut coastal towns keep a watch for British shipping heading south and be ready to give support to New York.[7]

There was a sense of urgency in McDougall's letters, for the political condition in the capital was worsening. The Second Provincial Congress, finally under way on December 6, 1775, recessed after only seventeen days, and the Committee of Safety acting in its place (to which McDougall was appointed) lacked a quorum to do business.[8] During the seventeen days in which the Congress sat, however, McDougall helped to head off a serious threat to the revolutionary movement. Governor William Tryon, in a public letter of December 4, had placed the Whig position in jeopardy by encouraging the people to discuss Lord North's plan of conciliation and make known their views to him in an effort to end the growing rebellion.[9] At a private meeting on December 7, a dozen members of the New York Congress conferred with William Smith on the possibility of having Tryon summon the moribund Assembly to consider another petition to the king and Parliament. McDougall learned of the meeting and was thus prepared the next day when Thomas Smith, William's brother, offered resolutions to request Governor Tryon to convene the Assembly to disclaim independence and to guarantee Tryon's safety ashore. McDougall knew that the Provincial Congress, struck with the thought of reconciliation, would not entirely reject Smith's proposals. Nevertheless, he and John Morin succeeded in persuading the Provincial Congress that New York's delegation in Philadelphia was properly informed and instructed on reconciliation; besides, they argued, if the Assembly was convened, it should be newly elected, not merely a resurrection of the body chosen in 1769.[10] When McDougall heard of Governor Tryon's secret plan to dissolve the standing Assembly and call for the immediate election of a new one, he sounded the alarm to protect against the danger of Tories being elected. Election broadsides appeared, John Holt's *Journal* carried Tory-baiting writing, and letters were sent off to country committees warning them of Tryon's plot.[11] Consequently, Whigs were nominated everywhere except in Richmond and Queen's, and thus the danger of having to deal with a potentially hostile Assembly, if it should meet, was overcome. McDougall was anxious to be elected, both to guard against future dangers from royal officials and to satisfy his role as revolutionary leader in New York. But he found time for a little campaigning. His chief opponent was John Morin Scott, who now sought to placate the city's conservative element by personally assuring Governor Tryon's safety in the capital. McDougall argued quietly that Scott's previous election defeats and his temper disqualified him for the Assembly, and on election day in February, 1776, the Whigs rejected Scott in favor of McDougall, along with John Jay, John Alsop, and Philip Livingston.[12] There is no evidence of an intense and personal campaign like those of the past, and even though McDougall and Scott had opposed each other, their future political relationship did not suffer. The Assembly election proved to be a tempest in a teapot, and McDougall's victory was an empty honor, except that it did demonstrate the strength of his revolutionary leadership in the city.

Such political concerns were quickly forgotten as military measures suddenly assumed an importance undreamed of by either the Loyalists or Whigs. New York's caution was being swept aside by events. McDougall's interests in January through March reflected the growing emphasis upon military action. His attendance in the Provincial

Congress fell off as he gave increasing time to army affairs. Still smarting from the criticism of his failure to lead his regiment into Canada, grieving over the death of his son, and following his instinctive impulse to be with the main action, he was determined to take part in the coming battle in New York.

George Washington had been warning New York for several months that a British army was expected, and Charles Lee thought the failure of the colony to prepare adequate defenses or to deal with its internal enemies was nothing less than criminal. As he implored McDougall late in October, 1775: "for heaven's sake, my dear sir, let your city no longer hold the honest in suspense by their shilly shally mode of conduct." In answer McDougall could only say that outsiders did not know the true condition of the colony, and he assured Lee that "the day is not very distant when this colony will act as decisive as any of its neighbours, and therefore I wish our friends in the army would suspend their opinion of us, for a few weeks." [13] The New York Congress, in fact, regarded overt actions against royal stores and officials in the colony as not to be worth the risk of provoking an attack upon the city. Lee was not reassured by McDougall's pleas for patience—New York made Lee "uneasy almost to distraction"—and his professional apprehension, matching his zeal for the cause, increased daily as the British made preparations to leave Boston. Lee urged Washington in early January, 1776, to take over New York's defenses, proposing that he be allowed to recruit a volunteer force in Connecticut and to join it with a New Jersey regiment under Lord Stirling. Together, the two units would be sufficient to protect New York and suppress the Tories on Long Island. Washington agreed with Lee's estimate of New York's importance and of the inability of local Whigs to seize the initiative, believing that it was crucial to "prevent the enemy from taking possession of the city of New York and the North River." The commander-in-chief, therefore, instructed Lee on January 8 to disarm the Tories, put the city into a condition of defense, and fortify the Hudson.[14]

While Lee recruited in Connecticut, with the ready concurrence of Governor Jonathan Trumbull and assisted by Isaac Sears, his assistant deputy adjutant for the expedition, New Yorkers received a taste of military action. New Jersey militia under Nathaniel Hurd, as directed by the Continental Congress, swept through Queen's County by the end of January, disarming the inhabitants unfriendly to Congress and

marching off to Philadelphia seventeen Tory ringleaders.[15] More ominous were rumors that an army under Lee was preparing to come into
the colony. Nothing official as yet had been received by the New
York Committee of Safety from either Washington or Lee, but the
capital took alarm from reports. More people left for the country,
fearing the city was soon to become a battlefield. The Committee of
Safety, consisting of only eight men and dominated by McDougall
and John Morin Scott, wrote to General Lee on January 21 demanding that he state his intentions and advising him to halt at the Connecticut border if he was coming with an army. Blandly assuring the
New York Whigs two days later that he had no hostile plans, Lee also
wrote to Washington that he expected little cooperation from New
Yorkers, who seemingly breathed the spirit of procrastination, timidity, and hysteria.[16]

McDougall agreed with Washington and Lee on the military importance of New York, but the political question of jurisdiction was of
equal concern to him. The fact that the problem of jurisdiction even
arose was symptomatic of the larger problem involving the authority
of the Continental Congress, its army, and its commander-in-chief of
less than a year, in their relations with local revolutionary groups.
Though he had earlier advised the use of armed forces from neighboring colonies to deal with New York's Loyalists, McDougall insisted
that the political integrity of New York required that such expeditions
enter only on invitation and come under the direction of the Provincial Congress.[17] When the Continental Congress learned from Lee
himself of the intended expedition into New York, New York's delegates immediately expressed the views similar to McDougall's and
demanded that a special committee be sent from Philadelphia to settle
matters of authority and jurisdiction. Thomas Lynch, Benjamin Harrison, and Andrew Allen thus arrived in New York on January 30,
1776, at about the same time that advance units of Lee's force under
Colonel David Waterbury were ready to enter the city.[18] For the next
two days, McDougall and Scott negotiated with the Congressional
Committee, demanding that Lee not be permitted to enter the colony
unless he accept in advance the authority of New York's Provincial
Congress. Only then could the question of jurisdiction be settled. Colonel Waterbury refused to concede anything, acting as though Lee's
troops comprised an army independent of all higher authority; he simply informed the Committee of Safety that he intended to bring his

McDougall's commission as a "Colonell" bore a familiar signature. —W. WRIGHT HAWKES COLLECTION, SCHAFFER LIBRARY, UNION COLLEGE

# In CONGRESS.

The DELEGATES of the UNITED COLONIES of New-Hampshire, Massachusetts-Bay, Rhode-Island, Connecticut, New-York, New-Jersey, Pennsylvania, the Counties of New-Castle, Kent, and Sussex on Delaware, Maryland, Virginia, North-Carolina, South-Carolina, and Georgia, to

*Alexander McDougall Esquire*

WE reposing especial Trust and Confidence in your Patriotism, Valour, Conduct and Fidelity, DO by these Presents, constitute and appoint you to be *Colonell of the First Battalion of New York Troops*

in the Army of the United Colonies raised for the defence of American Liberty, and for repelling every hostile Invasion thereof. You are therefore carefully and diligently to discharge the Duty of *Colonell* by doing and performing all Manner of Things thereunto belonging. And we do strictly charge and require all Officers and Soldiers under your Command, to be obedient to your Orders as *Colonell* And you are to observe and follow such Orders and Directions from Time to Time, as you shall receive from this or a future Congress of the United Colonies, or Committee of Congress, for that Purpose appointed, or Commander in Chief for the Time being of the Army of the United Colonies, or any other your superior Officer, according to the Rules and Discipline of War, in Pursuance of the Trust reposed in you. This Commission to continue in Force until revoked by this or a future Congress. *Philadelphia March 8th 1776*

By Order of the Congress

*John Hancock* PRESIDENT.

Attest. *Cha Thomson Secy*

*Number One*

men into the city and quarter them in the upper barracks. Tempers flared, and the situation was tense. Finally, the Continental Congress resolved the conflict by rejecting both New York's narrow view and General Lee's independent position; the troops coming into New York were placed under the higher command of the Congress and were told to obey accordingly. The arrangement represented an assertion of national congressional authority which proved satisfactory to General Lee and New York Whigs alike.[19]

Even though a case of gout detained Lee in New Haven until February 4, 1776, the general's harsh view of conditions in New York were well known to McDougall. As early as October, 1775, Lee had urged McDougall to seize Governor Tryon and his friends, and if the British warships bombarded the city in reprisal, the first burning house should be used as a "funeral pile" for the governor. Later, Lee asked McDougall why the city's women, children, and personal property had not been removed, if, as it was rumored, the Whigs intended to burn the city themselves rather than let it fall into the enemy's hands. "I know not whether you view these things in the same light with me," Lee wrote to McDougall, "but at least you must allow that hobbing on high heeled shoes and on low ones like the prince of Liliput gives you a mighty uncouth air." McDougall did not reply directly to Lee's blast, but he unquestionably disagreed that New York City should be destroyed in order to capture Governor Tryon. It simply was not worth the cost.[20]

Yet he could not deny the city's lack of action. For months he had labored to bring New York abreast of the other colonies, and he knew as well as anyone the difficulty of that work. His letters to Schuyler and Jay not only painted a bleak picture of conditions, but also revealed McDougall's sense of frustration at not accomplishing more. Perhaps McDougall contributed partly to New York's inertia by his sensitivity to the need of following middle-of-the-road policies that would keep Loyalists reasonably quiet while keeping New York behind the Continental Congress. But the danger that moderation might lead to inaction was clearly revealed in the desire of New Yorkers to safeguard the provincial capital at all costs. Fear of a retaliatory naval bombardment, if Loyalists or royal officials and stores were touched, seemed to paralyze New York Whigs. The city had to be preserved even if it meant inaction and the growth of loyalism. McDougall appeared to share that sentiment. As the special committee from the

Continental Congress reported from New York, "The strong apathy that holds Congress in fetters is still more forcible here."[21]

The city's worst fears seemed almost to come true on February 4, 1776, when General Lee did arrive with a large contingent of troops and announced that he would execute 100 Tories if the British warships opened fire. That evening a British frigate arrived with General Henry Clinton accompanied by two troop transports, and townspeople started immediately to evacuate the city. Fearing that shooting would start, McDougall persuaded the family of William Goforth, who was in Canada with McDougall's youngest son, to leave the city for the safety of the country; he also took charge of houses belonging to John Alsop and John Jay who were attending the Continental Congress.[22] Perhaps he even bundled his wife and daughter off to Connecticut. When no bombardment occurred, the panic subsided. But Lee stuck by his former policy; New York's Tories were to be hostages. All communication with the warships or royal officials was halted, and Governor Tryon's servant, who came ashore once a week with laundry, was seized and jailed. City Tories took flight, a consequence that McDougall could at least applaud. The city was finally rid of its enemies.[23]

Disarming Tories and harassing Tryon and the British navy were only part of Lee's responsibility. He had been ordered by Washington to build New York's defenses, and to Lee's surprise, the Committee of Safety quickly came to terms on what had to be done. McDougall worked with Lee in establishing the basic elements of New York's defense. Presumably drawing on McDougall's knowledge of the colony's waterways, Lee concluded that it was impossible to fortify New York City against a strong attack from the sea, for the surrounding water was too easily navigable to prevent heavy warships from approaching close to Manhattan. Fort George on the Battery, therefore, was useless to Americans, and if occupied by the enemy, it posed a threat to the city. Lee ordered immediately the destruction of the fort's walls facing the town and the construction of a barricade across Broadway, mounting four cannons, which were aimed at the old bastion of royal authority. Flanking barriers would be placed on every street leading into Broadway from the rivers on either side of the island, and redoubts facing the Hudson, from Trinity Church northward, would discourage warships approaching the city from the west. Lee agreed with the earlier decision of the

New York Congress that Kings Bridge over the Harlem River at the north end of Manhattan required a strong defense in order to protect the city's communication with the country and with Connecticut.[24]

But General Lee thought the possession of Long Island of greater importance than the provincial capital, which, if captured by the enemy, would be untenable without the supplies and protection of Long Island. He proposed to close off the East River by a series of cross-firing batteries. A major battery was planned for the heights at the Jews' Burying Ground along the East River where high ground jutted south and west and then became river bluffs, at the foot of which were the city's major shipyards. Further west was the island's highest ground, atop which a large residence belonging to the Loyalist Thomas Jones became the site of a large redoubt. A battery near the "Brookland" Ferry on Long Island was to provide supporting fire. Long Island's approach to the capital would be guarded by a chain of forts manned by four or five thousand men and anchored at either end by sea marshes to the south of the small parish of Brooklyn.[25]

Considering the fact that only a few weeks before General Lee's arrival New York seemed to be drifting back into support for the legitimate government, Lee's activities in the capital during February, 1776, represented an extraordinary change. Perhaps Lee's view that he received cooperation only because of the presence of American troops was correct, indicating how much more manageable an occupied city can be. In any case, the defensive actions McDougall had earlier thought impossible to begin because of the public's conflicting loyalties were started by Lee with a minimum of trouble. As in the days following Lexington and Concord, Loyalists either fell silent or sought refuge in more congenial localities. Isaac Sears outraged some Whigs by travelling through Queen's County administering a test oath and arresting those who refused to take it, but the hostility toward Sears was based more on his disregard for the authority of the Provincial Congress than his mistreatment of Loyalists.[26] Still, Sears taught the weak-kneed Whigs in New York a valuable lesson. The army's way of handling civil affairs, such as administering loyalty oaths, was not intended to safeguard individual liberties but merely to get a job done, and as John Jay warned from Philadelphia, "When the army become our legislators, the people that moment become slaves." "I am persuaded," McDougall replied to Jay, "it will be the last instance of their passivity on a point of so much importance to the liberty of a freeman." [27] General Lee remained in New York only a month, surrendering his command to Lord Stirling on March 8, who continued with equal vigor what Lee had begun.

As a member of the Committee of Safety and the Provincial Congress, McDougall's work was both military and political. One of the more serious problems arising from the army's presence was the continuing military challenge to the authority of the Provincial Congress. Both General Lee and Lord Stirling executed their command responsibilities with crispness that alarmed members of New York's political bodies. Of special concern to New Yorkers was who had the authority to deal with the problems of the Loyalists, royal officials, and the British warships in its harbor. The issue was whether the Provincial and Continental Congresses or the army ruled New York. [28]

McDougall was caught in a dilemma. He had spent too much time and energy in the Provincial Congress to be unmindful of that agency's legislative role in America's defense, but he also recognized that the new military commanders were intent upon preparing New York as quickly as possible for the British force that everyone feared would soon come. As a political leader and an army officer, though his regiment had been decimated in Canada and the remnants were still attached to General Schuyler's command, McDougall sought to bridge the gap between the two arms of the revolutionary movement, serving as a liaison between members of Congress and Generals Lee and Stirling. Through his efforts, the orders of Lee and Stirling were softened and made palatable to skittish members of Congress, who were afraid the British navy would destroy the capital. Most important, McDougall convinced the irascible Lee and the more pliable Lord Stirling to confer with the Congress on matters of mutual interest and concern, thereby reducing misunderstandings. [29] On the other hand, McDougall was useful to the military commanders in stimulating New York's efforts for its own defense. Working through the congressional committee system, he set about collecting military supplies of various kinds, locating living quarters for incoming troops, establishing a commissary department, and investigating those manufacturers needed for the colony's defense. [30] So much needed to be done in such a short time and with limited resources that McDougall's efforts in February and March appeared limited. But considering that the talk in the capital in early January, 1776, was of appeasement, reconciliation, and a return to the royal standard, soft attitudes which even infected the Provincial Congress, New York's military measures of early spring represented a change nearly as dramatic as that which occurred following the news of Lexington and Concord.

The change in British military strategy in late 1775 and early 1776 was instrumental in bringing about the altered tone of public sentiment in New York. As long as Britain confined her armed power to Boston, the dangers of military despotism seemed remote to New Yorkers, more a matter of probability than of imminent reality. Rumors were common of troops embarking from British ports destined for New York, or of European mercenaries and naval squadrons being under way. But the capital had lived under such threats before and still remained free of British regulars. Since the beginning of 1776, however, George Washington had been sending more frequent warnings from Cambridge that the British were making motions as though to leave Boston, with the apparent intention of landing at New York. That conviction had prompted Washington to approve Lee's occupation of New York when New Yorkers appeared to disregard the warnings. Now, in the early spring of 1776, the same fear prompted even more action. A council of general officers, meeting at Roxbury, Massachusetts, on March 13, decided to dispatch six regiments to New York, to be followed by others as the situation around Boston further changed.[31]

As soon as Lee and, later, Stirling received Washington's estimate of British intentions, McDougall carried the information to the Provincial Congress, and the pace of New York's military activity quickened. A particularly urgent message from Washington was received on March 13—the British were actually embarking. The Provincial Congress immediately appointed McDougall and five other members to confer with Stirling. The result was an agreement to use city and county civilians as workers on the capital's fortifications, so vital against a British attack from the sea.[32] Shortly thereafter, Washington led the Continental army from Massachusetts to New York, and military defense in the province had become a truly national affair.

When the commander-in-chief, George Washington, reached New York on April 13, 1776, to assume personal command, he found it a far different city from that which he visited nine months earlier on his way to Massachusetts. It was nearly like a ghost town compared to the summer of 1775. Its harbor was now empty of commercial shipping; ordinary business was slowed or stopped altogether. Everywhere, houses and shops stood empty or closed, and women and children and some men were continuing to leave for safe country places.[33] At first, 2,000 New York and New Jersey militia, rough country men and boys, controlled the city. But by mid-April, Continental soldiers were to be seen everywhere, some 12,000 of them, quartered in regular barracks or in elegant town houses vacated by Loyalists, drilling, digging, swearing, drinking, and whoring away the hours until the British came. It was necessary to maintain street patrols to protect civilians and town property, and in early April an evening curfew of eight o'clock was applied to military personnel and civilians alike. Military trials for drunkenness, insubordination, street fighting, housebreaking, and petty theft became common. Ladies of the street were equally as common, boldly penetrating the barracks until warned out "on pain of being well watered under the pump." [34]

The city's physical appearance was also undergoing change. According to Lee's plan, redoubts on the North and East Rivers were to be constructed immediately. Part of Fort George was torn down, the old battery along the south seawall became the Grand Battery, and ten foot barriers began to appear everywhere. The hard winter ground yielded slowly to pick and shovel as the militia were sent to work, soon joined on Stirling's order by half of the city's male inhabitants every other day and by all the slaves every day. Houses along the river bank southwest of Trinity Church were destroyed to make room for a major fortification, soon known as McDougall's battery, and further up the Hudson, on the estate of George Harrison, troops under Captain Abraham Van Dyck were at work on another battery, while Connecticut troops along the East River beyond the ship yards were building still another redoubt. A short distance beyond the city limits, a prominence on Nicholas Bayard's country property became the site for a major fort and battery, and on Broadway the hospital, still unfinished, was opened for military use. Rough shacks, rising wherever troops were at work, gave the city an even tackier appearance.[35]

By the time of Washington's arrival in April, military preparations in New York had superseded all else. McDougall was drawn willingly into these measures. He was convinced that reconciliation had been made impossible by the king's speech to parliament in October, 1775, declaring the colonies to be in a state of rebellion and vowing to crush the American rebels. But conviction did not guarantee McDougall's immediate importance in the new continental revolutionary movement. McDougall's prominent place among New York Whigs had been eclipsed by the greater weight and rank of Continental officers, who insisted that the burden of New York's defense was theirs. When Lord Stirling, a New Jersey colonel with a commission dated later than McDougall's, was promoted in March to a brigadier in the Continental service and promptly took charge in New York, McDougall's pride was deeply wounded. He hurried off letters to Philip Schuyler and John Jay demanding to know whether Lord Stirling's elevation was a political gesture to keep New Jersey content. "If the principle of his appointment is not to give New Jersey a general officer, as they have raised three batallions, I am ill treated, because he was a much younger field officer." [36] McDougall talked the matter over with Stirling and came away satisfied, but he nevertheless asked Jay in Philadelphia to ask members of Congress, without mentioning his name, about the reasons for Stirling's promotion. Both Schuyler and Jay responded quickly, assuring him that Stirling's promotion was indeed political; they appealed to his patriotism to stay on in New York.[37]

McDougall knew that his future course was already fixed by the need to vindicate his personal honor. He could not forget that he had remained at home while his regiment fought in Canada, where his men had suffered hardship and tragedy. He had been criticized in Congress and had required a defense from New York's delegates. To his greater mortification, his motives were also being questioned by his own officers and men in the field. Lieutenant Colonel Rudolphus Ritzema, who was in charge of the regiment in Canada, urged him to come north to quiet the talk, at the same time bragging to his father in New York City that General Montgomery had made him regimental commander in McDougall's place. In early February, 1776, McDougall learned that Ritzema's letter was known in the city, prompting talk about his absence from the expedition which had claimed one of his sons. Command of his regiment and its existence thus became a fixation with McDougall. Although it had been shattered beyond recognition, with some companies down to a dozen men and others simply no longer existing, McDougall was determined to bring his regiment together, fill its companies, and claim its leadership. It was a matter of honor. He revealed the depth of his feeling to Schuyler: "Although I am willing to spend and be spent for the country and have already ruined a good constitution and exhausted a great part of my little fortune in her cause, yet she cannot expect in addition to these the sacrifice of my reputation. Indeed this would render me unable to serve her." [38]

General Schuyler, in whose command McDougall still nominally remained, wrote a quick reply. Ritzema's contention was unfounded, Schuyler asserted. He had issued no such order, and neither had Montgomery, who was Ritzema's immediate superior officer during the assault upon Canada, for in both instances such a promotion would have required the approval of the New York Congress. Besides, General Montgomery, Schuyler concluded, "knew that you were absent with my leave, and the reason why I wished you to remain at New York. . . ." [39] The implication of Schuyler's letter was clear: McDougall was still in command of the New York First Regiment, even though that regiment's companies were riddled with casualties and desertions and the term of enlistments had expired. When McDougall learned that the Continental Congress had authorized New York to raise four new battalions, with their officers to be approved in Philadelphia, he sent letters to his friends asking for support. He even answered James Duane's letter, written months earlier, which had first warned him of criticism. McDougall wanted an active military command, a need that was fulfilled when the Continental Congress on March 8, 1776, appointed him colonel of New York's First Battalion. [40]

McDougall's decision to take an active part in the colony's defense ended his political activity in the revolutionary movement in New York. His change of directions was, in a sense, a measure of the capital's change over the past year. Until the spring of 1776, New York City had been the political nerve center, the pace-setter of the revolutionary movement in the colony. A year earlier four newspapers flourished, keeping the city and counties informed and providing ready opportunities, at a few shillings, for citizens to express their views. The city's 25,000 inhabitants were politically sensitive and often clamorous, alert to the nuances of local politics and the oddities of those personalities who dominated the public meetings and tavern discussions. Men disagreed, often angrily and occasionally violently, and fought by whatever means necessary to impose their views on the city. Still, there was a vibrancy in the capital to which men living in rural isolation responded. They looked to the capital for news and for leadership, and when they received neither, they wrote letters to their city friends and relatives to learn why. When New York's first revolutionary congress was born in 1775, it was only natural that county leaders should assemble in far distant New York City.

But the capital's political significance was rapidly diminishing by the time Washington opened his first New York headquarters in William Smith's house on April 13, 1776. In fact, Smith's absence—he had moved to Haverstraw two days after the British fleet sailed from Boston—was symbolic of the city's change from a political center to a military theater of operations.[41] When the Provincial Congress in March ordered new elections, McDougall did not stand as a candidate; he intended to fight in the coming battle, insisting that even "if congress had put the lowest sargent in my regiment over me, I am determined to serve this campaign." [42] He continued to serve in the Second New York Congress until it was replaced in May, 1776, but his military duties made his attendance irregular. John Jay, failing to note the temper of McDougall's earlier letters, was surprised by McDougall's decision, and he hurried home from Philadelphia to find out why.[43] McDougall's withdrawal from politics came at an interesting time, for Whig leaders like Jay were soon to face the difficult problems of formalizing the break with Britain and forming a new government. McDougall never had occasion to make known his views on these two questions, but his activities as a revolutionary leader placed him squarely on the side of rebellion. True, he had supported reconciliation as long as an accommodation seemed feasible, but when hope of a settlement vanished by the beginning of 1776, he accepted independence as both inevitable and proper. In the army, McDougall was, as John Sullivan described him to John Adams, "in the true way to happiness." [44] McDougall agreed with George Washington, however, that the problem of military defense was of greater immediate importance than expressions of political values and sentiments, and he stood ready to meet the British when they arrived.

# Chapter Nine

# Defending New York

The transition from politics to army life was an easy one for McDougall. New York's and America's need in 1776 was more for military than political leadership, and McDougall recognized that the country's political independence depended upon its ability to repel Britain's efforts to crush the rebellion. Thus, when McDougall's regiment was placed with the Continental army on May 1, 1776, the former New York City street leader was prepared to take on the demanding responsibilities of military command. Once in Continental service, McDougall raised a regiment of 536 rank and file by the end of May, 1776, and discovered, as he was to learn time and again, that his troops were a mixed lot, ranging in age from sixteen-year-old boys to men in their fifties, poorly clothed and totally dependent upon their army pay to support themselves.[1] His soldiers were probably no worse (or better) than those in other units, and consequently discipline suffered. Rude colonial troops exhibited a native immunity to military discipline; they abused their officers and occasionally threatened them, slept on guard duty, wandered away from camp, accosted women on the streets, and drank and swore too much.[2] Throughout the spring and summer of 1776, especially after the British army of 25,000 men under Sir William Howe finally appeared on June 29, McDougall's men worked steadily on the city's fortifications. It was a dreary business; the weather was hot and sultry, food rations were poor, and in July, the whole army seemed to be hit with the "bloody flux" of dysentery and fevers.[3] McDougall at least could still enjoy the occasional comforts of his own home on Chapel Street, and he also had the satisfaction of a promotion. In response to Washington's request for additional brigade commanders, the Continental Congress on August 9 named six new brigadier generals, among them McDougall.[4]

McDougall's promotion to brigadier general was hardly based on military merit. His command experience was quite limited and he was untested in battle. Rather, it was a recognition of McDougall's political stature in New York's revolutionary movement and of the state's military importance. In that early stage of the war, political factors weighed heavily in the selection of senior army officers. Since few men had previous military experience and fewer still could claim any sort of professional training in command responsibilities, the Continental Congress was forced to commission local political leaders whose commitment to and zeal for the cause were unquestioned. On that score, McDougall was well qualified, and his promotion to brigadier not only marked an important turning point in his life but was a personal triumph for him. The promotion signified that the army, not politics, would be his path to true importance in the American Revolution. Although he was to suffer crippling illness and barely to avoid bankruptcy during the war years, he never gave more than a passing thought to quitting the army for the comfort of civilian life. Eventually he would become the tenth ranking general officer below George Washington, respected and relied upon by the commander-in-chief and other senior officers, and involved in public affairs on the national level. McDougall's elevation to brigadier also meant that the ex-privateer captain had risen in seven years from an obscure street agitator in New York City, who had been ridiculed for his political and social pretensions, to the rank of a general officer, who could command attention and deference in society.

The Battle of Long Island was the first major clash between the American and British armies; it was also McDougall's first battle experience. When Sir William Howe finally set the British army in motion against George Washington, by landing on August 22 at Gravesend Bay, Long Island, McDougall's brigade of nineteen hundred men formed part of the American reserve. Smaller than other brigades, it remained in New York City to assist Jonathan Brewer's Corp of Artificers in constructing vital fortifications in the city's center. McDougall's old regiment was dogged by misfortune. The night before Howe's army moved from its base on Staten Island to Long Island, a violent thunderstorm raked the area and lightning struck three officers in McDougall's camp, melting their swords and the loose coins in their pockets.[5] Two days later the regiment's commanding officer, Lieutenant Colonel Herman Zedwitz, was arrested for treason, charged with offering military information to Governor William Tryon and, even worse, expressing a willingness to poison certain water wells used by the American army. The charge was especially alarming because of rumors that ten soldiers had died from poisoned chocolate distributed by Tories. A court-martial was ordered immediately, even though the battle of Long Island was beginning.[6] These vicissitudes reduced McDougall's brigade to two effective regiments, the New York Third under Rudolphus Ritzema and Charles Webb's Connecticut unit.

As the British attack on Long Island unfolded on Tuesday, August 27, McDougall's men were drawn into the battle. The exact time of his arrival on Long Island is uncertain, but he probably crossed over no later than Wednesday, for Webb's and Ritzema's regiments were involved in that day's steady skirmishing. The real battle was already over, however. The day before, the American left and center had been out-maneuvered by Howe and then pushed back to the forts and breastworks of Brooklyn Heights. Only Lord Stirling's brave men on the right, dying and drowning in Gowanus Swamp to hold off a superior force, earned honor in the American army's first major encounter. The battle was short of a disaster, but Washington's army had suffered a blow to its morale more serious than the loss of strength in numbers. Out of ten thousand on Long Island, American losses totalled 1,400, of which nearly 1,100 were prisoners, including two generals and 87 other officers.[7] Although the American positions at Brooklyn Heights were strong enough to withstand a frontal assault, the possibility of British siege operations combined with naval thrusts up the Hudson and East rivers were grave threats. Washington was forced to make the difficult decision of either retreating to New York City or remaining on Long Island and risking his divided army. McDougall assured him that it was possible for British warships to operate around nearby Governor's Island and to penetrate the East River defenses, which only a northeast wind prevented. Confronted by an enemy force twice as large as his own and appalled by the wretched condition of his own troops, Washington proposed an immediate retreat, and his generals agreed.[8]

The withdrawal from Long Island has been heralded as an accomplishment equal in importance to Howe's flanking movement of August 27 that had caught the Americans flat-footed and made their retreat necessary. From 7 o'clock Thursday evening into the early morning hours of Friday, Washington's army was shuttled across the East River without drawing British attention until the very end, by which time the Americans had escaped to the safety of New York City. Many men earned credit for the retreat's success: the indefatigable Hugh Hughes who assembled the necessary boats, and John Glover's tireless Marblehead regiment which supplied the muscle and sailing skill.[9] McDougall's role was coordinating the embarkation, drawing regiments out of the trenches as boats became available. It was dirty work for everyone. The rain was bad enough, but after two hours of progress, a strong northerly wind made sailing difficult and the troops were slowly rowed across the river. Only a few rowboats were at hand to make the exhausting two-mile round trip over the choppy river, and for a time McDougall did not think the army would make it. A wind shift to the south enabled Glover's men to use sailing craft once more and regiment after regiment was quickly ferried across. As daylight approached, a providential fog blanketed the bay and river, hiding the closing phase of the retreat. McDougall stayed to the end, but he was not the final man to leave the island; the sleepless commander-in-chief himself stepped into the last boat.[10]

The reunited American army lay exhausted in New York City, proud of its herculean feat, but the battle of Long Island had been lost. Many lessons were still to be learned. Although the individual British soldier had no greater claim to bravery than his American counterpart, he was superior in military discipline and obedience and was skilled in formations and mass maneuvers. British officers from subaltern to generals knew their craft, while Americans like McDougall had barely entered their military apprenticeship. Long Island was a campaign of movement, a forecast of the next twelve months. For the time being, Washington's amateurs could only dig trenches, throw up breastworks, and wait for Howe and his professionals to make the next move.

Following the retreat from Long Island, McDougall's brigade headquarters was located at Mrs. McGowan's farmhouse on the post road a little south of the fork leading into the village of Harlem. A council of war was held there on September 12 to determine whether an attempt should be made to hold New York's capital. It was a perplexing question, but one for which nearly everyone had an answer. Nathanael Greene advocated burning the city, thereby denying its use by the enemy as a winter base. The Continental and New York Congresses wanted the city to be held if possible but to remain undamaged if a general evacuation became necessary. Five days earlier, on September 7, 1776, a council of officers decided to defend the city, and now on September 12, in response to the second thoughts of six generals, the question was reconsidered.[11]

Actually, as Charles Lee had seen back in February, the city was indefensible; Colonel Rufus Putnam, Washington's chief engineer, made the same judgment. The Hudson River and Long Island Sound provided means by which the British could attack the American rear and cut off the inland escape route over Kings Bridge, and without the possession of Long Island, the low lying left bank of the East River invited an amphibious landing. When Montressor's Island, far up the East River near the mouth of the Harlem River, was seized by the British on September 10, the city's vulnerability received dramatic emphasis.[12] Only three officers, George Clinton, Joseph Spencer, and William Heath—a trio McDougall was later to refer to as "a stubborn, honest man, one a fool, and the other a knave"—opposed a withdrawal to Harlem Heights, nine miles north of the city.[13] In a campaign of movement, it was almost too little and nearly too late; three days later, on September 15, the British landed at Kips Bay and barely failed to trap 5,000 Americans still in the city.[14]

McDougall's troops were not involved in the general flight of the American army on September 15 to the protective cover of Harlem Heights. Assigned to guard the Hell Gate area after the Long Island retreat, his regiments, now including William Smallwood's Marylanders, were five or six miles north of Sir Henry Clinton's landing place. The day was so filled with confusion, broken units, panicky men, and abandoned equipment that it is impossible to determine which regiments behaved in an orderly fashion. In any case, safety was eventually reached, and McDougall's new position was primarily a flanking one, across the post road to the Harlem River in the general area of the present 135th and 145th Streets.[15] Washington's army salvaged some honor on September 16 in the Hollow Way fight, immediately to the south and below the Heights. Thereafter, the campaign was reduced to skirmishes between picket guards and parties harvesting grain and scavenging for lumber, of which McDougall's men received their share. It was a waiting game that lasted a month, during which McDougall, along with the entire army, witnessed the devastating fire of September 21–22 which destroyed nearly a quarter of

New York City, stopping only two doors away from the house formerly occupied by McDougall.[16]

Since the retreat from Long Island, the American army's condition had worsened considerably. At first optimistic of their chances against the British, one defeat and one thorough rout made the Americans less sure of themselves. The army was low on ammunition and much of its artillery and other equipment had been lost during the shameful panic of September 15. Physically, the soldiers were in poor health, tired and on a short diet, lacking adequate clothing and shelter for the coming winter season. Sickness was everywhere, with thirty percent of McDougall's brigade lost by illness. Desertion was also a major problem, especially among the militia units, and even Continental regiments were affected.[17] McDougall's brigade of over eleven hundred men fit for duty was only a third of its authorized strength, yet it was regarded as one of the stronger units in Washington's army of fifteen thousand.

On the second Saturday of October, the 12th, Howe resumed his campaign to destroy Washington's army. Passing through the fog-shrouded Hell Gate during Friday evening, Howe landed four thousand men on Throg's Point the next morning, at a point where the East River converges into Long Island Sound only eight miles east of Kings Bridge. While a small detachment of Edward Hand's Pennsylvania riflemen held the British landing party at bay, Washington ordered McDougall to reinforce William Heath's militia force protecting southern Westchester County. The battle was now near. As William Smallwood of McDougall's brigade wrote home, "There is nothing left but to fight them." McDougall's men arrived on the scene Saturday evening, but they saw little action in the next five days.[18] By choosing Throg's Point for a landing, Howe found himself on a low peninsula that became an island at high tide, with only two passable routes inland. The Americans quickly blocked Howe's path from behind a network of stone fences; rather than risk the heavy casualties of a frontal assault, Howe flanked the American positions on October 18 by a second landing three miles north of Pell's Point. Even before this move, it was evident that Washington's main position south of Kings Bridge was in danger, and a council of war attended by McDougall agreed on an immediate withdrawal northward toward White Plains, while a small force under Robert Magaw would hold Fort Washington as long as possible.[19]

The situation was fluid, and the American army was badly scattered over an area stretching from Manhattan Island into Westchester County. Yet there was some reason for hope. The fact that it had lost many of the cumbersome essentials of military camp gave the Americans mobility as the British sought to complete their turning movement, and the return of Charles Lee on October 4, fresh from his triumph at Charleston, South Carolina, was also regarded as an advantage. He was given "the flower of the army," consisting of John Nixon's, John Glover's, and McDougall's brigades, to watch Howe's movement and guard the American withdrawal from Harlem.[20] Instead of attacking Washington, Howe moved northward up the east side of the Bronx River toward White Plains, while Washington to the west of the river headed for the same destination. McDougall's men, as part of Lee's division protecting the American rear, were some of the very last to reach the new American position. A day later, on October 27, the vanguard of Howe's force also arrived at White Plains.[21]

Detachments from the armies of Washington and Howe fought at White Plains on October 28, and McDougall was the principal American commander in the limited but bloody action. Howe's army of twelve thousand men had moved north along the Old York Road through hilly and wooded countryside, dissected by numerous stone fences, streams, and by the larger Bronx River, which ran on a generally north-south line. Washington's defense line ran some three miles along the upper Connecticut road, with the American left secured by a small lake, and the army's right over against the Bronx River, which curved eastward toward White Plains. The army's right flank was dominated by a large hill, Chatterton's, rising one hundred and eighty feet above the flood-swollen Bronx River, which flowed around its eastern base. As the main body of Howe's army approached White Plains on October 28, McDougall's brigade occupied a nearby woods as a covering party in advance of the American right, about a mile northeast of Chatterton's Hill. In front of McDougall's brigade was a screen of militia under Joseph Spencer, posted to harass and slow down the oncoming British.[22]

By all accounts, that Monday was a beautiful day, a welcomed relief from the bone-chilling fall rains of the previous week. It was a good day for a fight, and Colonel Rall's leading Hessians were the first to attack the militia screen on McDougall's front, forcing the Connecticut men to retreat westward over the Bronx and up Chatterton's

Hill, where they were able to hold their ground. When the skirmishing began at mid-morning, Joseph Reed, Washington's adjutant, ordered McDougall's men, reinforced by Haslet's Delaware Continentals, to defend Chatterton's Hill. Arriving on the high ground at noon with his force of twelve hundred men, McDougall placed his old regiment and Charles Webb's on his left; Smallwood, Ritzema, and Haslet in the center; and Brooks' and Graham's militia far to the right. McDougall's combined force of regulars and militia was still not more than fifteen or sixteen hundred men, and they were supported only by Alexander Hamilton's two field pieces. Opposing him was General Alexander Lislie's division of four thousand British redcoats and Hessians who marched up in disciplined order in a wheat field below the hill.[23]

To McDougall's ragged farm boys, the attack division and the remainder of Howe's army presented an awesome spectacle of glittering metal and gawdy color. Even more awesome and frightening was the artillery bombardment that plastered the hilltop and its southern and eastern slopes, throwing great clouds of smoke and debris over the battle scene, obscuring the view from Washington's main camp. Hamilton's artillery replied, but little could be expected from inexperienced men and two cannon, one of which quickly became disabled. While British artillery played over Chatterton's Hill, McDougall calmly sat on his horse and ordered Smallwood's regiment, supported by Ritzema, to take position half way down the hill's southeastern slope, using fences and timber for cover. Meanwhile, reinforcements were gathering in the main American lines, but the British were also preparing for the final assault.

When the Hessians attempted to throw a rough bridge over the Bronx River, the Marylanders and New Yorkers cut them down. Later they dispersed two British regiments, holding the hill's base, which had tried to climb the steep slope.[24] The acrid smoke from small arms fire added to that of burning brush, dust, and artillery. To a distant observer, Chatterton's Hill was enveloped in a swirling cloud, cracking and booming with the noise of battle. When Smallwood and Ritzema could no longer prevent several thousand of the enemy from crossing the Bronx River and ascending the hill, all of McDougall's men except the militia on the far right were drawn into battle. British artillery fell silent, and the fight became a struggle between men, first at musket range, then at bayonet point.

McDougall's advance parties gave ground grudgingly to the climb-
ing force, but suddenly the battle scene shifted to the hill's western
flank where Brook's and Graham's militia were smashed by Johann
Rall's Hessians and the British light horse. The militia took flight,
some not even pausing to fire their weapons, even though Haslet's
Continentals tried vainly to stop the oncoming Germans and cavalry.
But the center of McDougall's line simply could not fight in two
places at once. With his right crumbling, McDougall's whole force
was endangered, and he ordered a withdrawal. It was not a panicky
retreat. Haslet's men, as well as other Continentals, left the hill
slowly, while McDougall led his men down the northern slope to the
Connecticut road a half mile from the main American line.[25]

The battle of White Plains, as the clash was called, lasted the whole
day, ending near dusk when McDougall pulled out. But the main
British assault up Chatterton's Hill, including the flanking movement
on the right, had actually lasted no more than thirty minutes of
furious fighting; and Howe's troops suffered twice as many casualties
as the one hundred and forty downed in McDougall's command.
Rufus Putnam compared the battle to Bunker Hill, both in British
losses and in the way it was fought.[26] McDougall, along with his
men, earned credit for stiff resistance to a superior enemy force. As
Charles Lee commented on the battle, "McDougall, it is true, in the
last affair was obliged to retreat by the superiority of their artillery,
but he lost no credit. . . . In short he is a sensible brave officer." [27]
Still, it was costly to the American side. Smallwood's Marylanders
took nearly a third of the loss with forty-three dead, wounded, and
missing, while thirty-four of Ritzema's regiment were listed as casualties. Webb's Connecticut Continentals, whom McDougall later mistakenly thought had failed in their duty, and the militia under Douglas,
Silliman, and Brooks were also cited for their brave stand. Colonel
Morris Graham, on the other hand, was promptly court-martialed,
with McDougall in charge of the trial, for running away from the
enemy.[28] Chatterton's Hill, however, meant more than the loss of
men or the incompetence of officers like Graham; Washington's position at White Plains was now untenable, and he was forced to retreat
to the protective heights of the North Castle area. Howe stayed a
week around White Plains before poor weather caused him to retire to
the comfort of New York City.[29]

The weeks and months following the White Plains action was a

period of crisis for the American army. Outmaneuvered and out-
gunned, except when small detachments fought, Washington's forces
had proved themselves unequal to the task of stopping Howe. When
the British returned to New York to establish winter quarters, the
ragged and sickly American army divided into smaller units to cover
the Hudson Highlands, the North Castle district, and the Jerseys,
while McDougall's brigade remained a part of Lee's division with the
responsibility of keeping the British from crossing Kings Bridge into
Westchester County. Reinforcements were also sent to Fort Washington atop Harlem Heights. The coming of winter only added to the
army's suffering, further demoralizing field officers and men in the
ranks.[30] A final blow came in November when Howe forced the surrender of Fort Washington after a short siege, and then four days later
sent Lord Cornwallis across the Hudson against Fort Lee, which the
Americans prudently evacuated without a fight.[31]

New Jersey became the major theater of operations following the
loss of Fort Lee as Cornwallis followed Washington across the state
and over the Delaware River. Responding with agonizing slowness to
Washington's call for reinforcements, Lee finally crossed the Hudson
in early December, and McDougall found himself once more on the
road. He allegedly said, before leaving the Highlands, that he was
prepared to live on chestnuts for ten years defending American independence rather than give it up. If true, it was an apt statement, for
he found conditions no better on the west side of the Hudson.[32] At
Haverstraw in New York's Orange County, a severe case of rheumatism brought on by the early winter rains forced McDougall into bed,
while his brigade continued on with Lee's division. McDougall's case
was common, however, for most of the brigadiers in Lee's division,
Washington complained to Congress, were "left sick at different
places on the road." [33] Eight days later McDougall was fit enough to
ride, but it was a discouraged New York brigadier who reached Morristown on December 14. There he learned that Charles Lee had been
captured by the British the day before. Without a command, hobbled
by illness, and situated in a Tory-infested area, McDougall's spirits
faltered. For a moment he thought of resigning, but he realized that
his quitting the army would be interpreted as a political defection and
thus would injure an already flagging cause. Still, as he informed
Washington, his physical condition made an active field command impossible; he required the warmth of regular quarters to soothe his

crippled body. Washington could not afford to lose McDougall, and luckily an assignment existed in the Highlands that could suit both McDougall and Washington.[34]

Command of the Hudson Highlands, as McDougall was to observe on several later occasions, was a risky proposition, fraught with administrative headaches, political interference, and tactical dangers that could ruin an officer's reputation. It was a sprawling command, stretching from Westchester County at its southern limit to Fishkill on the north; it was dominated by rugged and heavily-timbered mountains, hills, ravines, and river bluffs. Between Newburgh and Peekskill, the Hudson River bisected the Highlands, twisting and turning its way to the ocean and offering a number of advantageous points on either bank from which artillery could hold back a British river expedition. Since the Hudson was recognized as a strategic waterway which, if controlled by the British, could separate New England from the remainder of the united colonies, control of the Highlands concerned both the Continental Congress and General Washington. In later years West Point was to become the center of this area's defense complex, but in 1776 Washington counted on three forts located in the mountain vastness at the narrows of the river: Fort Independence, just above Peekskill Creek, and Forts Clinton and Montgomery, farther north on the river's west bank.[35] Formidable to view, and perhaps even more so to consider from the perspective of the distant Delaware, those defenses were intended primarily to repel a river attack. But in early 1777, as McDougall quickly learned, the war in the lower Hudson was more irregular action than formal assault, and he saw his task as one of assuring the continued support of interior New York for independence by protecting the Hudson and preventing the British from sweeping the countryside.[36]

Much needed to be done when McDougall arrived at Peekskill in early January, 1777, but he found others more demanding of his assistance than prepared to give him help. To begin with, Washington at this time viewed the Highlands as a strategic reserve from which he could draw additional regiments for the main army. When McDougall asked for more Continental troops, especially artillerymen, he was reminded that New York was expected to provide militia garrisons for the river forts; regular regiments recruiting in Connecticut and Massachusetts, and even in New York, were needed in New Jersey and at Ticonderoga.[37] McDougall already knew, as did every other continental officer, that militia were unreliable; they failed to appear when needed, did not stay long enough to do any good, and were unwilling to stand and fight. The Massachusetts militia in Westchester County ran true to form. By the middle of March, McDougall had only four partially filled Continental regiments, whose company officers were still enlisting men in Connecticut and New York, to garrison the forts and protect the military stores below Peekskill.[38] He had little doubt that the British would soon have a full report on his weakness and would probably send out a strong raiding party as soon as the river ice broke. Washington, though faced with larger problems, finally heeded McDougall's warnings and encouraged William Heath, now at Boston, to hurry on the new Massachusetts regiments to Peekskill. New York authorities ordered the supply depots moved out of Westchester, thus reducing the need for a large American force so far away from the river forts. Militia from Connecticut and Rhode Island were also on the way.[39]

Still, the Highlands' vulnerability was an open invitation to the British, and on Sunday, March 22, 1777, a strong river expedition of twenty armed vessels and six hundred redcoats passed Verplancks Landing just below Peekskill. It was the first in a series of river raids during the war, and even though later attacks were to be stronger and more menacing, none gave greater emphasis to the Highlands' importance than this first British thrust up the Hudson valley. What had been earlier recognized as a possibility became a present danger to be reckoned with for the next six years; if the Highlands fell, little else would stop the British from reaching Albany and beyond. For the moment, fortunately, General Howe wanted nothing more than to probe the Hudson defenses and gather supplies for his own army. Landing at Peekskill Creek around noon on March 22, the British found the town deserted and McDougall's meager force posted on high ground. There was little McDougall could have done to oppose the attack. His total strength was fewer than three hundred men plus two or three field pieces, and Henry Beekman Livingston's regiment did not even arrive until an hour after the landing. While McDougall's small force watched, now joined by Marinus Willett's small detachment from Constitution Island, the enemy destroyed the commissary stores still in Peekskill. The next day, Monday, McDougall moved his troops north to block the main road to Fishkill where more supplies were kept. The British sent an advance guard to check him, and late

*West Point as it appeared at the close of the Revolution, showing the famous barrier chain in place in a rare view of the fortress from the north. Engraved by C. Tiebout for the* New York Magazine, *March 1791.*

—NEW-YORK HISTORICAL SOCIETY

Monday afternoon, McDougall gave in to Marinus Willett's request to drive back the enemy's outposts. The action so alarmed British officers that they quickly embarked their men and set sail for New York City.[40]

Following that weekend, express riders carried the news of fighting and calls for help in all directions. Governor George Clinton at Poughkeepsie ordered out three militia regiments and rode hard for Fort Montgomery, arriving at 3 a.m. Tuesday. After he received second-hand accounts of the raid, Washington, too, ordered reinforcements; the tension at headquarters was heightened by McDougall's failure to send in an immediate action report. When McDougall finally did write a week later, offering no apology for the delay, he criticized the "weakness or supiness of this country" and complained that he had not been readily reinforced. His force was simply too small to risk a fight with an enemy twice his number. If he had attacked and lost, "the country would have been struck with universal panic," and nothing would have prevented the British from marching to Fishkill and destroying the more important artillery and ammunition located there.[41] With first-hand details before him, Washington's alarm faded, and he assured McDougall that he "was satisfied from the first, that you had done everything that prudence could suggest, and that as much opposition as your numbers would admit of, had been made." [42]

What Washington did not know at the time was that a serious rift had appeared in McDougall's command during the Peekskill raid. On Monday afternoon, March 23, after he had pulled back from the village, McDougall and Colonel Henry Beekman Livingston quarrelled violently at brigade headquarters. Livingston was immediately arrested on charges of "traducing" McDougall's conduct, of neglecting to bring his regiment to Peekskill on time, of using abusive language against McDougall in the presence of many brigade officers, and for several minor matters. Trouble between the two men had been developing for weeks over small questions of military routine, but for McDougall, the issue was his authority as a Continental brigadier over that of a lieutenant colonel. When the British attacked Peekskill and Livingston's regiment was slow in coming up, McDougall's patience ran out. In the hearing of other officers, a short-tempered McDougall blasted Livingston, who replied that he had only followed orders. Each man accused the other of lying. At one point McDougall nearly lost complete control of his temper by offering to give Livingston a gentleman's satisfaction, but Livingston wisely retreated from the room onto a porch. In a rage, McDougall shook his fist in Livingston's face, telling him he was a "pest" to the army, making more trouble than all the regiments put together and more than Livingston could ever make amends for. Livingston replied that if McDougall were not his superior officer, he would not stand for such treatment. McDougall exploded. He shouted that Livingston was fortunate indeed that he was in military service, otherwise McDougall would "put an end to his existence." [43]

The violent quarrel must have been entertaining to men in the ranks and embarrassing to the officers who witnessed it, but more was involved than the irritability of two men who were obviously feeling the strain of the moment. At bottom, their differences were symptomatic of changes in New York's social and political structure brought about by the revolutionary movement and the war. Henry Beekman Livingston, son of Robert R. Livingston of Clermont and brother of the state's first Chancellor, was a product of the old landed aristocracy, whose notions of society divided men into those born to rule and those to be ruled. Livingston's commission had come through family connections. McDougall, on the other hand, was a self-made man who had won high military rank because of his political importance to the independence movement and war effort. [44]

In the view of some members of New York's gentry, men of low birth from city and country were being preferred over sons of good families in matters of military rank. As Gouverneur Morris complained, "A herd of mechanics are preferred before the best families in the colony. . . ." [45] Once commissioned, officers from the lower class became intractable. Robert R. Livingston, Jr. reported to John Jay: "You can not conceive the trouble our generals have had, petitions, Mutinies, & a request to know the reason of every maneuver without a power to suspend or punish the offenders. . . ." [46] While recruiting his regiment earlier in the year, Henry Beekman Livingston told Washington that finding good officers was difficult. Those who were the leading contenders lacked the character of gentlemen and were, in his judgment, unfit to command. Captain William Goforth, for example, a former shoemaker and friend of McDougall who performed bravely in the Quebec campaign, had influence, in Livingston's opinion, because of his earlier political activity, but he was still ineligible for military command because he lacked the qualities of birth and breeding. Livingston's solution for the shortage of officers, which Washington never endorsed, was to bring from Canada young gentlemen adventurers who would give the army a higher tone.[47]

What Henry Beekman Livingston could simply not forget was that McDougall's origins, like those of William Goforth, were humble—indeed, lowly—and that McDougall's rise to influence and importance was meteoric and opportunistic. Too young to have associated with McDougall in politics, Livingston unquestionably heard the details recited in his own circle, and observed the end-product of the rags-to-riches process. Months after their bitter quarrel, Livingston distributed an unsigned handbill in the Highland camps which revealed the indignation he felt over McDougall's higher military rank: although McDougall was now a general, the fact remained that he had once delivered milk about New York City, had served as a tailor's apprentice, and then had gone to sea. Livingston remembered McDougall as a "poor contemptible mean half starved Scotchman" who had "so sensible an impression of the lowliness of his station that when passing a person who appeared to be above him in circumstances, was glad to lift his hat as a mark of obeisance while his other hand was employed in preventing the companions of his morning, evening & noontide hours from disturbing his noxious parts of his filthy and infected person." The French War, Livingston continued, made McDougall a wealthy man, but otherwise he remained "unpolished in manner rough as his profession & mean as the meanest of race." McDougall purchased "some foolish foppery of dress which on this idea of an ignorant sailor" constituted the character of a gentleman, and "puff'd up with pride & perswaded by his partners the banditti of the town," he entered politics and became "one of the scribblers of the age." Now McDougall was a general officer, and Livingston etched the ex-privateer's character in acid. "Unaccustomed to that company which his present intitles him to keep," Livingston contemptuously remarked, "& ignorant of that politeness which is necessary to constitute a part of the character, he uses the phrases of his original & best suited character the tar." McDougall might wear an officer's uniform, but dinner and conversation with him, according to Livingston, revealed his true nature: He was a common seaman acting in a role far beyond his capacity.[48]

When he obtained a copy of the handwritten diatribe, McDougall identified the author as Henry Beekman Livingston, but did nothing against the young officer. "Poor boy," McDougall informed Governor Clinton, "if he knew how little pain his scribbling gave me he would have saved himself the trouble of composing it." [49]

While McDougall did tolerate Livingston's haughty attitude to a degree, perhaps out of respect for the younger man's family background, he refused to overlook Livingston's contemptuous response to military discipline and order. Performance rather than breeding was the key to McDougall's social consciousness, and he applied the principle to army life. As he remarked early in the war, if state authorities failed to appoint officers who could actually lead other men and exercise at least common-sense judgment in battle, the war was as good as lost; family connections could not excuse incompetence and negligence nor compensate for failure.[50] The war for independence was too important to trust to young boys or old men, and, by implication, those who saw the army as glamorous and heroic; only men who possessed ability to match their courage should be commissioned. Henry Beekman Livingston was both able and courageous, and in later years McDougall recommended him to Washington. But in March of 1777, his notions of class subverted military effectiveness, and McDougall could thus no longer ignore Livingston's snobbish insubordination.

During that spring of 1777, McDougall's command on the Hudson was barren of satisfactory results. Frustration seemed to be as much a part of the Highlands as the area's bleakness and isolation. The British had forced him to make an embarrassing withdrawal; his pleas for men produced few additions; the commissary departments were bare; and his proposals for armed river vessels went unheeded.[51] At every turn he seemed unable to strengthen the Highlands against an expected return of Howe's redcoats. Washington, New York Governor Clinton, and the New York Congress did as much as they could, but they faced the same problems. The army's manpower as a whole, Continentals and militia, was at its lowest point. When Governor Clinton ordered out the militia, only a third of some county regiments appeared; and when Washington urged Governor Jonathan Trumbull of Connecticut to sent two thousand men to Peekskill, fewer than nine hundred were willing to march to the Hudson. According to William Heath's reports, recruitment in Continental regiments was no better. And those few who were willing to fight, whether in New York with McDougall or in New Jersey with the main army, were poorly fed, clothed, quartered, and armed. At one point, McDougall accused the deputy commissary, who worked in Philadelphia, of mismanagement and failure to supply the Highlands adequately.[52] By contrast, Tory regiments were enlisting on both sides of the river, especially in Westchester County, which became a no-man's-land raided by both sides. To combat the increasing Tory boldness, the New York Convention established the death penalty as punishment for aiding the enemy, but McDougall was hesitant to apply it without substantial evidence.[53]

General Howe's unknown intentions that spring gave McDougall his severest headache. Washington urged McDougall to make the Highlands "as defensible as time permits," and until Howe's campaign plans became known, to hold all troops coming to Peekskill. The strain of waiting was magnified by reports of a large British contingent embarking from Staten Island, and a few days later, there were reports of twenty-two sails on the Hudson off Dobbs Ferry. For the moment, an unfavorable wind kept them from ascending the river, but it was realized that Howe might be masking his real intention to move against Philadelphia, and readiness was necessary to meet either contingency.[54] McDougall did not know that a third objective the American supplies at Danbury, Connecticut—was the British goal for the present. While his patrols kept watch on the river, another British force of 2,000 Tories and redcoats led by Governor William Tryon coasted the Long Island Sound to Fairfield, reaching Danbury, twenty-three miles inland, on April 26, without resistance. News of the unexpected destruction of precious supplies reached McDougall early on the 27th, and he at once sent express riders to warn Washington. He then set off himself to cut the British line of march back to the coast. After a forced march of eighteen miles, McDougall reached Bedford in western Westchester County, only seventeen miles from the Sound. There he saw that it was impossible to catch the fast-marching enemy, and so he decided to return.[55] His major responsibility, after all, was still the Highlands, which remained a prime British target.

One suspects that Washington, while approving McDougall's "judicious" decision to halt, was disappointed in McDougall's inability to catch Tryon's raiding party. Washington wanted American victories in the field, and he hoped that McDougall could give him one.[56] In any case, by the beginning of May, 1777, McDougall was back at Peekskill trying to guess Howe's next move. Whatever the British general decided, the Hudson situation was rapidly changing. Progress was being made on the fortifications; new regiments from Massachusetts and Connecticut were swelling the river army; and the area was fast becoming a major command, with another brigadier, Samuel Holden Parsons, already on the scene, and two others, John Glover and John Nixon, on the way. Washington was behind the major build-up, and sent Henry Knox and Nathanael Greene to join McDougall in surveying the Highland defenses. McDougall recognized the need for the changes, that it was time for a major general to take charge, and he asked to be reassigned.[57] At first Washington thought of the energetic, recently promoted Benedict Arnold but settled finally in May on the more senior general, Israel Putnam. Until the summer campaign began and McDougall was called to the main army, Washington counted on McDougall's acquaintance "with the old gentleman's temper" and his advice and assistance to Putnam to make the new situation on the Hudson a happy and strong one.[58]

# Chapter Ten
# Defending the Highlands

Although McDougall yielded his command of the Highlands to Major General Israel Putnam, he remained in the area for the next four months. His primary role was to assist Putnam in the continuing development of the Hudson defenses against whatever moves General Howe might decide to make in 1777. McDougall echoed Washington's belief that only two British movements were really feasible: an attack up the Hudson River for the purpose of joining forces with the expedition out of Canada, thus dividing the new nation, or an attack upon Philadelphia to demoralize the American rebels and force a negotiated end to the war. Since it was evident that the American army could withstand a major attack in only one area, Washington vacillated on which attack to anticipate. At one moment he thought the Hudson was Howe's first interest, the next he was sure the British wanted Philadelphia. With only ten thousand effective soldiers against three times that number of British and Hessians, Washington was compelled to wait for the British commander to make the first move, while keeping his army ready to meet a major attack wherever it might develop. Moreover, from his headquarters at Morristown, New Jersey, Washington was never wholly confident that the Highlands could be held against a British thrust up the river. He consequently ordered as many troops to that area as he could spare from his meager reserves, urging Putnam and McDougall to complete the fortifications at Fort Montgomery quickly.[1]

The capture of Fort Ticonderoga at the north end of Lake George by General Burgoyne in early July, 1777, increased Washington's anxiety and misgivings.[2] The path to Albany was now apparently open. McDougall was also pessimistic about conditions in New York because of the uncertain military situation. America in the early summer of 1777 seemed to lack a willingness to fight or to make the sacrifices necessary to defeat the British. The pugnacious brigadier predicted that unless New York's new state government intensified recruiting efforts, the state's regiments would consist chiefly of officers. "The strength of the enemy never gave me a discouraging thought," he wrote to William Heath in Boston. "But I confess that the supiness [sic] of the country has many." For the moment he took comfort in his belief that God would "extricate this land from the cruel and unprovoked oppressor." [3]

As the summer weeks passed, Howe's strategy remained "dark and mysterious." Commanding a brigade under Putnam, McDougall twice led his troops over the Hudson in response to Washington's orders—once in mid-June when Howe marched into Jersey, and again at the beginning of August when Howe's army, now at sea, appeared off Delaware Bay. Each time McDougall was sent back to Peekskill, the first time after being gone from the Highlands only two days, and the second time before he could even send his heavy baggage over the river.[4] Much of the time, however, he had little to do. From Peekskill he sent patrols toward Kings Bridge to probe British strength; he obtained information from British deserters, Tories, and strangers coming up the river; and he drilled his men.[5] Finally, developments in late August and early September raised expectations of a successful showdown with the enemy to the north and south. Howe finally landed on the Chesapeake Bay and started for Philadelphia; above Albany, an American force under Horatio Gates offered stiff resistance to the advancing Burgoyne.

McDougall played only a small role in the critical events of the late summer. Sir Henry Clinton, in command of a small British force in New York, launched a raid into New Jersey on September 12, and Putnam sent McDougall's brigade over the Hudson once more. By the 15th McDougall came within four miles of Clinton's main body and then stopped at Tappan. Despite Putnam's declaration that McDougall had between twelve and fifteen hundred men, McDougall actually had only 731 Continentals and 200 militia, which were, in his words, "illy provided with ammunition, and badly officered." Yet inaction gnawed at the restless general, and though he did not know the exact size or disposition of Clinton's forces, he proposed a night attack. But his regimental officers opposed the idea, arguing that it was too hazardous since Clinton was already alerted to their presence and probably had two or three times as many men. McDougall accepted these warnings. When the brigade did advance at morning light Clinton had already decamped. Despite efforts to catch his opponent before he could reach safety, McDougall accomplished little except to hasten Clinton's withdrawal.[6]

It was just as well that McDougall did not risk his brigade in an action of limited value. Washington needed the men to try for bigger game in Pennsylvania. Rebounding from the thrashing Howe had given him on the Brandywine, Washington's army had regrouped and was preparing to take the initiative if an opportunity presented itself. Washington sent urgent calls to New York and elsewhere for reinforcements; knowing that McDougall was operating in New Jersey, he instructed the New York brigadier to "join the army under my immediate command with all possible expedition." When McDougall on the 18th saw that Clinton had returned to New York, he collected provisions and the next day began the long march over the Delaware.[7] It took McDougall's men nine days to march the ninety miles to Washington's camp at Pennypacker's Mill. Washington daily urged him on, sending route instructions and even guides to lead him safely past Howe's outposts around Philadelphia. McDougall finally arrived at Pennypacker's Mill on the 27th, just in time to attend a council of war the next day. Since a total reinforcement of only twenty-six hundred men reached his camp that week, Washington needed every available man for his planned assault on the British at Germantown. For the moment, his general officers disagreed with the plan, and McDougall joined the majority in recommending a delay until more men arrived or a better opportunity presented itself. Washington bowed to the arguments of his senior commanders. He moved his army about nine miles closer along the Shippack Road to Germantown and waited a few days longer.[8] While the commander-in-chief sought his opportunity to fight, McDougall enjoyed the company of old friends— Greene, Knox, Sullivan, Lord Stirling—none of whom he had seen since White Plains the previous winter. It was a short rest, for Washington decided to attack on October 4.

As one of Washington's authoritative biographers has pointed out, the battle of Germantown was one of the American commander-in-chief's most elaborately conceived plans.[9] He intended a concentric movement similar to his successful move at Trenton, with his Continentals under Sullivan and Greene attacking the British center and the militia striking the enemy's flank and rear. If all went well, Howe would be crushed between anvil and hammer. As detailed in his general orders of October 3, 1777, Washington's plan of attack called for four columns to converge simultaneously on Howe's camp the following morning. Sullivan's division would follow the main road into Germantown to strike the British left, while Green's column, consisting of two-thirds of Washington's eight thousand Continentals, would take a longer route to the north, turning south on the Limekiln Road to hit Howe's stronger right flank. McDougall was to be in command of one of the lead brigades in Greene's division. Two militia columns on the extreme flanks of the American advance were to strike from the south and the north. Lord Stirling had the reserve which would follow Sullivan. Pioneers armed with axes were to be at the point of each division to cut through fences and other obstructions. Only battle essentials were to be carried by the men: packs and blankets were to be left behind. The whole army was to move into position during the night, ready to begin the attack at precisely five o'clock on the morning of the 4th.[10]

It was a bold plan, requiring close attention to detail and skillful execution on the part of all officers and men. The attack depended upon exact coordination of movement, sure knowledge of terrain and roads, reasonably good communications, favorable weather, and, not the least important, fresh, disciplined troops. In each instance, circumstances worked against success. McDougall's men, for example, were already foot-sore after their long, shoeless march from New Jersey when they were ordered to march another nineteen miles over strange roads and rough terrain through "marshes, woods, & strong fences" that same night to reach their position on the British right flank.[11] The militia screen, farther to the left, which was supposed to attack the enemy's rear, was guided by a local inhabitant who lost his way in the area's labyrinth of roads and lanes. Thus, William Smallwood and David Forman never did reach the battle in time. Moreover, seven miles separated Washington, who remained with Sullivan, from his main body of troops on the Shippack Road, so neither Greene nor Washington heard from the other until the battle was over. Finally, an early morning ground-fog reduced visibility to a matter of yards, muffling and distorting the sounds of battle and making visual observation impossible. Thus, Adam Stephen, on the west of the Shippack Road commanding one of Greene's units, became confused by the noise of musketry and cannon on his right and drifted over in that direction. His men collided in the fog with those of Anthony Wayne fighting in the center, causing an unfortunate exchange of shots and a movement to the rear before Greene or anyone else realized what had happened.[12]

It was nevertheless a good fight, demonstrating Washington's tenacity of spirit and the resiliency of the American army following Howe's victory on the Brandywine.[13] Sullivan and Wayne, with Washington watching as best he could in the fog, nearly smashed the British left before their ammunition ran low and the obscuring mist thoroughly confused the exhausted men. McDougall also appeared to be successful on School House Lane, where he and Peter Muhlenberg's Virginians fought their way to the village center before enemy reinforcements threatened to envelop their flank. Even after panic caused many American units to retreat, McDougall's men provided cover for the general withdrawal ordered by Washington.[14] On the whole, the British had been strongly challenged and were fortunate to have escaped defeat.

Now convinced that its earlier defeat at Brandywine was retrieved, Washington's army licked its wounds at its camp at Pennypacker's Mill. Although morale was high, the regiments were in poor physical condition after two major engagements. Casualties, loss of equipment, the hardships of temporary camps, and the seemingly endless marches had worn down the army. The officer corps also suffered. Describing the army's problems to Congress on October 7, 1777, Washington called particular attention to the shortage of general officers to lead brigades and divisions. The insufficient number of available brigadiers and major generals, he insisted, meant "that the government of the army cannot go on with that energy, which is essential to its well being and success." At the moment he lacked the time to write more, but he wanted to recommend the immediate promotion of Alexander McDougall to major general. "This gentleman," Washington wrote, "from the time of his appointment as brigadier, from his abilities, military knowledge and approved bravery, has every claim to promotion." When general officers had been promoted by Congress during the preceding March, Washington explained, McDougall was passed over in preference for younger men. But his strong attachment to the cause of independence kept him from resigning. "This I think gives him a peculiar title to esteem," Washington concluded, "and concurs with the opinion I have of his value as an officer, to make me wish it may appear advisable to Congress, to promote him to one of the vacancies." [15]

Even though Congress did not approve Washington's recommendation until the 20th, the commander-in-chief refused to believe that it would not be accepted and accordingly assigned McDougall new duties. On the 10th, Washington named him to a "court of enquiry," with Lord Stirling as president, to investigate the battlefield performance of Anthony Wayne at Paoli, John Sullivan at Staten Island, and Adam Stephen at Germantown. It was unpleasant duty for McDougall to sit in judgment on fellow officers whom he admired, and he was relieved when the court unanimously agreed that Wayne and Sullivan were innocent of any personal misconduct. Adam Stephen's case was another matter. He was generally blamed for precipitating the retreat at Germantown that cost the army a full victory, and the court recommended that Stephen be dismissed from the service for "unofficerlike conduct" and drunkenness during the recent battle.[16]

A more agreeable assignment for the new major general was a divisional command consisting of the seven Connecticut and Massachusetts regiments from Peekskill, which were organized into two new brigades under James Varnum and Jedediah Huntington. Twice in October McDougall crossed the cold Schuylkill as Washington sought to check Howe's moves around Philadelphia.[17] When Howe sent part of his army to reduce the American forts blocking the Delaware to British shipping, Washington countered by moving McDougall and Greene into lower Jersey in late November. Both expeditions were unproductive. Once again without shoes and now without warm winter clothing or adequate food, McDougall's tired troops were unable to quick-march over hard and icy roads to prevent a British sweep southwest of Philadelphia.[18] Nor were the men the only ones to suffer. McDougall's own health also deteriorated under the rigors and privations of winter field duty. By the second week of December, 1777, when Washington began moving the army from Whitemarsh to its winter quarters at Valley Forge, McDougall's health had failed completely. Washington allowed him to seek warm quarters at Morristown, where he nursed a "nervous fever" for seven weeks. The move helped. By mid-February, 1778, McDougall could report to Nathanael Greene that he was over the fever but quite weak, and several weeks more were necessary before he could mount a horse.[19]

An internal disorder also gripped the army. At the time that Mc-Dougall set out for Morristown, the so-called Conway Cabal, that swirl of rumor, outrage, and politics that has intrigued historians, ate away at the army's remaining vitality. McDougall was already gone from camp when Thomas Conway's celebrated criticism of Washington, in a letter to Horatio Gates, became common knowledge. Nathanael Greene described the situation to his sick friend: a "faction" led by Horatio Gates and Thomas Mifflin, former aide-de-camp to Washington, Quartermaster General, and now member of the reorganized Board of War, were the chief promoters, according to Greene, of Conway's unmerited elevation to Inspector General of the army with the rank of major general.[20] Conway's promotion was not only distasteful to the commander-in-chief, it was also intended to be a means by which Washington's critics, in the army and in Congress, would be able to force the Virginian to step aside and to allow what they asserted would be a more competent person to assume command of the Continental forces. The faction's objective, Greene insisted, was nothing less than "to supplant his Excellency from the Command of the Army and get Gen. Gates at the head of it." For that and other reasons, many senior officers were unhappy and ready to leave the service. "Great numbers are gone," Greene claimed, "and others going daily." From James Varnum, McDougall learned that the brigadiers had sent a memorial to Congress against Conway's promotion and were thinking of a mass resignation to protest their mistreatment.[21]

McDougall was astonished and distressed by the news from Valley Forge. Replying to Greene on February 14, and writing again on February 28, 1778, he fumed over the thought of Conway being peddled as "one of the greatest generals of the age." He told Greene, "I have been on command with . . . [Conway] . . . and could not observe any extraordinary marks of Military Genius about him. If he has seen service equal to his years, his proficiency in Arms is but very moderate." As for Horatio Gates, the hero of Saratoga was only a child of fortune, his victory over Burgoyne made possible by circumstances created by the British general himself. "And was it not easy and obvious for . . . [Gates] . . . with a force so far superior to surround him? If General Gates' strength had been but a little superior to the enemy he would have found it a very arduous task if not impracticable to secure the enemies army." Clearly Gates' ability did not entitle him to first command and "he should therefore know himself, and not attempt a measure, in which if he succeeded, he would disserve this country. I could tell him, the Tories and the Enemy would be glad he could accomplish his views." [22]

Of greater concern to McDougall was the suspicion that a faction was at work to advance Conway and Gates over Washington. "I am not surprised," he informed Greene, "that European wickedness in politics appear amongst us." It was in keeping with the "great depravity of Human Nature" that "some would ingage in it, under the mask of Patriotism to serve their private ends." What worried McDougall was the work of the "Junto" to put Gates in Washington's place. If Gates thought he had the public's confidence, he was mistaken, and he would be "undeceived" if he tried to take over the army on that basis. In McDougall's opinion, "the removal of the General [Washington] from the comd. of the army, in the manner proposed by the Junto would be one of the greatest misfortunes that could befall the country." He hoped Greene could obtain hard evidence against Mifflin, Gates and Conway, then "we might soon take such measures as would not only put a period to their wicked and ambitious hopes, but render them odious to the continent, which their conduct justly merits." [23]

He admitted that in a larger sense the country as a whole was at fault. Little effort, so far as he could tell, was being made to recruit new continental regiments or to provide them with necessaries, and in the spring the army's officers will be "put off with militia or short levies as in former campaigns; and the country will wonder according to custom that the enemy is not defeated." The public seemed to be in a "state of perfect ease and supineness," unconcerned over the army's condition, and contemptuous of those officers who were sacrificing everything for the nation. He found that out, he told Greene, when he tried to rent shelter on the road to Morristown. "It was with difficulty I could get a house to cover me from the weather, altho I contracted my sickness in the service of the country." He was plainly angry, and like other officers thought of returning to civilian life. "Were it not that I had taken such a lead in public politics & the sacredness of the cause we are engaged in," he confided to Greene, "I would not continue one moment in the service." He therefore advised Varnum and other disgruntled brigadiers to stay in the army, perhaps sympathizing with the advice a friend gave to Greene, that "a few oz's of gunpowder diffused thro channels will answer a good purpose." [24]

Perhaps the presence of George Washington was another force which kept McDougall in the army. McDougall never fully revealed his feelings toward the commander-in-chief in the way that he did about other officers, but there is no doubt that McDougall was awed, as other men were, by the aristocratic Virginian. Whether because of his personal qualities or his social status, Washington commanded the respect of his military associates to a degree which appears unusual for the time. Certainly that was the case with McDougall, and it also seems true for the other general officers. Washington was mentioned in their letters as "His Excellency" in most instances, or less frequently as the "General." While the magic of Washington's hold upon his subordinates can be exaggerated, it can be said that the commander-in-chief's exalted notion of duty and service to the country was an inspiration to senior officers, especially the general officers who came to know him. The charisma of his leadership, his quiet and confident exercise of authority, his even-handed treatment of others— all influenced the senior officers to emulate Washington's determination to remain in the army in spite of criticism from friends and defeats by the enemy.

The quality of Washington's leadership evoked from men either a secret jealousy and hatred or an intense loyalty; there apparently was little middle ground on how men responded to him. Among those officers who were with Washington in Pennsylvania at the battles of Brandywine and Germantown and who then spent the winter suffering at Valley Forge, emotions ranged from the near-hatred of Anthony Wayne, who became a rabid partisan of Gates, to those of John Cadwallader, who provoked a duel with Thomas Conway for slurring the commander-in-chief. McDougall was counted among a small band of senior officers—the most conspicuous being Greene, Knox, Lord Stirling, and John Sullivan—who appeared to see Washington as the embodiment of the war effort. And as they looked to Washington as a model for their own conduct in the years ahead, he came to rely upon them to faithfully serve the cause he was committed to. Perhaps it was an intuitive understanding of McDougall's devotion which prompted Washington after Germantown to recommend McDougall's promotion to major general; perhaps it was that sense of loyalty and duty to Washington which prevented a disgusted McDougall from leaving the army in the spring of 1778. [25]

His health and strength returning by March of 1778, McDougall was called back to duty. At first he was asked to join Lafayette's Canadian expedition, but he declined because he was not strong enough for that sort of active field command. Besides, he believed another campaign on the St. Lawrence would only end in disaster, as had the first. He could not, however, deny Washington's request of March 16, 1778, that he return to the Hudson to take command of the Highlands defenses and to investigate the October, 1777, loss of the river forts by Israel Putnam.[26] It was a chance to return to more familiar and congenial surroundings, to his family and old political friends. It was also an unpleasant assignment, for many delegates to Congress were calling for Putnam's head, and it appeared that McDougall was expected to deliver it. In guarded phrases, Washington even admitted that "mismanagement" had taken place in the Hudson's defenses and expressed embarrassment that Putnam, as a senior major general "with so moderate a share of abilities," could have claimed such a vital command in the first place. He assured Governor George Clinton and other New York leaders that he was sending a man "who will be perfectly agreeable to the state and to the public." [27] McDougall was given the "general controul and direction of all the posts in the Highlands and their dependencies, and be answerable for them," a firm reminder that Washington expected more from McDougall than he had gotten from Putnam. The commander-in-chief also carefully spelled out McDougall's authority to investigate the loss of Forts Montgomery and Clinton and to complete the new works at West Point. Washington held out hope that if McDougall could put the Highlands defense "in a proper train by the opening of the campaign, so as that the prosecution may be assigned to other hands," he would give him a field command with the main army.[28] McDougall was no doubt glad that he had asked Greene to seek out some rum and wine for him; he might have need of it.[29]

McDougall, along with Jedediah Huntington and Edward Wigglesworth, left Morristown on Monday morning, March 23, 1778, and rode the eighty-odd miles to Fishkill in three days, crossing the Hudson at New Windsor. By Wednesday evening the new commander in the Highlands had set up his headquarters at Colonel Dirck Brinkerhoff's house, where he rested for the beginning of his duties the next day. Although it was only six months since he had left New York to join the main army, he was to find his second tour of duty in the

Highlands far different from his first. Gone were the familiar forts above Peekskill; they had been burned by the British in their October raid. He was farther up the river where the land on either side of the river was wilder, the mountains and river bluffs were steeper, and the countryside more barren of inhabitants and farms than below. The strategically vital defense works at West Point, which Washington demanded that McDougall complete, had barely been started. But McDougall's assignment was larger than before, his authority and power as a major general, supported by Washington's explicit instructions, would command attention noticeably lacking the previous year.[30] Comfortably situated at Fishkill, McDougall played the generous host to many visitors: to Governor Clinton, John Jay, and James Duane, political leaders of the state government; to his fellow general officers, James Clinton, Henry Knox, Samuel Holden Parsons, Benedict Arnold, and Nathanael Greene. Lafayette also paid him a visit, sweeping into Fishkill "with 7 horses and four domestics." Even Israel Putnam, whose conduct on the Hudson was to be investigated, was welcomed and shared McDougall's table. In other respects the situation on the Hudson had not changed even though the disposition of American forces was different. Too few men were available to dig and build and mount patrols, and supplies of every kind were scant. Rumors abounded of imminent British attacks upon the river's defenses; and the Livingstons, especially Chancellor Robert R. Livingston, still disliked the former privateer captain.[31]

Pleased that Washington should have such high confidence in him, McDougall was nevertheless not overjoyed by his new assignment. As he listened to the reports of various officers during his first days at Fishkill, McDougall judged that the Hudson was to all intents defenseless. Writing to Washington four days after his arrival, he admitted that a soldier must obey his superiors, "and I cheerfully take my lot, of the difficulties of the times," but a note of bitterness ran through his letter. The Highlands had been bad enough to administer when Forts Montgomery and Clinton existed and a supporting force had been in the neighborhood, but the forts were gone now and everything needed to be done at once. He warned Washington not to expect too much in the short time before the British might ascend the river, adding: "I have little hopes of maintaining my reputation, if the enemy should in force, pay us an early visit." And as if he did not have problems enough, he ended his letter with the terse comment that "Congress have ordered General Conway to this post." [32] But Washington knew his man. The Commander-in-chief recognized that McDougall was a grumbler, that his desire to protect his "reputation," common enough among officers, was complemented by energy, ability and a thirst for success that would drive McDougall to correct the bungling and inaction of others on the Hudson. Writing to Governor George Clinton about the problems on the Hudson, Washington commented, "as I have appointed Genl. McDougall to take the command, I hope matters will assume a more pleasing aspect." [33]

The inquiry into the loss of Forts Montgomery and Clinton, which really referred to Putnam's command performance in 1777, had to be disposed of first. By March 28, 1778, the principals were assembled at Fishkill, and on Monday, the 30th, the court began taking evidence. McDougall had no wish to unnecessarily embarrass his old friend, so the hearings were conducted in an atmosphere of informality, the court members and witnesses dining generally at McDougall's quarters each day. In the week that followed, more than twenty officers appeared and gave their version of the October debacle, each explaining his particular action. As McDougall, Huntington and Wigglesworth listened to the officers involved, it was clear that there were two basic causes for the disaster. [34] The mountain passes leading to the weakly defended western approaches to the forts were wide open to the British because no one thought the enemy could possibly attack from that direction; and Putnam, although a brave and eager fighter, was baffled, confused, and in the end made helpless by Sir Henry Clinton's strategy and movements. As George Clinton remarked a month after the 1777 debacle, the forts were lost because "of a bad head, no part to a weakened heart." [35] It was a simple case of not meeting problems which were too complex for a man of Putnam's abilities. McDougall and the court could see no cowardice or dereliction of duty, and Putnam was exonerated. Huntington and Wigglesworth left Fishkill on April 6, leaving McDougall to write the lengthy report to Washington. [36] But McDougall set aside that task and turned to what he considered more pressing business—the West Point defenses.

McDougall had reason to be concerned. West Point was still only an engineer's dream, without forts or artillery or supplies to defend the post. As in former times, disturbing reports that the British were stirring in New York caused alarm in Fishkill. On April 2, an American spy reported that the British intended to move up the river, intelligence that was confirmed two days later by the sudden appearance of three British warships at Tarrytown. Perhaps remembering his experience at Peekskill, and observing Putnam's present anguish, McDougall sent orders to Samuel Holden Parsons at West Point to expect an attack. He also sent a request to Governor Clinton for militia and asked for a personal meeting. To Albany he sent orders for three Continental regiments to be sent down at once.[37] McDougall was perhaps unduly alarmed, as a more experienced river-watcher, Governor Clinton, argued. The British wanted only to "amuse us by making alarms of that kind familiar & of course disregarded," Clinton wrote. "This was the case last year, and I hope we have sufficiently learned the moral that is to be drawn from the fable of the shepard & the wolf. . . ."[38] There were of course two possible morals in the fable, and Clinton could not fault McDougall's vigilance against the ultimate appearance of the real wolf.

One cause of McDougall's overreaction to the possibility of a British attack was that he had little first hand knowledge of the West Point defenses. At his headquarters, he had heard contrary accounts from General Parsons, an old acquaintance who was in charge of the new fortifications, and from the disgruntled French engineer, Lewis de la Radiere, who originally laid out the design but who was unhappy over the work being done under the supervision of the Polish engineer, Thaddeus Kosciuszko. McDougall invited Governor Clinton and his brother, General James Clinton, to join him for a personal appraisal and other business, and accompanied by Radiere, he crossed over on April 8 and had a first hand view of West Point for the first time.[39]

McDougall spent the better part of four days at West Point clambering over rocky slopes and hills and conferring with his officers and with Governor Clinton. What he found was not wholly displeasing. Barracks for several hundred men were finished, and small log huts were available to house additional men. A large amount of timber was on hand, and troops were already building two walls and a connecting bastion of the massive fort to be located on the plain's northeastern corner. Near the river's edge, a battery was nearly finished and ready to receive artillery. Additional redoubts were ordered for the higher ground southwest of the plain to protect the main fort. McDougall was also heartened by a set of energetic officers working to make West

Point the anchor of the Hudson Valley defenses. Before leaving on Saturday the 11th, he gave detailed instructions to General Parsons of work to be done, the disposition of his troops, and the defensive tactics to be followed in case of an attack.[40] From Governor Clinton McDougall obtained a promise of militia units to be used as a construction force.[41] McDougall and Clinton also talked over Washington's proposal of an attack on New York City, quickly agreeing that it was out of the question until West Point was stronger. Writing to Washington two days after the visit, McDougall could report that the work was moving forward and that the fort was now at least able to repel a "sudden assault." [42]

Satisfied that the new defense system of the Highlands was safely underway, McDougall's life settled down to a busy routine of administrative problems. "I am so harrassed with business of a trivial nature," McDougall complained to Governor Clinton, "that my mind is almost distracted and scarcely able to attend to the important concerns of the department." [43] Money had to be found to pay the regiments, forage purchased for the horses and cattle, additional troops located for the Indian-ravaged northern frontiers, prisoners disposed of, flags of truce regulated and British deserters interrogated, and recruits from New England inoculated and trained.[44] West Point still remained his first responsibility, but fortunately he could rely on the diligence of others to keep the work moving. By the end of April, 1778, the chain was across the river and the new redoubts were rising fast.[45] There was a corresponding lull in activity. Many of McDougall's entries in a diary kept for this period were nothing more than the laconic phrase: "Nothing of moment." The dull routine, however, suddenly ended. On April 25 McDougall learned that Congress had turned the Northern Department, including West Point, over to Horatio Gates; and by Washington's order, McDougall was to return to the main army as soon as Gates arrived at Fishkill.[46]

It was not a popular change along the Hudson. Many of the state's political leaders remembered only too well Gates' bad treatment of Philip Schuyler in 1777 when the latter had been removed from command of the Northern Department. When Governor Clinton learned of Gates' appointment, he commented bitterly, "If it was possible to ruin us by unwise & injudicious measures it must have er' now been effected." On the other hand, McDougall's performance was respected (if not praised), and Clinton told a friend, "the exchange, therefore, is not considered a favour." [47] McDougall was understandably angered by the appointment. His natural bitterness deepened as the days passed and Gates did not appear. "I think," he told Clinton, "I am not well treated by him and Congress." The Governor urged McDougall to be philosophical and to remember that "Genl Gates is a great man. Little people like you & me must submit to insults." [48] Several weeks later, John Sullivan at Providence, Rhode Island, sarcastically pointed out that McDougall's disappointment was his own fault, for he had failed to learn the art of flattery. Sullivan advised him to hold on; "perhaps we may be saved politically & have opportunity to do ourselves justice." [49]

While McDougall waited impatiently for Gates to appear, a number of visitors provided diverting entertainment. At the end of April, Simeon Deane, brother of the more famous envoy, Silas Deane, brought news of an alliance with France. Everyone was elated, and McDougall allowed his officers to plan a Saturday night celebration of roast ox and rum. The party turned into a hilarious drinking bout, with McDougall taking a back seat to no man.[50] Nine days later, May 11, 1778, after a four-day visit to West Point, McDougall welcomed Benedict Arnold, whom he regarded as the real hero of Saratoga and whose wounds from that battle (including those to his pride) were still not fully healed. At dinner that evening it is probable that, among other topics, the two men talked of Gates, his attempt to succeed Washington, and their own grievances against the putative victor of Saratoga. Before Arnold's departure two days later, McDougall took him on a tour of West Point, proudly pointing to the progress achieved in two months. Arnold no sooner left than Samuel Holden Parsons came up from West Point to stay overnight, and the next day Nathanael Greene, who had first warned McDougall of Gates, arrived for a two day visit. Sometime between Arnold's stay and Greene's departure on the 16th, McDougall exercised his privilege as commanding general to name the main fort at West Point, now rising above the plain, in honor of the courageous Arnold. Whether out of admiration for the one or to show spite to the other, McDougall nonetheless had his revenge on Gates earlier than his friend Sullivan suggested. He saw to it that as long as Gates remained in command of the Highlands, Fort Arnold would daily remind him of one of his enemies.[51]

McDougall quietly relinquished his command on May 21 and began a six-month period of duty with the main army that involved little action.[52] Washington, following the battle of Monmouth on June 28, 1778, pointed his men toward the Hudson, hoping to cooperate with a recently arrived French fleet in an attack on Sir Henry Clinton in New York City. Until Washington opened his new headquarters at White Plains on July 20, McDougall remained at Fishkill, without a command or specific duties, and Gates openly ignored him. Despite the circumstances, the period of rest was beneficial, for McDougall was apparently sick once more. He wrote the long overdue report on the loss of Fort Montgomery and enjoyed his wife's company.[53] Meanwhile, Washington continued to work on a plan for an attack on New York City, an operation which the commander-in-chief wanted McDougall to command if his health permitted. When McDougall finally moved to White Plains in late July, he attended a council of war which reviewed the plan and recommended that it be abandoned because New York's harbor was too shallow for the deep-drawing French warships. There was little else to do. When Washington moved troops into Connecticut to balance Clinton's threatening motions in September, McDougall's division of three brigades marched and countermarched and moved no farther east than New Milford. In mid-October, 1778, Washington again feared the British were moving eastward and sent McDougall toward Hartford. McDougall remained in Connecticut for two months, during which time his most notable achievement was to repair the road to Farmington.[54] He did manage to visit his wife and daughter at Hartford, and finally, in disposing the army for the winter months, Washington on November 24 ordered McDougall to return to the Hudson and once more command the Highlands.[55]

# Chapter Eleven
# Mission to Philadelphia

The army's condition was at its worst during the winter 1778–79. Suffering in the three main camps (Redding, Connecticut, the Highlands, and Middlebrook, New Jersey) and in more scattered outposts was far worse than the previous winter at Valley Forge. The weather was colder, the snow deeper, and the food scantier than ever before. Even though the army was to suffer even more, no winter would inflict greater hardship on American soldiers than that of 1778–79. Conditions in McDougall's Highland command were as bad as elsewhere. As the cold weather approached, the harried major general was still desperately trying to get his men out of tents and into weather-proof quarters of some sort. A shortage of straw for bedding in one brigade resulted in a short-lived mutiny. Draft animals were fast dying for lack of forage, and the men were forced to haul the wagons themselves or to go without firewood and provisions. Finding food was a continuously vexing problem, and it was not uncommon for the troops to be without flour or bread for days on end during the course of the winter. The weather only added to the misery of empty stomachs and shivering bodies.[1]

As a consequence of these wartime experiences, a dramatic shift appeared in the political outlook of a number of the country's citizen-soldiers. In its starkest form, the general officers came to doubt that the people of the thirteen states were seriously committed to the purpose of independence and the war, the establishment of a republican society. If, as political writers contended, republicanism was derived from and dependent upon the wide diffusion of virtue among the people—a collective willingness to subordinate private interests to the higher good of the whole society—American independence was then in deep trouble. Public and private virtue seemed nonexistent or at least a rarity to the frustrated senior officers as they sought to overcome the multiple problems of keeping the army ready and fit to fight the enemy. At one time the general officers had enthusiastically and confidently joined the armed defense of those republican ideals expressed in 1776. But as the war dragged on, as battles were lost, as shortages of manpower and supplies became continuous problems, and as currency depreciation progressively worsened, a feeling of betrayal and anger developed in the army's chain of command. The senior officers asked themselves why the war effort had gone sour, and they reached the conclusion that the source of the problem was to be found in the indifferent attitude toward the war taken by the new state governments and the public generally. They accused the representatives of the states in Congress of wrangling endlessly over matters of detail while the army suffered. And when the general officers turned to the state legislatures for help, they insisted that they encountered hostility, ignorance of the enemy's strength, and, generally, a greater concern for local matters than for the need to defeat the British. Particularly galling to the senior commanders was the fact that while their soldiers were in rags, civilians appeared to be benefiting from the wartime economy. In the end, Washington's generals became distrustful of the people's representatives in government. It was the state legislatures which had the responsibility of sustaining a war that was national in scope, but the new governments seemed reluctant to levy taxes, organize the militia, obtain supplies, stabilize prices, or stamp out profiteering, seemingly because those policies would tread upon the special interests of farmers, merchants, and artisans. "To the shame and scandal of America, and Human Nature," McDougall asserted, too many citizens placed their own interests ahead of the country's safety at a time when the country's very existence was in doubt.[2]

McDougall was as unhappy and frustrated over the slow progress of the war as any other general officer, and his aroused feelings shaped his actions in the months ahead. From the time of his arrival at Peekskill on November 26, 1778, McDougall's main concern was to keep his men tolerably fit for fighting. The fortifications at West Point were not ignored, nor were Washington's orders to fortify both banks of the Hudson at King's Ferry. McDougall even planned the construction of a new road over the Croton into Westchester County.[3] His command concerns, however, were distracted by the plight of the soldiers stationed in the Highlands, a condition which he saw as typical of the entire American army. The public expected the army to be everywhere at once when danger was near, but few were willing to make the sacrifices necessary to defeat the enemy. "Connecticut won't have us but in the hour of danger. New York is reluctant we should have any repose. New Jersey complain they have had too much of us. Where, my dear sir," the exasperated McDougall demanded of Governor Clinton, "are we to go?" [4]

McDougall's bitterness ran deeper than his complaints against the public for its treatment of the army. There were also personal matters involved, as he revealed in an angry letter to Washington two weeks after his arrival at Peekskill. His health was poor once more, which did not help his frame of mind. But most important, he simply did not want to be in command of the Highlands where he felt his "reputation" would be ruined by the enormous problem of defending the Hudson Valley with inadequate resources. Even before Washington made the assignment, McDougall feared that he might have to serve in New York under Israel Putnam, the "old general" who belonged in retirement.[5] McDougall's preference had been to remain with Washington's main force, as the commander-in-chief knew; instead Washington sent him to take charge of the Highland defenses, which were in a horrible condition. He would dutifully obey orders, he told his commander, but neither Washington nor Congress could expect him to perform miracles if his assignment lasted only a few months or if Congress failed to supply whatever was necessary to complete and arm the fortifications.

It was against Congress that McDougall expressed his deepest bitterness, and as he unburdened himself to Washington, it was evident that he had been seething for some time over certain congressional actions. First, Congress had promoted junior officers over his head, "Some of whom were unknown in the cause of this country, even before the sword was drawn; and what was known of them was their passivity." Second, in the spring of 1778 Congress, for no other discernible reason than "Athenian Caprice," had taken the Highland command away from him and had given it to Horatio Gates. The latter decision especially rankled McDougall because he thought he had performed his duties well and because he disliked Gates. "I have not merited this treatment of my countrymen," he complained to Washington. "When it has arisen I am at a loss to determine, unless it is that I have not meanly cringed or wickedly caballed; or that having had a halter about my neck thirteen years for my services to America,

Congress conceive themselves at liberty to treat me as they have done." But no more. "I am determined," he wrote belligerently, "not to be made the scape goat of any ignorant, wicked, or inattentive servant of the country, appointed by the cabals or intrigues of any set of men." He informed Washington that the military engineer at West Point would be required to keep a "journal of my orders directing the works, the strength and materials he shall have, and the progress of the work from day to day; and if the supreme council of the country will not enable me to execute their orders, they must take the consequences with their constituents." If West Point fell to the enemy for lack of defenses, it would not be his fault.[6]

Washington's response to McDougall's emotional outburst was a masterful demonstration of his ability to manage other men. Confident that McDougall would not quit the army, the hard-pressed Washington delayed two months before he answered McDougall's complaints, thereby giving the agitated New Yorker time to calm down. When he did write in February, 1779, Washington was sympathetic but firm. If McDougall thought his assignment to the Highlands was made because he lacked Washington's favor, he was wrong. "I persuade myself, my dear sir," Washington told him, "you need no assurances of my perfect confidence and esteem. The occasions are too numerous and unequivocal in which it has been testified to make the assistance of words necessary to your conviction." He further reminded McDougall that winter duties were assigned "as far as circumstances would permit, where the nature of the service in my judgment made the talents and qualifications of a good officer, requisite." What the Highlands required in 1779 was an energetic administrator who was also familiar with the leaders and circumstances of the New York government, and McDougall was the man for that position. "My opinion of your merit," Washington assured him, "has had a principal share in regulating my choice of the stations you have been appointed to fill." The implication of Washington's words was unmistakable: He was relying upon McDougall to do an unglamorous, dirty but necessary job. The West Point fortifications must be completed and the Hudson defended.[7]

As Washington expected, McDougall energetically attacked the problems of his command. But as the weeks of winter passed, McDougall's dark mood over public affairs was deepened as he encountered what seemed to him to be a self-serving public, indifferent to the needs of the army. There were farmers who sought British gold for their wheat and flour; landlords who disliked the presence of soldiers seeking warm rooms and dry beds; impatient legislators who wondered why the army did not drive the British out of New York; strong young men who eluded military service by hiring boys or old men as substitutes; fair-weather Whigs who continually talked of the imminent peace which made further military efforts unnecessary; and merchants, jobbers, and speculators who revelled in their wartime profits. At one point in December, 1778, when he sought temporary quarters for some soldiers in Poughkeepsie, which served as the seat of the state government, an irritable McDougall even exchanged sharp words with his friend Governor Clinton over the legislature's opposition to the presence of troops in the capital city.[8] McDougall interpreted these experiences to mean that the people felt the war was someone else's problem, not theirs.

In an exasperated and resentful mood, McDougall became convinced that the war could not long continue under those circumstances. "Can the country expect Spartan virtue in her army while the people are wallowing in all the luxury of Rome in her declining state," McDougall asked. "If they do, they are novices in the science of Human Nature." [9] If the public could not—or would not—see what was needed to win the war, the army then had an obligation to compel the shortsighted, selfish citizenry to make sacrifices for the greater good. The army, McDougall seemed to be saying, might be required to intervene in civil affairs in order to win the war. But he was not comfortable with the prospect—indeed, perhaps the necessity—of using the army for non-military purposes. "It is one of the first wishes of my heart," he insisted, "to see the civil at all times superior to the military, and the most permanent foundation laid to perpetuate this blessing to the latest posterity." [10] He recognized that however limited and well-intentioned a military interference in governmental affairs might be, it still would result in a diminution of the representational principle of civil authority and thus constitute a danger to the rights of the people. Clearly, he preferred to see the states and Congress adopt whatever policies were necessary to secure independence; but if government did not act, then bold measures were justified. McDougall drew upon the history of Republican Rome, which he apparently found instructive in America's time of crisis, to show that it was "right that the citizen to obtain the object of war, resigns

Washington to McDougall in the Commander-in-Chief's own hand, outlining a route for McDougall's approach to the enemy at Potts Grove, Pa., September 24, 1777.

—W. WRIGHT HAWKES COLLECTION, SCHAFFER LIBRARY, UNION COLLEGE

his personal liberty, and exposes his life, for the safety of his country." That same history also proved that the citizen who remained at home, "protected and left to the enjoyment of his personal liberty & property," had to make a temporary surrender of each in order to secure both to the whole country.[11] If any citizen in the present war with Britain expected the full enjoyment of all his rights, he must prepare "to bow the knee to the tyrant," for such a citizen cannot have both at the same time. Either the public's own generals would seize power to achieve a military victory, McDougall believed, or the people would be conquered by their enemies. Civil government must do what was necessary to win the war, or the army would. "If not," he predicted, "all our toils & perils are lost; and lost forever."[12] Such were McDougall's views on the perilous condition of the war in early 1779.

If a specific plan existed in 1779 among the general officers which outlined the form and extent of a potential military intrusion into government, McDougall's correspondence does not reveal it. His letters referred only to the urgent need for action to save the war and the possibility that the army might have to do more than fight the enemy. He did not advocate a military dictatorship, even by George Washington, as some of his military friends wanted. He was too committed to the principles of liberty to wish civil government displaced and destroyed. McDougall believed that "no man is fit to be trusted with the sword, who wishes for more power than to call her [the country's] means out, on extraordinary occasions, and pressing emergencies, and these should be such as common sense will easily perceive."[13] He favored the Roman model, by which generals were given great authority during war and "exercised the power at the risque of their heads." The republicans of antiquity clearly understood the uselessness of discussing the nature of freedom without providing for its security, while Americans had apparently rejected that lesson of history. In America, generals "are held amenable to the public for its safety, and exposed to the clamour of all without the power of saving the former or doing justice to our own reputations."[14]

It was his powerless position as a general officer which disturbed McDougall. The people expected the army to defend the country, but the public apparently lacked the faith to entrust its military officers with sufficient power to defeat the enemy. Although army leaders had been telling government authorities that greater military support was

needed to achieve victory, such warnings went unheeded. Yet whenever the army sought additional power to finish its job, "the cry is instantly raised, the army is having designs to enslave the country, and
to be superior to their creators." "Would to God," McDougall exclaimed, "the hearts of all the citizens of America were as jealousy and
honorably attached to the interest of their country, as those of the
Army." For McDougall, however, the issue was not whether army
officers or political leaders were more attached to republicanism. At
stake was republican government itself, for without an effort by all
the people to defeat Britain's intention to crush the American rebellion, independence was a dream. It was now a time of crisis, and Mc-
Dougall warned that the army must not be blamed if independence
was lost. "It is time the American generals to be on their guard," he
warned, "and not apt to be made the scapegoats of any public bodies,
however dignified or respectable they may be." [15]

In some respects, McDougall's view of the war effort involved more
than an alarming pessimism over the prospects of victory. His own
faith in republicanism—in the people's ability to rule themselves—which he had so vigorously expressed in earlier times, now
seemed to be weakening under the weight of the army's misery. The
war was nearing the end of its fourth year, yet the prospects of American success were seemingly little better than in 1775. The British
seemed to be as strong as ever, content to wait in the relative comfort
of New York City until the rebellion collapsed. America, on the other
hand, "is asleep, & dreaming the enemy will evacuate the United
States," McDougall wrote to George Clinton. "She, or too many of
her silly sons, imagine the struggle is at an end. Today reconciliation,
tomorrow the interference of France is to terminate the dispute . . .
Now it is said Spain's acceding to the independency is to effect it—"
anyone, apparently, rather than the Americans themselves.[16] There
existed a notion among the people that a war to defend liberty against
"a cruel and arbitrary enemy" did not require unity and sacrifice at
all. The war, it seemed, was the army's problem. Shortsightedness
became public policy as governments responsible for directing the
army's actions responded to the people's desire to be burdened as little
as possible. Yet the army, as McDougall frequently said, was commanded "to make bricks without straw," to fight a war without an adequate supply of money and manpower. Instead of accepting the responsibility to sacrifice in defense of the liberty that was the war's

principal goal, America was in a "profound sleep." Despite the new constitutions which established representative government, the people acted in self-centered ways which suggested that they lacked that collective virtue upon which republicanism depended. The situation could not continue, and McDougall was fearful that republicanism might fall victim to the critical circumstances of the war. Something must change. "While we are pleasing and amusing ourselves with spartan constitutions on paper," McDougall told Joseph Reed in Philadelphia, "a very contrary spirit reigns triumphant, in all ranks, [and] we may look out for some fatal *catastrophy* to befall this people. Our political constitutions and manners do not agree, one or the other must fall—give way—otherwise America is a phenomenon in civil society." [17]

The army's plight required a political remedy, a conclusion McDougall shared with most of the other general officers. If the collective frustration of the general staff might have fostered a conspiratorial design, most generals were restrained by the example of George Washington's uncomplaining self-sacrifice. McDougall in particular was awed by Washington's determination to remain as head of the army and to fight the enemy as best he could to the very end. The commander-in-chief's example reinforced McDougall's own decision to stay with the army. But McDougall's experience and political temperament told him that complete inaction would be fatal to the cause, so he found matters that he could act on alone. In response to Walter Livingston's lament that "never were a set of men in more profound ignorance of the numbers of their foe," he wrote the New York legislature, for instance, furnishing members of both houses with an account of the enemy's strength in New York. His purpose was to remind the legislators that the war was far from over and that greater effort was needed to win independence. He filled his letters to Governor Clinton with the same arguments, asking for laws or executive orders that would help the army survive.[18]

Although McDougall did not want a general military takeover of government, he did believe that the military should be used to enforce civil laws. He did not hesitate to use his soldiers to compel local authorities to obey wartime regulations when those officials proved unwilling or unequal to the task. Two problems, flour exports and horse stealing, were symptomatic of the malaise and thus received particular attention. McDougall was convinced that enough wheat and flour existed in the state to feed both the military and public, but while his division lived on short rations, farmers hid their surplus grain from commissary agents and exported those commodities out of the state, in violation of an embargo dating from 1776. Jobbers and British agents outbid and outwitted local authorities, causing flour prices to soar and forcing the army to scrounge for food. On January 20, 1779, McDougall reported to Governor Clinton that the situation was so bad that he was forced to "act arbitrary [sic] in many cases where necessity require it for the preservation of this state, and the common cause." [19] He established an elaborate system of permits and sent army patrols along the Connecticut border and deep into West-chester County to prevent flour from illegally leaving the state. But evasions continued despite these precautions, and by the spring, Mc-Dougall opened a "custom house office" with a military guard to stop New York wheat and flour from entering Connecticut.[20] "Divine, Civil, or military law," he told Governor Clinton, "is not in this day regarded. God only knows what will be the consequence. The enemy and the line, of our army, takes up but very little of my time, com-pared with what is engrossed by internal enemies, and pretended Whigs." [21] For a time even a state confiscation law was ineffectual in supplying McDougall's division. Commissary officers had wagons but no horses, and local justices of the peace and constables proved un-willing to enforce the law.[22] The situation was intolerable, and Mc-Dougall complained that "a soldier receives thirty nine lashes for ab-senting himself without leave; and yet a citizen, no better born than him shall pass without corporal punishment, altho he shall do his ut-most to starve that very soldier." [23]

The deficiency of horses in McDougall's command was also a serious problem. Everyone in the Highlands felt the pinch. Mc-Dougall's flour patrols on the Connecticut border, for instance, were on foot while the suspects they sought, rode horses.[24] He feared that his troops would soon have "scarce a horse to draw a wagon or an ar-tillery piece" because of the shortage.[25] It was a maddening problem. Without forage the army's draft animals died or were rendered use-less, but without horses and oxen the commissary men could not collect the hay and feed needed to keep the animals alive. Fortunately this aggravating situation had a humorous aspect, since those horses which did survive were promptly rustled away by horse thieves. It seemed that an officer could not dismount without running the risk of having his horse stolen. In addition to his other responsibilities and problems, McDougall thus became a sheriff in pursuit of horse thieves.

His first reaction was to apply lynch law. He issued orders to his continental guards in Westchester County to court-martial and hang on the spot anyone caught stealing cattle or horses for the British. He was tired, he wrote an approving Governor Clinton, of his command serving as a supply depot for the enemy's cavalry.[26] A large, strong jail was constructed at West Point, capable of holding "fifty of the strongest horse thieves in the country" and ready for use by February.[27] McDougall was proud of his new jail and the fact that he quickly filled it and hanged a few guilty parties. But he knew it would not be enough. "All the American army, disposed in guards, in the covered and rocky country of this state, will not totally prevent the mischief," he wrote, "and far less will the small corps of the army under my command effect it." He needed the assistance of local and state authorities and threatened to take "decisive measures" if government did not help stamp out horse stealing. "It is a hard condition for me to be placed in," he informed Governor Clinton, "to be obliged for the security of this state, and the general security, to act as a despot and then to be subject to the caprice and calumny of the times." He threw a last dart at the legislature, which he blamed for most of his problems. "I hope my countrymen will take the honor to themselves, and not compel the military to do acts, which will come with a better grace from a watchful legislature." [28]

The American army somehow survived the winter of 1778–79, and became a tougher fighting force in the process. But few men would forget their hardships, and there remained among those in the ranks a smoldering discontent over conditions that would later erupt in serious mutinies. McDougall had also changed, growing more irritable and intransigent. His declining health no doubt accounted for part of his peevishness, while the country's political condition made him uneasy. He was less sure than before that the American public wanted to continue a war that promised only sacrifice to its supporters; instead, he told John Sullivan, the people believed in "false hopes." [29] There is no evidence that he thought of giving up the cause of independence, but it was clear that he wondered whether the pledge of 1776, "of our Lives, our Fortunes, and our Sacred Honor," retained its meaning.

The routine of garrison life and the strengthening of West Point were not neglected during McDougall's periods of gloom from December, 1778, to April, 1779. The work load was heavy, as he complained to Governor Clinton. "I have done a great deal of business in the course of my life, but at no period have I been so hard pressed." [30] Guarding against a surprise British move up the Hudson was particularly important to McDougall, who could not easily forget his brush with defeat at Peekskill in 1777 and Israel Putnam's debacle a few months later. McDougall sought information of British plans through a spy network authorized by Washington and financed by congressional gold. He reacted quickly, therefore, when he learned in late May that the British intended to assault the Highlands once more. [31] The British easily captured the new forty-man forts at King's Ferry on June 1, but McDougall hurriedly moved his troops into a blocking position. Washington sent reinforcements and followed with the main army to foil whatever further objectives Sir Henry Clinton might have had. [32] While the two armies watched each other through June and part of July, McDougall continued to command at West Point, and from his perch in the Highlands, he was a spectator to Anthony Wayne's daring recapture of Stony Point on July 16 and the subsequent withdrawal of American forces from King's Ferry. There was little other military business for him to do. [33]

Except for Wayne's success, followed a month later by Henry Lee's raid against the British at Paulus Hook, New Jersey, Washington's army remained inactive. With little campaigning in prospect, the army became restless, grumbling over deficiencies that were more noticeable and intolerable than before. A rapidly depreciating continental currency generated a monetary crisis so severe that Washington and his generals saw little hope of a change in the army's temper. Indeed, the problem was so alarming that Washington feared his army might have to disband if Congress failed to find a solution. [34] The financial pinch was no less severe for general officers like McDougall than for other levels in the army. Depreciation made the liberal wages of 1775 inadequate, the officers were forced to draw upon their personal resources to support themselves. Months earlier Washington had hoped to quiet their complaints by sponsoring a proposal of half-pay for life after the war ended, a measure that would at least assure them of a comfortable retirement, but congressional response was less enthusiastic than Washington had hoped for. [35] In fact, Congress recommended a compromise measure. It had been recommended to the states that officers be provided with half-pay for seven years if those officers remained in service and held no public office during the seven-year term. But by spring, 1779, this partial remedy was unacceptable to the generals. What at first may have seemed an acceptable compromise had been made meaningless by the crushing currency depreciation. Army officers needed and demanded immediate relief; they also wanted half-pay for life.[36]

Congressional reaction to the army's plight was divided, and it was mixed with a sense of futility. The army was suffering and making ugly noises about quitting, but congressmen recognized that resolutions ordering changes and increased benefits were of little value when Congress lacked the economic resources to support those measures. Moreover, the demand for lifetime half-pay revived the republican hostility exhibited by some members in 1778 when the proposal was first debated. The proposal would establish a military caste in society, some members argued, and would raise army officers above other citizens who were sacrificing as much in the common cause. Rejecting a committee report recommending the principle of life-time pensions, Congress instead passed the measure along to the states for action, along with a limp encouragement for the establishment of any other rewards a state deemed appropriate. The next day, August 18, 1779, Congress agreed to a subsistance allowance of $500 per month for officers to the rank of colonel, but refused to give additional money to general officers.[37]

The army's general officers were ignored by Congress that summer, and the neglect politicized them for the remainder of the war. Since they had never really been on good terms with Congress, discontent smoldered among the army's highest ranking officers: first there had been congressional mishandling of promotions; now general officers were apparently meant to be kept impoverished. Or so it seemed to McDougall and others. To McDougall, no less than to other senior officers, the problems of rank, compensation, and future rewards were symptomatic of a war effort subverted by poor policies, political manipulation, and private interest. Political activity appeared to be the only method left to obtain satisfaction. Although he was in poor health, McDougall attended several meetings in September, 1779 (probably held at West Point), to decide on a course of common action. A memorial to Congress pleading the officers' case was an obvious first step, and with Washington's blessings, one was ready for Congress before the end of the month. In rich prose the generals outlined the nature of their complaint. General officers had to keep their own horses, clothe themselves, and provide a table and entertainment suitable to their military rank but costing far in excess of their depreciating pay and allowances. By contrast Congress had voted pay raises and had established depreciation adjustments for subordinate officers who were now better off financially than major generals. From the private to the colonel, "Congress have been pleased to hold out . . . some object beyond the war—but to general officers— nothing." The generals asked for "no extravagant advantages." They merely wanted a pay increase and some other type of reward at war's end so that they would not return "to the arms of those who depend upon us, in a worse situation than when for public service we left them." They intended to rely on the candor and equity of Congress, "from whose benevolence we are certain of receiving every reasonable attention and relief." Eleven major generals and fifteen brigadiers, some of whom were not in camp, put their names to the memorial with Washington's tacit approval. Robert Howe, who protested to Washington about the proceedings, was the only general officer in camp who refused to sign.[38]

While Congress considered the memorial, McDougall spent the winter months of 1779–80 at Fishkill nursing his "complaint of the stone" which made him unfit for winter duty. He indirectly asked Washington to be relieved. Already in a sick bed, he wrote the commander in chief, "I shall not long be able to be of much service to the country or myself, besides the distressing & dreadful prospect of grazing thro the future part of life in pain & misery." Washington agreed and named William Heath to succeed McDougall, who was finally relieved of his command at West Point on December 4, 1779.[39] But absence from active command did not mean that McDougall no longer fretted over military problems or the country's condition. He warned Governor Clinton that the soldiers at West Point were in an "ill temper" because of the chronic shortage of food, and he insisted that the legislature must act to save the state from disaster.[40] In a brooding letter to an old friend, John McKesson, he revealed his wintry mood. "America is truly democratical in some respects to her servants and appears as cruel to them as the Egyptians were to the Israelites of old, when they were commanded to make brick without straw," he wrote.

"The most rigid virtue is expected of the army while the country at large pursue property as the primary object. How long this principle and democracy will exist together is a question of importance to the civil sages." He concluded ominously: "Some of the military ones are of [the] opinion your constitutions and manners do not accord that therefore one or the other must give way." [41] If McDougall was again hinting at the possibility of a military intervention in government, as he had the previous winter, he stopped short of making the prediction.

To the old complaints was now added that of the congressional action—or inaction—on the generals' memorial of the past fall. From Nathanael Greene, McDougall learned that Congress was as "calm and easy as if all things were in the most flourishing and prosperous train." [42] Little could be expected on the memorial, Greene wrote bitterly, for Congress was "determined to keep the general officers poor, to prevent their obtaining an extensive influence." McDougall was outraged. "If the general officers had not halters about their necks they would not have been so often insulted and neglected," he fumed to Greene. "To be exposed to the calumny incident to our office, at the same time unsupported slaves is a condition too much for human nature to bear." [43] But he could only be philosophical. America's problems were at "the disposal of that God, who has hitherto extricated America out of various difficulties, apparently insurmountable." [44]

By late spring McDougall was healthy again and he rejoined the army. When the British crossed over into New Jersey in force in June, 1780, Washington ordered him to West Point to command five brigades in support of Robert Howe, post commandant, where Washington expected McDougall's presence to calm the fears of New Yorkers about Howe's competence. [45] When the army assembled in June of 1780, a crisis existed as serious as that of the previous summer. Depreciation was still severe, and, even worse, a drought in New York and New Jersey threatened the crops upon which the army depended for winter provisions. Nor had the generals' memorial to Congress elicited a response. Congressional inaction was unquestionably a topic of conversation among the general officers at Washington's headquarters, and McDougall was drawn into the discussion of the next move. Invited to Washington's camp at Preakness, New Jersey, McDougall arrived on July 3 to explain the harbor approaches to New York City.[46] Either before or during his visit to headquarters, a second memorial to Congress was drafted. Just who was involved in writing this new memorial is not known. Nathanael Greene was in camp, as were portly Henry Knox and several other generals, and it seems probable that they talked with McDougall about their futures, all the while damning Congress and the politicians. In any case, these generals crowded around a table in Greene's tent on a hot Tuesday and signed a second petition to Congress. First Greene, then Lord Stirling, followed by McDougall, Knox, and the others. Once again, only Robert Howe refused. It was decided that this time the address must be personally delivered to Congress by one of their own. McDougall was chosen. He was told not to "return to the army without a definite answer." [47]

The document entrusted to McDougall was a clear recital of the intolerable grievances suffered by the general officers. Assuming that the "ample and unequivocal proofs of their patriotism and self-denial" entitled them to consideration, the officers demanded an immediate payment of an allowance to cover depreciation of their pay, a pension system for widows and orphans of fallen comrades, and an increase in payments for their living expenses. Further justifications for their claims were not offered; those had been given in the first memorial. The new document contained a thinly disguised threat: if Congress ignored their complaints as it had last year, and "the army, exposed as they are to the rapacity of almost every class of the community, should be obliged by necessity to quit the service, and ill consequences should arise to their country, they leave to the world to determine who ought to be responsible for them." [48] Congress could hardly mistake the generals' threat to leave the army if their demands were not satisfied.

It was two weeks before McDougall was able to start for Philadelphia. He remained at Preakness and worked on a lengthy report to Washington containing his own pessimistic assessment of the possibility of a successful American attack on Sir Henry Clinton's forces, then set off for West Point to collect his belongings. Accompanied by a body servant and his son Stephen, he was on the road by the 26th and reached Philadelphia on the last day of the month. Except for the extreme heat and a delay caused by a lame horse, it was an uneventful trip, and on the first day of August, 1780, McDougall found lodging at the home of Mrs. Sarah Clark. He quickly went to work.

Congress already knew about the general officers' memorial and Mc-Dougall's mission. A copy had been given to a congressional committee at headquarters, and it was sent to Philadelphia on the 23rd with a recommendation by the committee that Congress act quickly on the demands.[49] But any hope for promptness was futile. McDougall found Congress in no hurry to act on the petition.

But Congressional leaders could not completely ignore McDougall's presence or the memorial he brought with him. The times were too critical to permit a repetition of the previous year's tactic of ignoring the general officers. On the other hand, the members of Congress refused to be stampeded by the generals' threat to quit the army.[50] For seven weeks McDougall dickered with Congress. At first he requested permission to address the whole body, demanding it as a right of the army. This request was denied by President Samuel Huntington of Connecticut. McDougall then had to settle for a committee of five to consider the petition. It was not a friendly group, even though McDougall knew three committee members, Samuel Adams, Roger Sherman of Connecticut, and Henry Laurens of South Carolina. Through long, uncomfortably hot days and nights, Mc-Dougall discussed in plain language, "but with prudence and decorum," the generals' case with the committee, and with other members of Congress. But he held little hope of success. Reporting a week later to Greene, he thought his performance would "no doubt give me a place with others on their blame list." [51]

Except in two instances, his arguments were familiar to congressmen. General officers had not received a pay raise or an increase in their maintenance allowance since the war began. Now, even if they received the fifty percent advance earlier wanted, currency depreciation was so great that they would still have less purchasing power than in 1776. In comparison to provisions made for officers in foreign armies, the half-pay policy recommended to the states in 1778 was inadequate in length of time, "clogged" with unjust stipulations, and dishonorable to the generals. Widows and orphans of officers killed in service were entitled to the country's support "and not be exposed to indigence or want or cast on the parish for a mean subsistence." Since a general was called upon and expected to entertain fellow officers and "strangers," table expenses had to be increased to keep pace with inflation. Finally, for their "toils & lost time" and to prevent being "marked out to their countrymen or her enemies as conspicuous beggars," the generals were entitled to still another reward—land.

These requests were familiar. But McDougall's presentation also included two new views, apparently shared by his military friends, which must have startled the politicians. As he saw developments and public policy since 1776, a conflict of interest had emerged in America. At the outset of the war the people had adopted constitutions based on principles of liberty and freedom and had created a republican army to defend those principles. But the war had also unleashed greed and corruption among those who did not fight. Making no pretense of honor, some men had abandoned the virtue and simplicity of their first principles and now lived in comfort off their new wartime riches, while demanding that the military adhere to a policy of dedication and sacrifice. The army, McDougall argued, would not object to its hardships if the public were suffering equal privations. But it clearly was not, as, the generals insisted, every man with eyes should be able to see. The object of the war was no longer a vindication of the political beliefs and values of republicanism; it was instead a war "for Empire and Liberty to a people whose object is Property." And with an emphasis that could not be missed, McDougall stated boldly that "the army expects some of that property which the citizen seeks, and which the army protects for him. . . ." McDougall had been blunt. Half-pay for life and generous land grants out of America's "Empire" were required to compensate the army's general officers for their sacrifices.[52]

The demands of the army's senior officers divided Congressmen, as they had in the previous year. Some members were impressed with the justice of the army's grievances, prudently recognizing both the army's power to do harm and the country's dependence upon it to secure independence. Other members were suspicious of the generals, fearing that they intended to set themselves up as a privileged class in American society. References to the generals' request to be as well-kept as French officers prompted one member to comment sarcastically, "Aye! the demand is reasonable—a warrant moreover should be issued for furnishing them with equipages, good breeding and education equally with the French nobility. . . ." America's officers, in this view, were simply not equal to those in Europe's armies and therefore ought not to expect the same benefits. And beyond these factors, McDougall's embassy came at a bad moment, since Congress was seeking to settle the military supply system and doing it at a time when its financial resources were exhausted. But irritation over the generals' poor timing was less than the fear that the officers might seize by force what they could not secure by petition.[53]

The fear of the consequences of inaction probably stirred the committee to action. Its report to Congress was generally sympathetic on everything but half-pay for life. But Congress as a body was apparently less moved by fear. After an initial debate on August 12, there was a delay of twelve days before the committee's report was again taken up.[54] In a series of resolutions, Congress made its position clear: General officers were as well paid as their station warranted, and unless the new emission money failed to curb inflation, it should remain at its present level. The recommendation of half-pay for seven years made to the states on May 15, 1778, was regarded as the proper mode to adjust for currency depreciation and price inflation. Congress did agree to extend the principle of half-pay to military widows and orphans and to remove the prohibition against office-holding during the seven year term. The general officers could expect no more for themselves, except for a depreciation adjustment on their rations if that became necessary.[55]

Congressional action was far short of what McDougall hoped for, and although he continued to work, especially by protesting the inadequacy of the depreciation provision, little more could be done.[56] He could only counsel patience to his friends and stress what had been accomplished. Congress had obviously given all that it intended to give. Even a stern warning from Washington on August 20, that unless something was quickly done the army could dissolve at the end of the campaign, had failed to move Congress to further concessions. Ironically, Benedict Arnold's treason and Horatio Gates' defeat at Camden—two dramatic illustrations of the army's problems—accomplished what McDougall and Washington could not. On October 21, weeks after McDougall went home, Congress approved the principle of half-pay for life for senior officers.[57]

But that was in the future. Before McDougall left Philadelphia on September 19, 1780, he settled a bit of personal business with Congress. With his own finances in shambles, barely able to support himself and his family, he had petitioned Congress on August 14 to settle his pay for the periods when he had commanded on the Hudson. Near the end of the month, after negotiations with the Treasury Board, McDougall was successful in obtaining more than $1,900 from

Congress, even though it denied his petition for his expenses in Philadelphia. As it turned out, it would be the last money he would receive until the end of the war.[58]

# Chapter Twelve
# Delegate to Congress

On September 19, 1780, McDougall made his way back to the grim isolation of military life in the Highlands. It had been four years since he had enjoyed the advantages of being in a major city, but he probably left Philadelphia with few regrets. His observations of wartime life in the country's capital only confirmed his belief that the war was in danger of being lost because of the gulf between the people's professed ideals and the reality of their scramble for profit. He was shocked by Philadelphia's extravagance, as Nathanael Greene had told him he would be, and his revolutionary faith was shaken by the political inattention to those ragged and hungry officers and privates who were fighting to stay alive while they defended that freedom which all men claimed. Even the weather offered no relief. August was so hot that "there is no comfort for mortals at night or day." [1] What McDougall had learned in New York about the public's nonchalant attitude toward the war was magnified many times by his experience in Philadelphia. And his dealings with Congress only added weight to his view that the country's salvation was now more a political problem than a military one, that the quickest and perhaps easiest way for the army to obtain the material support necessary to fight the enemy and win the war was by means of a modification of the distribution of political power in the country. It was time for the old revolutionary to return to politics.

McDougall reached West Point some time on Monday, the 25th, the day of Benedict Arnold's desertion to the British. There is no record of his immediate reaction to Arnold's treason, though it must have been one of shock and disbelief. He had admired the man's fighting spirit, convinced as were other general officers that Arnold rather than Gates was the true hero of Saratoga. Whatever his initial reaction, McDougall was soon angered over Arnold's flight from adversity and his betrayal of comrades whose suffering and personal sacrifice had been no less than his. When emotions cooled, West Point's security became McDougall's greatest concern. The Hudson River was still the vital link between east and west, north and south. The Highlands was still the best defensive line on the river, and Washington had to make it secure. Fearing the worst, Washington braced for a British attack and called upon those whom he could trust and depend. Greene's division was ordered to King's Ferry, Colonel John Lamb of the Continental artillery was sent to West Point, and McDougall was directed to take temporary command of the Highlands until the arrival of Arthur St. Clair.[2]

McDougall remained at West Point only a week. Relieved by St. Clair on October 4, McDougall rode to Poughkeepsie for a week-long visit with the state legislature and Governor George Clinton. When he arrived, he found that he had been elected a delegate to the Continental Congress from New York.[3] The records do not reveal the circumstances of his selection to serve in Congress, whether he sought the post, or who supported him. In any case, because of his concern over the country's political condition, he welcomed an opportunity to become actively involved in government. It was a chance to help bring about the political reformation he felt was so necessary to the country's survival. A discussion of issues and policies vital to the war effort and the state's liberation from the British occupied his time in Poughkeepsie. In talks with Governor Clinton and state legislators, he repeated conclusions he had reached over the past year, alarming everyone with his frank, pessimistic view of public affairs. His recent experience in Philadelphia, he explained, had confirmed his belief that members of Congress were too preoccupied with petty administrative details to give much time to those larger policies that would win the war. Somehow the Congress must be reformed and reinvigorated to deal with the problems of the war. Until that was achieved, the state legislatures, through their control of the taxing power and local affairs, must assume greater responsibility for supplying Washington's army with the sinews of war, with money and men.[4] No longer could the country afford the luxury of passing "laws of an utopian government" which protected every man in his freedom and liberty at the expense of everything else, including a military defense of that freedom. The army's condition was too weak and critical, and the public's attention was too completely focused on pursuit of private interests, to follow the ideal of republicanism. McDougall believed that it was "much safer and wiser to adopt rules of government to the present times than to change and bend the manners (which must always take a longer period and depend on nice causes) to the laws of a utopian government." In short, it would be quicker to reform government than to reform society. New York must act at once to defend herself against the British, but the larger solution was to broaden the powers of Congress so that it could obtain from all the states whatever was necessary to win the war.[5]

As he later informed Washington, his remarks had a good effect. Before adjourning, the New York legislature enacted laws to fill the state's quota of longterm enlistments and to raise greater tax revenue. It also appointed delegates "of enlarged minds fully informed of our civil defects" to attend a convention meeting on various war problems at Hartford, and it instructed the delegates to work for the establishment of a national executive with broad powers. With obvious approval, he enclosed a copy of a state legislative resolution calling upon Congress to exercise "every power which they may deem necessary for an effectual prosecution of the war" and to use Washington's army to compel any delinquent state to furnish "its quota of men, money, and provisions or other supplies" required by the war. In short, sir," he wrote Washington, "a great majority of the legislature have a proper spirit for the times, and so far as our safety depends on their exertions we have nothing to fear." [6]

Washington was pleased with McDougall's election and urged him to attend Congress even before the new congressman sought a release from his immediate military duties. Congress was considering ways and means of supporting the next campaign, and McDougall could not "so essentially serve the public as by going there; the moment is singularly critical; and the determination depending must have the greatest influence upon our future affairs." [7] With the understanding that he would continue to hold his army rank and return whenever Washington needed him, McDougall rested with his family at Fishkill before starting out for Philadelphia at the beginning of the new year of 1781.[8] While he waited, he received a warning from Philadelphia. Nathanael Greene, on his way south to revive the shattered American forces in North Carolina, reported that some members of Congress did not approve of McDougall taking a seat in that body. Greene suspected that some congressmen drew a sharp distinction between the citizen and the soldier and disapproved of McDougall's active army commission, which made him subject to Washington's immediate recall, while serving in Congress.[9]

When he claimed his seat on January 17, 1781, McDougall was surprised to find that Congress now seemed infused with energy and determination to overcome the political and financial problems of the war. "I find," John Sullivan reported, "that Congress and assemblies begin to rouse from their slumber and individuals are now alarmed for the public safety who have for years past been employed in amassing wealth." [10] Although political leaders were confident that the country had the basic resources to win independence, the possibility that Washington's army might collapse for lack of support suddenly seemed real and frightening. The mutiny of the Pennsylvania line troops in late December, 1780, was alarming evidence of discontent in the ranks over the army's lack of funds.

Many things had been wrong, but the root cause of congressional difficulties was political localism—the insistence that the fundamental power to govern remain as close as possible to the people. The First Continental Congress had initiated the principle that the national government existed at the sufferance of the states; the Second Congress proclaimed it in the Declaration of Independence and then wrote the concept into the Articles of Confederation. Thus state governments alone possessed the requisite taxing and spending authority, while the national congress (in what was, according to James Duane, "perhaps a novelty in the history of mankind") could only coordinate, recommend quotas, and plead for the means to make war. This might fit well with sound republican principles, but it certainly hampered the direction of continental warfare. The consequence of setting local self-government above all else had been to plunge the country into an ocean of inefficient government, worthless currency, and debt. As James Duane commented, "The deliberate power exercised by states individually over the acts of Congress must terminate in the common ruin; and the legislatures, however, reluctantly, must resign a portion of their authority to the national representative, or cease to be legislatures." [11]

Various remedies were proposed by men in and out of government. Some were quite extreme, such as New York's recommendation to use the army against negligent state governments; others were sweeping in scope, such as the calling of a constitutional convention to make a fresh start. But of the several options open to them, delegates to Congress in late 1780 and early 1781 were interested primarily in two reforms which were practical yet far-reaching. First, some members advocated overhauling the administrative functions of congressional work by creating departments for foreign affairs, finance, war, and marine matters. Each department would be managed by a secretary who would be elected by Congress and who would have reasonable power to act. Much of the old committee and board systems of administration, cumbersome and time-consuming at best, would be replaced by a civil service responsible for executing congressional policy.[12] The second matter of interest was a revenue plan by which the states would vest in Congress the power to levy an impost on trade, thus establishing a national revenue to finance the war and freeing Congress from the parsimony of state legislatures controlled by local interests. If both reforms were successful, the war as a national concern would be directed more efficiently by a Congress with a degree of independent national fiscal authority.[13]

By the fall of 1780, McDougall had become part of a growing effort to strengthen the central government. At the time of his entry into Congress, he was rapidly becoming an extremist in what would eventually be known as the nationalist movement. He had not entirely abandoned his faith in the power of the people as the basis of good government. He now felt, however, that there were times when man's right to freedom had to be constrained and controlled. War time was one of these. The basic flaw of American society was the absence of civic virtue in a time of crisis, the ascendancy of private interest over public good, even when all men were in danger. It was now necessary to put into public office stern men committed without reservation to the war, men who had sufficient power to act decisively and who would be held accountable for their actions. But it was also a time to wrest from the states a sufficient taxing power so that the central government could adequately finance military needs. His experiences as a military administrator in the Highlands had shown McDougall the tragic results of inadequate support for the army; those same experiences also increased his suspicions of state governments and his doubts about their willingness to raise and spend the taxes needed to achieve victory. His readiness to use the army to compel the state legislatures to surrender to Congress a portion of their absolute control over public finances suggests the depth of McDougall's sense of crisis in the country. Desperate times required desperate measures, but McDougall's militancy was too extreme for Congress. Even James Duane, fellow nationalist and New York delegate, thought that New York's proposal to use the army against state governments (which was adopted by the Hartford Convention) was too impractical and dangerous. As a newcomer to Congress and a militant nationalist, therefore, McDougall did not bowl over the older leaders with his eagerness to lecture them on what needed to be done. His military dress did not help matters, as Greene had warned him it would not and in his duties as a member of Congress, he was recognized simply as "Mister" McDougall.[14]

As an experienced politician, however, McDougall knew the virtue of patience, and for the moment he was content to observe while other nationalists took the lead. He did not have long to wait for favorable developments, for the first three months of 1781 was a productive and optimistic period for the national Congress. First, the Articles of Confederation were finally ratified by the thirteenth state, Maryland. That event was shortly over-shadowed by the passage of an impost plan providing Congress with an independent revenue. Finally, the administrative reorganization of the central government was begun. These developments seemed to reaffirm the national purpose of the Revolution and to point to a more vigorous and determined effort to win the war. McDougall's role was slight, since he served only thirty-seven days in Congress, from January 17 to March 2, 1781. He introduced no measures, and his committee assignments from President Samuel Huntington dealt with the details of the voluminous military correspondence of Congress on such matters as salaries for army clerks, personal petitions, British prisoners, and the southern campaign.[15] Still, he was an important addition to the movement seeking greater power for the national legislature. He was, in an unofficial sense, a spokesman for the army as much as he was a delegate from New York. His wide friendship with the senior officers and the experience he had gained during his 1780 mission to Congress enabled him to speak authoritatively on the army's expectations and dissatisfactions. In addition, he supported the winning side on the vital question of establishing a federal revenue: he favored an enlargement of congressional authority by vesting in Congress the power to levy import duties, rather than securing an impost through state tariff legislation, as some proposed. When, after days of debate, a vote was taken on a plan that would give Congress the right to collect a five percent duty on American imports, McDougall willingly cast his vote for the measure. He also agreed to the resolutions creating four new executive departments. He made only one substantive proposal on congressional procedures. Like his old army friend, John Sullivan of New Hampshire, McDougall quickly became weary of the endless debate and discussion on every question when the country's condition cried out for action. Thus, he sponsored a resolution restricting debate to one speech per man on a single issue until all other delegates had an opportunity to speak.[16]

Weary or not, McDougall was recognized as an important member of the nationalist forces. He was consequently elected Secretary of the new Marine Department. Compared to War or Foreign Affairs or the Treasury, the Marine Department was the least important office of the new executive organization and dealt with the least important side of America's military effort. Yet it was part of the plan to relieve the congressional committee structure of administering the war effort and place that responsibility in executive officers. McDougall was willing to accept the appointment, but he had two conditions. Since the navy had few ships and only a limited budget, and since the administrative work of the department would probably not require more than six to eight months' work a year, McDougall insisted that he be allowed to continue serving in the army during the summer season. He said he would have time for both responsibilities.[17] Besides, he informed Congress, "I cannot, in the present critical condition of the United States in general, and that of the state of New York in particular; and considering the early agency I have had in stimulating the opposition to the tyranny of Great Britain, think of retiring from the toils and perils of the field entirely to an office secure from danger." [18] His second condition was that his rank and pay of a major general run concurrently with his secretaryship.

McDougall believed that these demands were just. In conferring with a committee of Congress on this conditional acceptance, he stressed his financial hardship. Nearly destitute after using his personal fortune to support several regiments in 1775 and 1776, he simply could not afford to lose the present and future benefits of his army rank.[19] To his disappointment, Congress refused. Some members were willing to allow him to retain his rank and to rejoin the army if Washington should need him, but a majority insisted that he choose between the two responsibilities: he could not have the full economic benefits of both. McDougall was informed that, under the circumstances, Congress did not expect him to accept the Marine secretaryship.[20]

McDougall remained in Philadelphia another seven weeks before returning to New York. Despite the encouraging administrative reforms and the final ratification of the Articles of Confederation, his experience in Congress could not have been a happy one. The endless wrangling over detail, the clashing state interests, the petty jealousies, and the scant prospect of an immediate relief for the army combined to make him pessimistic about the war effort and added to his growing sense of personal frustration. Congress turned down his petition to Congress for a recovery of money he had lent in 1775–76 to support the four New York battalions and two artillery companies. He was again in poor health himself and concerned about his wife's condition, which added to his worry over his finances. He seemed to personify the army's deteriorating condition, and for both the future looked bleak.[21] In late April he wrote a friend that "a disposition appears in Congress to get rid of officers and the expense of attending them, in a manner I own, which does not altogether correspond with my idea of justice to them, however *I* may view those subjects thro too partial and interested mediums." By the end of May, in response to a call from Washington, McDougall was back on the Hudson.[22]

Six months had elapsed since McDougall was last with the army, and the nation's military situation had lost none of its gloom. Although Nathanael Greene, wearing a green cockade given him by Hannah McDougall, had withstood Lord Cornwallis in North Carolina, and the gnarled veteran, Daniel Morgan, had won brilliantly at Cowpens, the strength and well-being of the southern department was still uncertain. A large British force operated freely in Virginia, brushing aside the feeble resistance of Lafayette and a few Continentals. A French naval expedition sent to cooperate with Lafayette failed to close the sea lanes, and Sir Henry Clinton was consequently able to send reinforcements south from New York. By the spring of 1781 both Greene and Cornwallis were once more on the move in the south, and in May, Washington received reports of British activity far to the north around Lake Champlain.[23] What the movements and activities of the armies portended was unclear. The only bright side was the news that a second French naval squadron flying Admiral De

Grasse's flag was sailing for the West Indies and American waters. That gave Americans some hope. Perhaps the combined fleets of De Grasse and De Barras at Newport could end British naval superiority along the American coast; perhaps Washington could bring his dispersed forces together for a concentrated attack somewhere, without fear of the British navy. A week after McDougall was asked to rejoin the army, Washington met the French commander in America, Comte de Rochambeau, at Wethersfield, Connecticut, to formulate a plan of operation. But after they considered several alternatives, the only acceptable possibility for the moment was an attack upon New York City to ease the British pressure on Lafayette and Greene in the south.[24]

Preparations were already under way at the end of May when McDougall reached the old Robinson place across from West Point. When the ex-congressman was ready for duty, Washington assigned him temporarily to West Point, intending to bring him into the field army later. As it turned out, McDougall remained at the river fortress for the next fourteen months. The planned attack on New York City, in which McDougall was to participate, never fully materialized. In early June, 1781, Clinton obtained a hint of the operation and pulled in his outposts. Washington's force was not strong enough to break through the British defenses at King's Bridge, and the abortive enterprise proved to be just another example of Washington's frustration.[25] In mid-August Rochambeau's arrival in the Highlands and the news that De Grasse was sailing for the Chesapeake Bay with twenty-nine warships and three thousand troops gave Washington new hope that he could still mount an allied offensive. Virginia now became the object of Washington's strategy. On August 19 Washington offered McDougall the main division of New Jersey and New York regiments in a joint expedition into Virginia, but McDougall had to decline. After talking over Washington's plan with Henry Knox, McDougall decided that his health was too uncertain for an active command and a 450-mile march. The commander-in-chief understood McDougall's reason and appointed Benjamin Lincoln in his place. McDougall would remain at West Point, with William Heath in over-all command of the Highlands.[26]

This was McDougall's last assignment to West Point, and it proved to be the most distasteful. The garrison was unlike any other he commanded. Stripped of Continentals for Washington's Chesapeake campaign, the men at West Point were primarily youthful, inexperienced Connecticut militia, and the Corp of Invalids, old soldiers whose bodies bore the marks of the war. The latter group, he complained, were in a "truly wretched and pitiable condition, fitter subjects of a good hospital, than to compose part of this garrison. . . ." [27] When cold weather came, McDougall's men were too weak and poorly clothed to haul provisions and cut wood, thus forcing the few able-bodied men to do double fatigue duty. At year's end a smallpox epidemic made the garrison's health problems even worse. Reflecting a certain grim humor, McDougall made the construction of a hospital one of his major goals during the winter months. [28]

McDougall would have grumbled about his problems in any event, but the fact that he and the department's commanding general, William Heath, could not work together also made his last winter at West Point miserable. Their headquarters were widely separated and the difficulties of winter travel forced the two major generals to communicate in missives which tended to be self-justifying and contentious in tone, provoking personal controversies rather than clarifying their respective duties and responsibilities. As the weeks passed, such matters as bringing in the great river chain, granting clothing allowances, distributing rum rations, assigning fatigue and guard duty, utilizing lumber supplies, and locating provisions—matters vital to survival in the Highlands but of small importance to the total war— revealed a widening gulf between McDougall and Heath. [29] McDougall insisted that the West Point commandant was responsible only to the commander-in-chief and Congress, while Heath insisted that McDougall show a proper obedience to his superior officer's orders concerning many details of military administration at West Point. Both men showed the strain of a long war. Both were in poor health and were financially pressed; both were too sensitive about their personal rank to work together effectively. At bottom the two men had opposite personalities which intensified their differing military views. McDougall was direct and outspoken, too talkative perhaps, an affable drinking companion who made as much fun of himself as others, and who regularly invited his junior officers to share his table. Heath on the other hand was stiff, formal, and overbearing, insisting on the trappings and respect due his rank. He also had the reputation of doing more blustering than fighting. [30] Each was quick to lecture the other on the proper course to follow. By virtue of his previous experience in the Highlands, McDougall considered himself the best authority on command in that area. By the end of 1781, McDougall was accusing Heath of "unmilitary" practice when orders effecting McDougall's post were issued without prior consultation or information. He intended to ask Washington to settle the issues "in a more solemn manner, than can now be obtained." [31] Heath's replies invariably took the form of firm denials of any irregularities and preached to McDougall on the necessity of obeying one's commanders. [32]

The final break came when McDougall learned in early January, 1782, that Heath had closed West Point's ammunition magazine to everyone, including McDougall, without an explanation. [33] Up to that point, McDougall had confined his displays of temper to his letters, but now he lost control of himself. On at least two occasions in the first half of January, he openly criticized Heath's orders in the company of the garrison's officers and challenged Heath's competence to command the Highlands. How, he angrily demanded of his juniors, could he defend West Point, when Heath denied him powder and shot? Did anything more clearly demonstrate Heath's poor judgment and lack of military ability? The more McDougall talked, the angrier he became, and the deeper he slashed away at Heath's character: if Heath could not be called a coward, he at least was not known to have ever acted bravely. McDougall then told his audience how Heath had behaved in a council of war in September, 1776, when the evacuation of New York City was discussed. "None were opposed to it," he declared, "but a fool, a knave, and an obstinate honest man." The officers who opposed evacuation were in fact Joseph Spencer, George Clinton, and William Heath, and it is unclear whether McDougall meant to call Spencer or Clinton the fool. But he was emphatic about Heath. He was the knave, an officer who "carried two faces" by first arguing that the city was militarily indefensible and then voting against evacuation in order to gain popularity with local people who wanted the city defended. The insult quickly reached Heath's ears. Two days later, on January 18, Heath relieved McDougall of his command and placed him under arrest, charging him with seven counts of "conduct unmilitary and unbecoming an officer." [34]

Both men wrote to Washington, Heath to prefer charges and McDougall to demand an immediate court martial. McDougall branded Heath's accusations as "frivolous, mean, and wicked," and openly

Paris. March 1st 1780

Dear Sir

It is with great Pleasure that I take my Pen
to give the Viscount de Noailles, a Letter
to Such a Veteran in American Policy and
War, as General McDougal. This young
Nobleman whose military Ardour is equal to
that of his Brother the Marquis de la Fayette, is
going to America, and in Such Company as will
I hope insure his Welcome. I should be very
happy to return any Civilities you may shew him
to any of your Friends who may be travelling
to Paris.

I should moreover be greatly obliged to you for your
Correspondence, as Information from America
especially the Army is much wanted here. I am
with a long and firm Attachment, Sir your Friend
and humble Servant
John Adams

Major General James McDougal.

*John Adams to Major General James McDougal* [sic], *recommending the Viscount de Noailles for employment in the American Army.*

—W. WRIGHT HAWKES COLLECTION, SCHAFFER LIBRARY, UNION COLLEGE

expressed his feelings toward Heath. "In short," McDougall exclaimed, "he has treated me like a Bastard, and his conduct to me and this post in a manner absurdly unmilitary and extremely different from that line of conduct observed by your excellency, and every other officer that hath commanded in this department." Although Heath did not issue the customary order to McDougall to confine himself to his post during his arrest (in fact he told McDougall that he could go anywhere he wished within the state), McDougall was so furious that he intended to reject any favors from Heath. McDougall told Washington that he would remain at West Point until his trial was over or until Washington directed otherwise. In Philadelphia, an embarrassed Washington appointed Lord Stirling president of a court martial to judge McDougall's alleged breach of military discipline.[35] "Had I had any previous notice of this disagreeable affair," Washington wrote McDougall, "I should as the common friend of both and for the reputation of the service, have offered my private interposition." But now it was too late. A court martial must take place.[36]

McDougall's trial was a lengthy affair. From the end of January, when Washington ordered the court martial, to the third week of July, when a verdict was reached, the Highland command was preoccupied with the charges and countercharges of the two major generals. McDougall worked feverishly on his own defense. He busied himself collecting evidence and testimony to prove that it was not he but Heath who was guilty of unprofessional behavior. His Scottish temper riding high, he objected to Fishkill as the trial site; it was too expensive and inconvenient for witnesses to cross over from West Point. When the court opened on Monday, February 18, he maneuvered to get a delay because his defense was not yet fully developed. He challenged the competence of Lord Stirling to serve as court president and the qualifications of three junior members. He bluntly informed the court that Lord Stirling had committed so many "capital defects" in Charles Lee's trial that he was unfit to preside in the present case.[37] The unprecedented question of defense "challenges" of court members in a military trial had to be referred to Washington for decision, a delay which allowed McDougall to continue his defense preparations; the challenge also opened a rift between McDougall and Stirling that never healed. Two months later Washington gently put Lord Stirling aside and appointed Robert Howe as court president, but Stirling never forgot the insult and later tried to bring McDougall to a personal accounting.[38] In addition to criticizing the court's membership, McDougall also claimed that Heath's charges against him were too general; as a "free man and an officer" he demanded that they be made specific. "If this is not done," McDougall threatened, "and that without delay, I shall be under the disagreeable necessity of bringing his Excellency Major General Heath to a bar from which there is no appeal." [39] When he heard that Heath might take a furlough, McDougall asked Washington to keep him in the Highlands in the event that McDougall decided to file charges of his own. By the first week of April, Washington, wearied of the delay, directed Robert Howe to assemble the new court and to get on with the trial.[40]

McDougall's defense was ready when the court convened on April 13. His case had been reviewed by his brother-in-law, Daniel Roberdeau, the old Pennsylvania extremist and militia general, and it was undoubtedly touched up by his son-in-law, John Lawrance, former Judge Advocate of the army. But its broad outlines were McDougall's own.[41] A great deal of evidence was presented by both sides on the number of boards, ammunition stocks, clothing supplies, and rations in the Highlands, and testimony was taken on McDougall's orders and remarks. McDougall's defense against six of the seven charges was simple: he sought to prove that a junior officer, whatever the rank involved, had an obligation to his country to disobey the orders of a superior officer when those orders contravened common sense, the good of the army, and humanity. Thus, McDougall argued, if Heath had the right to order the ammunition magazine closed at West Point, thereby depriving McDougall of the means necessary for defense, then Heath could also order McDougall to surrender the post to the British, spike the cannon, or otherwise render the forts useless. Heath's orders violated common military practices, and McDougall had no choice but to disobey them even though he technically violated the Articles of War.

On the seventh charge McDougall exerted himself to prove that Heath was in fact a "knave." McDougall repeated the story of Heath's opposition to the evacuation of New York City in 1776 on the grounds that it would shock the people, even though Heath openly admitted at the time that city could not be defended. It was a strange situation, McDougall insisted, for an officer to argue that a position was not defensible and then demand that it be defended. "I leave General Heath with all his little facts to reconcile this contradiction and absurd opinion to the army," McDougall told the court. But how to explain Heath's behavior in 1776? It could only result from a "want of sincerity and candor," McDougall concluded. "And is not a want of these qualities a want of honesty? And is it not a want of honesty, knavish and crafty? And is it not obvious it was in this sense I used the word knave?" The logic was tortured and the proposition difficult, and though some officers might have agreed, McDougall failed to persuade the court.[42] In the end McDougall was fully acquitted on six charges, but on the seventh he was found guilty and a reprimand in general orders was recommended. Washington dismissed the court on August 1 and sent the trial proceedings to Congress which approved the verdict on August 15.[43] From Congress, James Duane wrote a letter of support to McDougall to take some of the sting out of the official reprimand; members of Congress Duane reported, saw McDougall's "fool, a knave, and an obstinate honest man" remark as simply something said in a "*social* hour." [44]

The trial sapped McDougall's energy, and by late August he was bed-ridden again. He was low in spirits, too—depressed by his poverty and by the announcement that Henry Knox was to command at West Point. Writing a private letter to Washington on August 26, 1782, he described his condition. Within a few months he would be completely out of hard money for necessities, and in order to economize, he and his wife were living off the vegetables from Beverly Robinson's farm. He wanted to know what assignment Washington intended for him. Since he had only one good horse, a division command would be a hardship: "For I am but ill provided with means or health to take the field; and I own I feel a dread on my spirits, at the idea of my condition, being unable now to appear in character and thereby exposed to the allied army." McDougall asked for West Point, which, he said, would enable him to support himself off his rented farm.[45] Washington replied at once that he did not expect nor wish McDougall to join the army in camp if his health was impaired, but he suggested that since the army would be stationed at Verplank's Landing, only a short distance below West Point, McDougall might not find it too inconvenient or expensive to be stationed there. But the commander-in-chief did not offer to remove Knox from West Point, and McDougall was assigned a division of two brigades. McDougall remained at Robinson's house throughout the autumn, nursing his health and declining Washington's wish that he and Knox arrange the details of a prisoners exchange with the new British commanding general, Sir Guy Carleton. But more and more that autumn, McDougall wondered about the security and future of himself, his family, and his country.[46]

# Chapter Thirteen
# Philadelphia and Newburgh

Actually, by the time McDougall's trial concluded in August, 1782, there was reason for the American military leaders to be optimistic. The allied army under Washington and Rochambeau had won an extraordinary victory at Yorktown on October 20, 1781, and by spring of 1782, there were indications that the British government's will to fight was disappearing. Unanimous state approval of the five percent impost providing the Confederation with a modest permanent income seemed likely, since only Rhode Island's concurrence was needed. Ironically, however, improving conditions added to the country's problems. Confident that peace was near, state legislatures rapidly lost interest in complying with congressional requests for money and supplies, and Robert Morris's fiscal policies only temporarily hid the fact that Congress was bankrupt. Rhode Island's delay on the impost grew into an obstinate refusal. Even the new contract system of supplying the army proved no better than the old methods of commissionary agents. The army's condition in 1782 was worse than ever before.

Morale in the army was dangerously low by the springtime of 1782. The grievances—poor rations, little clothing, and no pay—were as old as the war, but the prospects of peace and the disbanding of the army gave new urgency to the general complaints and increased the demands for settlement of old accounts. "Minds soured by distresses are easily rankled," Washington warned.[1] Officers grumbled over the new contract system of issuing rations, which, according to Washington's many letters on the subject, was nothing more than a device benefiting a few suppliers at the army's expense. Especially galling was the fact that others in the service of government received their salaries when the army did not. An additional grievance developed over the method and timetable for demobilization. Informal meetings among the officers were common, and talk of mutiny was heard once more among the sergeants and privates. Desertion was also greater than in past years.[2] Circumstances worsened by autumn. Writing to the Secretary at War, Benjamin Lincoln, Washington went over all the old complaints. He warned that Congress's failure to settle past claims or to establish future benefits, even as it was ordering a reduction in the army's size, was causing discontent among the officers. The commander-in-chief was confident that as long as the army remained in the field the discontent would not erupt "into acts of outrage," but it would be a different matter when the regiments were sent into winter quarters. "I cannot be at ease, respecting the consequences," Washington concluded.[3]

The army's patience ran out in the winter of 1782–83. Grumbling had turned to thoughts of political action, and appeals to justice were replaced by threats of coercion. From regiment to regiment in the Highlands, officers met to hammer out a common plan of action. The result was a second grand memorial to Congress; and once again McDougall was asked to make the long ride to Philadelphia with two regimental colonels to present it.

McDougall was as bitter and angry over the army's condition as anyone in military service. Even throughout his long court martial, his own financial difficulties had never been far from his thoughts. His physical infirmities and shabby circumstances were daily reminders. Other officers were in similarly bad straits; most agreed with McDougall's view that Congress was helpless without a revenue, and that the states showed little inclination to offer compensation.[4] Yet political lobbying at the state level was still necessary, for only the states had money to make good on congressional promises of half-pay and depreciation allowances. The lobbying had to be done quickly, before the war officially ended: once the army was no longer needed, the states could more easily ignore the officers and soldiers with little fear of the consequences. McDougall urged the officers of New York regiments to seek out the state's legislators and press them on the point. "It is therefore a duty we owe to ourselves and our families," he wrote to a New York colonel, "to know of our legislature, whether they consider those acts [of Congress] binding on this state or not." [5]

Following his own advice, he wrote to Governor Clinton pleading his own cause as well as that of his fellow officers. McDougall's story was probably familiar to the governor, but McDougall reviewed it once more and, in the process, revealed something of his state of mind. McDougall's particular case involved the New York law of 1780 allowing a settlement of military pay according to a scale of currency depreciation.[6] The difference between nominal pay received and currency depreciation was to be compensated by interest-bearing certificates. McDougall pointed out that he had been paid only twice since the beginning of the war, but according to the law, his claim therefore could be no more than $500 in real value. Contending that the law operated to his disadvantage by not providing for those who had received no wages at all, he asked the state to make good his entire salary since August, 1776—a balance of $6,900 in his favor. It was evident that, as McDougall spelled out his financial problem, he was angered by the thought of his own sacrifice and the activity of speculators who were already buying up the depreciation certificates at a fraction of their face value. "Although my services have not been brilliant," McDougall conceded, "yet neither the state of which I am a subject nor the army of which I am a member have been disgraced by them. . . . Whatever my services have been, I will not yield the palm to any subject in the state, in attachment to it, nor in regard to its honor and safety." Self-sacrifice, McDougall continued, had been his guiding principle from the very beginning when he had supported four regiments with his own money, and that principle had been maintained throughout the war. Junior officers in his command always drew their pay first by his order, and if any money was left in the "military chest" he would then take his.

While his previous petition to the legislature for compensation in 1780 had been received with an "inattentive contempt" by the state government, "some of the most unworthy of the community" were using depreciation certificates, bought at fractional values, to claim lands and estates confiscated from Loyalists. Men "who never risqued a scratch, or a shilling during the whole contest" were reaping benefits from the war, McDougall contended, "while I have not a hovel that I can call my own, out of the enemy's lines, after spending an easy fortune in the service of the state; and grown gray in it's [sic] service." [7] McDougall was not as open as he might have been with his old acquaintance George Clinton, but a suspicion of wrong-doing was evident in McDougall's letter: a conspiracy of selfish men seemed to be hindering satisfaction of the just claims of the army, which had fought and died for the common liberty. Since the sense of betrayal was common in the army, perhaps McDougall felt as Samuel Hold Parsons did, that liberty was "imaginary" and independence a "phantom." [8]

McDougall's court martial had prevented him from giving further attention to his own financial problems or those of other officers. But he undoubtedly knew of the rising dissatisfaction among the officers of the Massachusetts regiments during June and July of 1782. As commandant of West Point before his arrest, he had known of the New Englanders' deplorable condition and with difficulty had quieted talk of mutiny; he also listened to their alarm over New England's attitude toward the army. Two of McDougall's close military associates, Henry Knox and Rufus Putnam, were responsible for drafting a memorial to the Massachusetts legislature in July, 1782, requesting, among other things, enactment of either the half-pay for life recommended by Congress or the conversion of that principle into a lump sum payable at the close of the war.[9] The origin of the plan for commutation, as it became known, is hard to detect, but McDougall had advocated it as early as July, 1781, and had drawn support from a number of general officers, including Knox, who agreed to accept it as an alternative if legislative leaders resisted the idea of a pension.[10] When a deputation of Massachusetts officers—Rufus Putnam, John Brooks, and William Hull—reached Boston to present their case in early September, 1782, they encountered open hostility to half-pay for life. Various arguments were offered against it: it would be too expensive; it would cause a rise in taxes; it would create a class of idle pensioners; and it was unjustified on grounds of merit. Rebuffed, the three officers had no choice but to return to their regiments in the Highlands and report their failure.[11] McDougall no doubt shared their frustration and anger.

Throughout the remainder of 1782, the tension mounted in Washington's army on the Hudson. The commander-in-chief had intended to winter in Virginia for the first time since the war began, but the army's condition kept him at Newburgh. Compounding the personal hardships inflicted by the severe money shortage was the congressional order to reduce the size of the army. Although this order was issued by Congress on August 7, demobilization was a slow process, deepening the discontent of those officers and men in the ranks who were to be discharged and sent home with empty pockets. Warned by Washington of the army's grumbling, Secretary at War Benjamin Lincoln hurried to Newburgh in October to "calm the rising billows" and to explain how demobilization would take place.[12] Lincoln's visit may have prevented serious outbreaks for the moment, but his assurances that the discharged officers would not lose their benefits and that Congress would make some provision for everyone were of little solace to men whose needs were immediate and overpowering. Hotheads talked of mutiny; some insisted that the army should refuse to lay down its arms and disband unless all accounts and promises were settled; still others plotted to have the army start for home immediately and leave the politicians to face the British alone. Regimental meetings of officers of the Massachusetts and Connecticut lines, under orders to consolidate and eliminate units, instead discussed grievances and means of securing relief.[13] Describing the army's mood, Henry Knox wrote that "expectations of the army, from the drummer to the highest officers, are so keen for *some* pay, that I shudder at the idea of their not receiving it. The utmost period of sufferance upon that head has arrived. To attempt to lengthen it will undoubtedly occasion commotions." [14]

The primary result of this latest and worst crisis in the army was another petition to Congress. Prepared at Henry Knox's West Point headquarters, the petition expressed the immediate demands of the hospital corps and of regiments from five states. For the moment at least, the Northern Army was willing to stay in channels, and Washington, alarmed over the "irritable" and "soured" temper of his men, gave the address his tacit approval.[15] There is no reason to suppose that McDougall, living on Robinson's farm across the river, was not involved in the memorial's drafting stages. Regardless of whether he participated in the planning, however, he was asked once more to represent the army before Congress. With John Brooks of Massachusetts and Matthias Ogden of New Jersey, who were selected as the army's spokesmen, McDougall received instructions on December 7, 1782, to present the army's demands "in that ready manner that is expressive of the characters of officers" and to "continue with Congress until you obtain their full determination on our address." [16] Financing the trip to Philadelphia proved to be a problem. In 1780 McDougall had paid for his mission out of his own pocket, never recovering his expenses from Congress or from his military friends; it was a sign of the hard times that he was now forced to solicit contributions before he could begin this new journey. The fact that it took him nearly two weeks to collect enough money to send the military delegation on its way is eloquent testimony to the financial state of the army. Finally arriving at

Philadelphia on December 29, McDougall took up quarters at the Indian Queen and began his work.[17]

The memorial that McDougall brought to Philadelphia was different in several respects from the address he presented to Congress in 1780. The earlier plea had concentrated on two demands, a depreciation allowance and half-pay for life, and had been the particular representation only of the general officers. It had been backed by an open threat of resignations unless Congress acted promptly. Two years later, the army's demands had increased. The new memorial asked for action on back pay, and on clothing, ration, and forage allowances, as well as the half-pay measure adopted in 1780. The demands were those of nearly all the regiments of the Northern Army, and this fact was made clear at the outset. Regimental officers who signed the memorial were seeking redress for their "brethren the soldiers" no less than for themselves. An ominous tone pervaded the whole document, shading the meaning of every sentence. While Congress had offered "shadows" in the past, the memorial asserted, the "substance has been gleaned by others;" the "exigency" of the army's "extreme poverty" and "distresses" were "now brought to a point" and the "uneasiness of the soldiers, for want of pay, is great and dangerous—any further experiments on their patience may have fatal effects." Congressmen could not have missed the implication in the concluding paragraph that an explosion was dangerously near: "It would be criminal in the officers to conceal the general dissatisfaction which prevails, and is gaining ground in the army. . . ." [18]

The memorial was written for effect, but, as McDougall quickly discovered, political conditions in Philadelphia were little changed. Congress faced financial problems of immense proportions. Public creditors clamored for payment, while state legislatures were either tardy or claimed an inability to furnish money for national expenses. The Superintendent of Finance, Robert Morris, had already exhausted existing foreign loans and, in order to pay the most pressing demands, was forced to draw upon additional European credits yet to be negotiated. He joined his voice to others in demanding that Congress provide a sound remedy. Throughout the continuous discussions of its revenue difficulties, the one sustaining hope in Congress was the five percent impost proposed in 1781. Only Rhode Island's persistent refusal to ratify the plan frustrated the establishment of a permanent national fund. Then, even as McDougall was riding toward Philadelphia, the prospect of establishing a general revenue in this way was put beyond reach. Virginia, for inexplicable reasons, repealed its approval of the impost. For those nationalists who had labored since 1781 to strengthen the Confederation and to give it the economic substance of a national government, Virginia's action was a staggering blow. Thus driven by political desperation in early 1783, some men in Philadelphia began to explore the possibility of a military solution for the nation's financial disorders.[19]

It was among the nationalists, then, that McDougall found support for the army's demands on Congress. By championing the army's cause, nationalist leaders in the Confederation government—men like Robert and Gouverneur Morris in the Finance Office, and Alexander Hamilton, James Wilson, and James Madison in Congress—saw an opportunity to turn the army's discontent into political advantage. It might be possible to use the army's anger to impress upon Congress that, despite the opposition of Rhode Island and Virginia to the impost plan, it was imperative to continue the effort to obtain an independent congressional revenue in order to settle the country's affairs. At the same time, McDougall found that public creditors who wanted to end the country's financial instability welcomed his mission to Congress. He was in Philadelphia hardly a week when he received an invitation to merge the army's demands with those of government creditors. As Arthur Clairy, a local businessman, explained the strategy to McDougall, "If the debts due to, and the provision to be made for the army can, conjointly with the other public debts be, in the present moment, thrown upon the continental [Congress] at large, paradoxical as it may appear, the hands of Congress will be strengthened—the army may be kept together, and the continental government take some tone, and be able to speak with proper authority, to any single refractory state, and be sure both of being heard and attended to." Only by that joint effort, Clairy informed McDougall, could America's "national faith and national character" be established.[20] The prospect of using military power to support plans to end financial chaos in America was not new to McDougall; he had argued that necessity during the winter of 1780–81. What was new was the sense of urgency and of desperation which prevailed at both Newburgh and Philadelphia. Until the end of January, it was hoped both in the army and in Congress that political pressure would produce sound revenue reform; by the end of February, it seemed that stronger measures might be necessary to save the country.

McDougall did not immediately present the army's memorial to Congress, for he wanted time to inform individual members of the urgent conditions at Newburgh and the purpose of his mission. In particular he wanted to explain the proposal to commute half-pay for life into full pay for a limited term or a fixed sum. It was also necessary to sound the political waters. From Robert Morris and others, he learned that a majority in Congress were "seriously disposed to do everything in their power, for the fulfillment of all their engagements to the army." McDougall recognized, however, as he had in previous months, that the question of half-pay or commutation was irrelevant unless Congress had a permanent revenue. Everything depended upon what the states were willing to underwrite, and their record thus far was poor. What use was it, he asked, for Congress to make strong recommendations if the New England states (which McDougall thought were especially at fault) failed to respond favorably? McDougall saw that the army's officers needed political allies, and the public creditors formed a willing group to work on Congress. In a private letter to Henry Knox January 9, 1783, he posed the question: "What if it should be proposed to unite the influence of Congress with that of the army and the public creditors to obtain permanent funds for the United States which will promise most ultimate security to the army?" He suggested that Knox and Jedediah Huntington consider the possibility and be ready to give him directions if the need arose.[21] The letter to Knox was McDougall's first report on the political situation in Philadelphia, and it was evident that no strategy had yet emerged. Discussions of how best to achieve the quite similar goals of the army, the public creditors, and the nationalists were still in a preliminary stage. By the end of the second week of January, 1783, however, the situation began to clear.

Congress formally received the army memorial on Monday, January 6, and promptly instructed a committee representing every state to bring in a report. At the committee's request, Robert Morris, Superintendent of Finance, appeared the next evening to discuss the government's ability to make some sort of payment to the troops. Morris was able to inform them that he had already initiated steps to provide the soldiers with some pay, but as everyone well knew, the treasury was empty and there was scant chance of securing new funds. Thus, Morris argued, a general revenue from the states was vital and should be secured before Congress made permanent provision for the army.

The fact that Morris ranked a revenue first and the army second was to become a sensitive political issue in the weeks ahead, but of more immediate concern to the committee were "the consequences to be apprehended from a disappointment of the mission from the army." It was agreed to confer with the army deputies on Friday evening. McDougall's rheumatism kept him in bed on that day, so he asked the committee to meet in his quarters at the Indian Queen. At first sympathetic, the committee's members decided finally that it would be "derogatory from the respect due to themselves" for the committee to accept McDougall's invitation. Claiming that bad weather prevented some members from attending, the committee adjourned to the following Monday.[22]

Although still disabled, McDougall went with John Brooks and Matthias Ogden on January 13 to argue the army's case. McDougall knew most of the committee members. Oliver Wolcott, Samuel Osgood, Daniel Carroll, and James Madison had been in Congress during his brief term in 1781. He had served with Philemon Dickinson in New Jersey during the campaigns of 1776 and 1777, and Richard Peters, former secretary of the old Board of War, was well known in the army. McDougall was undoubtedly best known to Alexander Hamilton, to whom he had loaned books and given political lessons nearly a decade before, during the revolutionary turmoil in New York City. As the committee session got under way, McDougall began his presentation calmly enough, but his Scottish temper rose as he described the army's sacrifices and disappointments throughout the war. In "very high-colored expressions," as James Madison put it, McDougall warned the committee that "serious consequences" could be expected unless Congress made an immediate advance of pay. When questioned specifically on what the army might do if it was not paid, all three officers replied bluntly: "There was sufficient reason to dread that at least a mutiny would ensue" and that it would probably have the sympathy of regimental officers. The army's situation, McDougall said, was such "to make a wise man mad," and John Brooks, knowing best the temper of the Massachusetts regiments, told the committee that the soldiers could no longer "reason or deliberate cooly on consequences and therefore a disappointment might throw them blindly into extremities."

McDougall also discussed two other points of greater significance to him than an immediate advance of pay. He insisted that Congress and the states had an obligation to give security for all overdue pay and allowances, and to take appropriate action to make the 1780 pledge of half-pay for life a reality. Only then, McDougall stated, could the officers, now broken and destitute, look back on the war as a worthwhile sacrifice and look forward to peace as a blessing. He repeated an observation often made in his correspondence—that everywhere he looked the people lived in ease and affluence while the ragged and penniless officers and their families faced a future of poverty. Expressing "indignation" that Rhode Island and Virginia had refused to approve the impost, thereby denying Congress a "federal revenue for discharging the federal engagements," McDougall emphasized that the army's patience had limits. He admitted to the committee that the "intelligent and considerate part of the army" realized that the basic problem was an "unwillingness of the states to cement & invigorate" the Confederation; but he also reminded them—with "peculiar emphasis" according to Madison—that if the union dissolved because of its weaknesses, "the benefits expected from the Revolution [would] be greatly impaired, and as in particular, the contests which might ensue [among] the states would be sure to embroil the officers which respectively belonged to them."

James Madison, who recorded McDougall's presentation to the committee, thought that McDougall's last comment deserved "the greater attention" than his main speech. Did the major general mean that officers would not stand behind the Confederation government which refused its support to the army, Madison pondered, or that a civil war among the states which might involve the officers was possible? McDougall's remark was ominous, but before he could be questioned on his meaning, he moved on to the question of half-pay. McDougall's arguments were timeworn and familiar to the committee. He stressed that he and the other officers were authorized to negotiate a commutation in order to overcome public objections to military pensions. The evening session ended on that issue. McDougall, Brooks, and Ogden had made their point to the committee: Unless immediate steps were taken to resolve the army's grievances, there was no telling what the consequences might be. The committee directed Hamilton, Madison, and John Rutledge to "report arrangements, in concert with the Superintendent of Finance," for the consideration of the full committee.[23]

After eight days of discussion and analysis of the army's demands, the committee returned a favorable report, written by Hamilton. Congress received it on January 22, 1783, briefly debated the issues the next day, and then took up the report in earnest on Friday and Saturday, the 24th and 25th. Considered on its merits, the report was probably not displeasing to McDougall. It recommended an immediate month's pay to the army and the issuance of certificates at six percent for the remainder accumulated since August of 1780. The officers were to be given the option of half-pay as originally passed in 1780 or a commutation into a lump sum payable one year after the war in money or in interest-bearing securities. This was as much as the committee could recommend at the moment. Additional time was needed to study the question of clothing and ration allowances. While admitting that all of Congress' creditors were justifiably angry and entitled to immediate settlement, the committee urged that the first order of business ought to be an "immediate & full consideration of the nature of such funds & the most likely mode of obtaining them." [24] Claims for payment were pointless without revenue.

As Congress pondered the report, the nationalist objective emerged more clearly. The cost of acceding to the army's demands was added proof of the need to strengthen the Confederation by means of funding the public debt. To give emphasis to the urgency of the problem, Robert Morris informed Congress on the 24th that he would be unable to continue as Superintendent of Finance after April unless a permanent government income was established. Congress's hand was forced. In addition to Morris's intended resignation, fear of mutiny on the Hudson hung like a pall over Congress. Congress promptly approved an earlier secret provision made by Morris for a month's pay to the army, with an order to Morris to settle the rest as he thought best. How to finance the national debt, including army claims and commutation, was another matter, a question of the utmost importance requiring the attendance of all members and, as James Madison admitted, involving the "necessity of proceeding with more caution." [25] After a test vote, commutation was referred to a special committee and Congress agreed to take up the question of general funds at its next meeting.[26]

McDougall stood on the sidelines as the nationalist strategy of strengthening the Confederation unfolded and Congressional discussion of a general revenue droned on. It seemed likely that commutation was in danger of being lost in the tangle of congressional politics, since the nationalists insisted on linking it inextricably to their demands. "The terror of a mutinying army is played off with considerable efficacy," one congressman commented.[27] Intending to use the "terror" of a military revolt to stampede Congress into fiscal reform, the nationalist leaders—the Morrises, Hamilton, Wilson, and to a lesser extent Madison—apparently had little intention of allowing the military to get something from Congress without first achieving a fundamental change in the Confederation.

This put pressure on McDougall. He agreed in principle with the nationalist position on a general revenue, but his goal in Philadelphia was to obtain certain specific benefits for army officers. Perfectly willing to join cause with other public creditors if it would help the army's chances, McDougall was unwilling to see commutation succeed or fail only as the public creditors in general succeeded or failed. McDougall, Brooks and Ogden reported to Henry Knox on February 8 that it was far from certain that Congress would be able to get a general revenue from the states, and that they intended to stand clear of the politics in Congress over that issue. McDougall's own reason for being in Philadelphia was to secure commutation for half-pay and the "obtaining of that is necessary, previous to our particularizing what fund will be most agreeable to us." He did not want the army's discontent and just claims to become merely another weapon in the nationalist attack on the weakness of the Confederation. Let Congress first approve commutation, then, "if Congress get funds we shall be secured." But, "if not," McDougall reasoned, "the equivalent settled, a principle will be established, which will be more acceptable to the eastern states than half-pay, if application must be made to them." The actual source of funds (which McDougall believed "must be determined by circumstances") was of secondary importance to the object of securing the financial future of discharged officers.[28]

McDougall was on a political tightrope, but he kept his balance. The nationalists (probably Robert and Gouverneur Morris and Hamilton) privately pressed McDougall to declare openly that the army would accept commutation only if it was funded out of continental revenue; others in Congress argued that the matter should be referred to the states for decision. McDougall kept silent. It was plain that opposition to commutation was mixed with opposition to the nationalist objective of creating a stronger central government. Congressional politics, McDougall wrote to Knox, "induced us to conceal what funds we wished, or expected, lest our declaration for one or the other might retard a settlement of our accounts, or a determination on the equivalent for half-pay." [29]

Though he was experienced enough in politics not to be trapped in the labyrinth of Congressional rivalries, McDougall was nevertheless caught in a dilemma. If he took the nationalist side, their opponents in Congress would kill commutation. If he agreed to have the issue referred to the states, the nationalists would prevent Congress from establishing the principle of equivalency. In either case the army would be the loser. There was nothing to do but wait. Until the direction of events became clearer, McDougall would stand firm upon the narrow ground of justice to the army first and solution of the national revenue problem second.

By the middle of February, 1783, rumors of an impending military uprising swirled through Philadelphia. Trading on the public's fear of a mutiny, the nationalists hoped to benefit from the tension and sense of danger created by the army's discontent. But since they had been unable to bring McDougall to support their position, they had already begun to deal directly with army leaders at Newburgh. To Henry Knox at West Point, Gouverneur Morris expressed the conviction that regimental officers would be served best by uniting with domestic and foreign creditors "to urge the grant of general permanent funds" instead of "looking wildly for a redress of grievances to their particular states." The army must influence the state legislatures to yield to Congress.[30] Writing the same day, February 7, Alexander Hamilton said essentially the same thing to Washington. Searching for the right words, he hinted to the commander-in-chief that he should assume direction of the military dissatisfaction to keep it "within the bounds of moderation." The nationalists looked to Washington to guide the army, "so as to produce a concurrence in the measures which the exigencies of affairs demand." The establishment of general funds, wrote Hamilton, "alone can do justice to the creditors of the United States (of whom the army forms the most meritorious class), restore public credit, and supply the future wants of government. This is the object of all men of sense; in this the influence of the army, properly directed, may cooperate." Hamilton thought that Knox, possessing the army's confidence, "may be safely made use of" in the nationalist cause.[31]

McDougall also sent messages and a messenger to Newburgh. Not to be outflanked by the nationalists, he outlined their strategy for Knox, emphasizing that they opposed referring the army "to the states for a settlement and security, till all prospect of obtaining continental funds was at an end." [32] John Brooks, carrying McDougall's letter, and probably those of Morris and Hamilton, was sent back to Newburgh by McDougall to give Henry Knox a fuller personal account of congressional politics. On February 12, McDougall wrote again. Interestingly, he used his old pseudonym of "Brutus," but if he intended to hide his identity from the nationalists by that disguise, it was a futile gesture. Even a cursory look at the surviving corpus of McDougall's papers proves his authorship, and undoubtedly many in Congress, as well as most officers at Newburgh, could identify the angular handwriting as McDougall's. His primary purpose in writing was to inform Knox that the reports of peace being received in Philadelphia might complicate matters for the army. He had questioned members of Congress, he said, as to what would happen to the soldiers if the peace rumors proved true. "Will they dissolve them without settling with them, or money to carry them home?" He was relieved to find that "the idea is becoming more and more familiar every day to members of Congress, and the citizens of this place, that the army will not disband till justice is done to them." His hope, he told Knox, was still that "the country have yet so much sense of justice and policy left as to do justice to the army without any violent declaration of their part." But McDougall recognized, as he had in years past, that whatever political influence the officers and soldiers might exert upon public policy resulted from their existence as an organized force in the field. News of peace threatened that solidarity. Soldiers and officers, already anxious to go home, would simply leave the army if peace was declared, and he feared that both Congress and the states would think it politically safe to ignore military claims once the regiments dissolved. It was therefore necessary, McDougall warned Knox, that "the army ought not to loose a moment in preparing for events—and for the worst that may happen to them." [33] The regiments *must* not be disbanded until some resolution had been achieved.

Letters from Newburgh and congressional debates proved frustrating to the nationalist leaders and McDougall alike. Henry Knox, like McDougall, basically sympathized with nationalist aspirations to endow the Confederation with powers sufficient to remedy national problems. "A hoop to the barrel," Knox said, was a favorite army expression. But what could the army do to remedy the country's political situation? "As the present Constitution is so defective," Knox asked Gouverneur Morris, "why do not your great men call the people together and tell them so; that is, to have a convention of the states to form a better Constitution?" [34] To McDougall he urged caution. As a pressure group, the army could properly send a memorial to Congress, but its reputation of submission to civil authority must not be sullied by coercive action or even the threat of it. McDougall should continue efforts to establish the principle and rate of commutation and to settle old accounts, so that the regiments could then seek funds from their respective states if Congress lacked a revenue of its own.

The advice was unnecessary. McDougall had sought those very goals with little progress for nearly two months; irked and tired of dealing with obdurate politicians, he remained in Philadelphia only because a chance still remained that commutation might be won. [35] But it was a slim chance. Discussion in Congress showed that army officers would not receive half pay or its equivalent apart from a general settlement for all public creditors, and Congress could not agree on the exact nature and scope of a revenue plan. On February 28, commutation fell short of the necessary votes of nine states. After two months of wrangling, it was clear that time was running out for the army. [36]

Everyone knew a formal end to the war was near. McDougall and other officers feared that the public's interest in the army's problems would vanish once peace was certain and officers and men were discharged. Near the end of February, McDougall heard (and reported to Knox) rumors that the regiments quartered in the Highlands were to be sent to various parts of the country to lessen the danger of a military uprising. The army, he thought, was about to lose its influence as a unified political pressure group, and old claims and promises would fade quickly from memory. [37]

While debate continued in Congress during the first half of March, 1783, events at Newburgh changed the picture completely. Scholars do not concur on the exact nature of the developments at the army's main camp, but supposedly a military conspiracy, conceived in Philadelphia, was hatched at Newburgh. Although the conspirators' designs and the dimensions of the plot are not wholly clear, it was apparently planned that the army's senior officers would ask Washington to use the army to arbitrate a political settlement between Congress and the states along nationalist lines. If he refused, which was likely General Horatio Gates was to take Washington's place and lead a mutinous army into direct political action. Circumstantial evidence points to Robert Morris and Gouverneur Morris as the principals in Philadelphia, while at Newburgh Colonel Walter Stewart, Major John Armstrong, and Timothy Pickering, along with Gates, were the army's leaders.[38] There is no direct evidence to associate McDougall with what has become known as the "Newburgh Conspiracy." True, he was financially desperate and politically militant and wanted the army to remain together until all claims were settled, but McDougall's lifelong republicanism and his dislike of Gates were too deep for him to join such a plot. Almost nothing could have induced him to cast Washington aside.

Instead of helping to bring about a coup d'etat, if that was indeed the plan at Newburgh that March of 1783, McDougall continued to lobby in Congress. He found new hope in the arrival of Delaware's representatives, who raised to eight the number of states supporting the army's claims. Eliphalet Dyer, who had previously prevented Connecticut from voting in favor of commutation, appeared to be wavering, offering another ray of hope. For a time, McDougall thought Dyer had been persuaded of the justice of commutation; but on March 10, when Congress voted the issue once more, Dyer remained in opposition and commutation lost, defeated by one vote.[39] Even this failure did not stop McDougall. He assured his friends at Newburgh that he would keep trying, and he proved it by informing Dyer "in plain terms, in what light the army and all honest men must consider his conduct, if he persists in it." If he failed again, however, McDougall intended to leave Philadelphia at the end of the month.[40]

What McDougall was unable to accomplish in the nation's capital by persuasion and appeals to justice, the nationalist leaders, working through the army at Newburgh, did for him in a week's time. Beginning on Monday, March 10, anonymous addresses appeared in camp. Arousing the emotions of the officers, the notices called on them to meet and consider a new course of action in the light of Congressional indifference to their memorial. It was intimated that Washington approved of strong action.

The implication was misleading. Forewarned of possible trouble,

Washington was angered by the audacious suggestion of the broadsides, which seemed to say tht Gates would take over and that under his leadership the army would secure its own justice by force of arms.[41] To undermine those trying to plunge the country into political chaos, Washington himself directed the officers' council to assemble on Saturday, March 15. The meeting was a disappointment to those who planned to use the army for political ends. With matchless skill, Washington brought a majority of the officers over to his position that the army's record as the nation's keeper of republican liberty must not be destroyed by an attempt to coerce a free government. The officers had to maintain their patience and their faith in Congress. After Washington withdrew, a committee headed by Knox obtained approval of five resolutions thanking McDougall for his efforts, expressing confidence that Congress would settle accounts and approve commutation, and condemning the recent anonymous addresses.[42]

In one stroke, Congress surrendered. Grumbling at Newburgh did not immediately end because of the March 15 meeting, but Washington's report to Congress, which reached Philadelphia on March 17, brought everything the army demanded. According to Madison, Washington's account of the sitation at Newburgh was given to members opposed to commutation, in order "to saddle with this embarrassment the men who had opposed the measures necessary for satisfying the army." Eliphalet Dyer gave up his opposition and swung Connecticut over to commutation, and on March 22, a frightened Congress commuted half-pay for life into five years at full pay for those officers of the state lines who, as a group, chose that option.[43] It was hardly a victory for the nationalists, who were still short of their goal of establishing a national revenue, but to McDougall the March 22 vote made his mission successful. The army had won a measure of justice, a balm to soothe the sting of sacrifice, and a reward to rescue ruined fortunes.

It is difficult to evaluate the Newburgh Conspiracy and McDougall's role in it. Was there actually a plot underway among nationalist leaders to use the army to force some sort of governmental reorganization? Did they actually intend to unseat George Washington if he refused to aid them? An especially troublesome question is why the whole affair ended so abruptly in mid-March. These, and other questions like them, have not been satisfactorily answered by historians. We cannot draw a firm conclusion on whether America nearly experienced a coup d'etat in early 1783. Perhaps we will never know the full story of those tumultuous weeks.

As for McDougall's role in the whole affair, he apparently saw himself solely as a military spokesman to Congress whose responsibility was to secure a satisfactory settlement of army demands; there is no evidence that he or the other principal army leaders intended or approved of any other objective. Still, McDougall was quite willing to stimulate fear of a mutinous army among congressmen, which, of course, it nearly became. Perhaps he even agreed that the army should refuse to lay down its arms until it received justice, thereby demonstrating to the doubtful the gravity of the situation; at least this was what "Brutus" implied. To that extent—intensifying tension and cultivating a fear of violence—McDougall's behavior in Philadelphia was not much different from his activities as a revolutionary leader on the streets of New York City. It was part of his political style to impress upon his political opponents that violent consequences might result from their continued opposition. Whether the political situation involved a faction-ridden state assembly, timid community leaders, or parsimonious legislators, McDougall sought to exploit his opponents' dread of violence to achieve his goals. He seemed always willing to take his case into the streets, or onto the battlefield, as a last resort. Although there is no certain way to determine whether his political brinkmanship was carefully contrived or was simply a visceral response to actions which he could not alter, the latter seems most characteristic. Success could not obliterate his rugged background. He carried over into his political and military roles the two-fisted toughness required to prosper along the waterfront or to stand on the quarter-deck of a privateer. In New York City before 1776, McDougall's old shipmates gave substance to his threats; in 1783, a disgruntled army was the instrument of implied coercion. He was more experienced, confident, and sophisticated in the politics of intimidation by 1783 (and, of course, the danger was greater). But his tactics in Philadelphia differed only in degree from those he had used in the streets of New York. Thus, although McDougall did not conspire with the others at Newburgh, he must share the blame for leaving the impression with Congress that the army was capable of mutiny if its demands were not met. And there can be little doubt that while McDougall would have thought such a mutiny horrible, he might also have considered it justified.

Remaining in Philadelphia until mid-May, McDougall waited only for decent travelling weather before returning to New York. When he arrived in the Highlands, the war was officially over but not all was well at Newburgh. Sergeants and privates were restless over the delayed payment of their accumulated pay, and officers had difficulty keeping their men under control. Still, the army melted away. Eager for home, some soldiers quietly packed off without waiting for their pay, while others were granted furloughs to reduce the tension in camp. McDougall willingly fell in with Henry Knox's plan of an association, the Society of Cincinnati, to perpetuate the friendship and protect the political interests of the army's senior officers.[44]

Like others who had served throughout the war, McDougall longed for the ease of civilian life, yet he faced the future with a certain misgiving. Seven years of military service had brought profound changes in his life. His health and wealth were gone, replaced by the nagging miseries of rheumatism and kidney trouble and by poverty; even his personal possessions were gone, destroyed by enemy raiders. Only his land holdings in North Carolina and upstate New York remained.[45] No longer young, McDougall was without an estate or profession to which he could return. Yet as a ranking senior officer, McDougall had acquired a high station in wartime society, served by aides and orderlies and treated with deference and respect by subordinates. Now that would be gone.

What would be his place in civilian life, now that he was penniless? Would it be lower than it had been for years past? Could he afford the trappings of his acquired rank? He knew better than most the economic footings upon which social stature rested: a man's house, furnishings, servants, horses and equipage, clothes, and table—all were regarded as symbols of taste and gentility, and all required a large income to maintain. Yet the war had impoverished him. Appearances counted a great deal to McDougall. He knew that a man's appearance influenced his standing. On several occasions near the end of the war, he had declined duties because he was financially unable to outfit himself in the manner his rank required; he simply refused to risk the ridicule of others. His insecurity about the future resulted in large measure from his near bankruptcy. His persistent pursuit of back pay, depreciation allowances, and half-pay and commutation, and his critical views about the wartime profits made by fair-weather Whigs were expressions of a deep anxiety over the loss of fortune and feared decline in status. During the war his financial straits had been irksome but not a social liability. In peacetime, however, it would be another matter. His proud military achievements might have earned him nothing.

# Chapter Fourteen
# End of a Public Career

When Congress officially proclaimed the war's end on April 11, 1783, exiled New York Whigs began returning to their old capital almost at once. Although southern New York was still in British hands, going down the Hudson became so fashionable, as one woman complained in April, that it was difficult to get boat passage. In late October, McDougall slipped into the city to look after two estates for which he was administrator and to locate housing for his family.[1] New York City was far different from the place McDougall remembered. Like McDougall himself, the city bore the marks of seven years of war. It had been charred extensively by great fires in 1776 and 1778, disfigured by sprawling forts and artillery batteries, and worn and dirtied by thousands of occupying troops and Tory refugees. "Everywhere there was ruin and desolation," one historian has written. "Streets, roads, and pavements had been torn up; lamps had been destroyed; wharves and slips had been neglected. And everywhere lay filth, dirt, and rubbish—mute evidence of the breakdown of municipal government." [2] For the hundreds of exiles who were returning to the city, decent housing was terribly expensive—when it could be found; employment was equally difficult to obtain; commerce had stopped; and money was extremely scarce. To those who, like McDougall, could recall the exciting opportunities of earlier days, the city was a tragic casualty of the war.

New Yorkers formally reclaimed their city on November 25, 1783, when the British finally completed their evacuation. Led by Governor George Clinton and General Washington, Americans paraded down Bowry Lane and the Broadway to the town's center. McDougall was among the soldiers who followed their commander-in-chief for the last time. Loaded with the honors of service, McDougall was a popular hero and an elder statesman of the Revolution. It was a moment of triumph for him. Throughout the seven years of his military service, he had sought no higher goal than defeating the enemy and establishing independence; now New York was finally free. But as McDougall and other exiled leaders surveyed the wreckage of New York City, they saw a multitude of problems demanding attention. First, the city had to be revived. It had to be cleaned up, and building had to begin. Its economy had to be stimulated to provide employment for demobilized soldiers, and basic municipal services needed to be reestablished. On a higher moral plane, the wounds of divided loyalties had to be healed; business had to adjust to the realities of peace; war debts had to be funded and paid; and some men thought the survival of the nation and the city depended upon an expansion of the Confederation's power to govern the country.[3]

For the remaining thirty-one months of his life, McDougall devoted his time primarily to the economic and political rehabilitation of southern New York. He approached the state's post-war problems, and particularly those of New York City, with no overall plan, except in monetary matters and in the need to strengthen the national Congress. His wartime experiences with currency depreciation had made him a firm opponent of any monetary system which was not solidly based on the convertibility of paper money into specie. Surprisingly, the anger of his late war years had cooled, perhaps as a result of the victory in the commutation fight and as a result of his steadily declining health. But no less important than his physical condition to the evaluation of his postwar years is an understanding of McDougall's basic political instincts. Despite his libertarian principles, he was never a social and political leveller, out to tear down entirely the structure in which some men were presumed to be more qualified than others to exercise power. When, for example, three hundred and fifty people asked that New York City's municipal government be wholly rather than partially elective, McDougall had no enthusiasm for such a change. He was evidently satisfied with the political system as it existed. McDougall was a man who relied upon common sense and personal experience to resolve public problems. It is tempting to label McDougall a pragmatist dealing in the realm of the possible. He was, at the minimum, a practical man, as perhaps all men of his time were to a degree. But his practicality was tempered by a political idealism which, despite his wartime criticism of state legislatures, was still founded upon the assumption that republican government was the best way to serve the ideals of justice and liberty for the people, even though he sometimes lacked faith in the strength of republican virtue among the people themselves.

The doubts as well as the hopes of wartime influenced McDougall's postwar activity. At first a temporary council governed the southern counties and New York City. Its purpose was to smooth the transition from British occupation to constitutional authority by supervising the election of municipal officials and members of the legislative houses, and by enforcing the laws, especially those aimed at the state's former enemies. Under Henry Knox, the remnants of the American army provided street patrols to keep order, but the city's mood was still tense in the weeks following November 25.[4] Whig exiles remained in an ugly mood, unable to forget that Tories had held their city for seven years, had taken their jobs, had lived in their houses, and had farmed their land. The peace treaty was particularly upsetting. Even before the British evacuation, grumbling over articles five and six of the treaty (which seemed to promise that Tories would be spared retribution and that confiscated Loyalist property would be returned) was widespread. A number of exiles expressed the intention of inflicting punishment upon all Tories for occupying the city, and a few even went so far as to talk of a general banishment of those foolish enough to try to remain. McDougall disagreed with such extremism. He parted company with Marinus Willett, John Lamb, Isaac Sears, and William Malcolm—all of whom advocated a hard line—favoring instead the moderate approach of allowing the law to work its course. At one point in December, 1783, a heated argument occurred between McDougall and Malcom over the issue, with Malcom insisting that vigilante action was necessary to drive Tories out of the city and McDougall arguing that the people must not take the law into their own hands.[5] Considering McDougall's revolutionary background, it must have been a surprise to his old friends to learn that he now supported law and order.

It is difficult to pinpoint the source of McDougall's moderate attitude toward his old enemies. Certainly his prewar political prejudices and his wartime experiences would logically seem to incline him toward anti-torism. Yet he opposed a general proscription, emphasizing the need to rely upon legislative judgment in the matter. Perhaps he felt that the Tories of 1775–76, who had fled early, were the Revolution's real enemies, while those who had remained during the occupa-

tion and did not leave when the British evacuated the city were simply unimportant people trapped by the circumstances of the war.
Perhaps he also agreed with Alexander Hamilton's estimate that the
state could not afford to lose men of wealth, even though those who
had been loyal to crown, and that it was time to heal the old wounds
in order to make peace a reality.[6]

In any case, McDougall's patriotism and long military service saved
him from the criticism of being too lenient. When the Whig exiles
organized on December 17, 1783, to nominate candidates for the legislative elections, McDougall was among those listed for a state senate
seat. The polls opened on December 29, and an event occurred the
next day which promoted the cause of all Whig candidates. Printer
John Holt, dead at the age of sixty-four, was buried. Holt's funeral
was a somber affair as the old Whigs paid their final tribute to the lit-
erary radical, but it also had political overtones. The eight pall-
bearers—Sons of Liberty from a different era—were candidates for
the Assembly, reaffirming their association with the Revolution and
emphasizing their opposition to the presence of Tories in the city.
They were all subsequently elected on a strong anti-Tory platform.
When the election polls closed on January 5, 1784, McDougall also
found himself elected to the Legislature from the state's southern senatorial district.[7]

Why McDougall accepted public office so soon after the war is difficult to explain. Considering his poor health and years of uninter-
rupted military service, he could have retired from public service with
honor and dignity to remain an elder statesman of the Revolution.
Certainly the meager salary of a state senator was not an inducement.
Probably, he just could not bear the thought of not being on the inner
counsels. It was time to return to politics. He had settled his personal
finances before he returned to the city, so the problem that rankled so
deeply during the last years of the war was apparently resolved. Settlement of back pay, depreciation allowances, and commutation provided McDougall with a block of securities valued at £4,000 sterling.
He had also obtained a loan (negotiated through John Vanderbelt, a
future stockholder of the Bank of New York) which brought in hard
money, and James Duane had worked out an arrangement with Mc-
Dougall's wartime creditors.[8] McDougall also collected a few prewar
debts. Even though his wealth was less than it had been before the
war, he was saved from the near-bankruptcy of the war years.

Perhaps McDougall's compulsive need to achieve social recognition made public office a natural postwar activity for him. After nearly twenty years of involvement in public life, he had grown accustomed to the distinction of being at the center of affairs, and exclusion or even retirement now would mean a loss of stature. McDougall made it known that he was not interested in an office requiring great labor (such as being mayor of New York City) but a place in the legislature—preferably the Senate, which possessed a higher status than the Assembly—would provide a public role which would not unduly tax his failing health. And there was certainly work to be done. The times were uncertain and the reconstruction of the southern part of the state required attention. Politics formed a common public diet for the people who returned to New York City. Political and social values may have changed as a result of the Revolution, but it was still expected that men of broad experience and proven leadership would participate in governmental affairs. McDougall willingly accepted that civic responsibility.

The powerful figure of Governor George Clinton dominated New York's postwar politics. After being elected the new state's first governor in 1777, Clinton compiled an incomparable record as a wartime leader. Year after year throughout the war, he defended his state's independence and its interests against all opponents, whether British, Loyalists, Indians, or land-grabbers from neighboring states. Plain-spoken and unassumingly dressed, Clinton lived comfortably but without display at New Windsor, where he reflected the interests of the landed gentry along the Hudson's west bank. He was perfectly at home among the prosperous farmers of the state's middle counties, and no less friendly with the great landlords of the valley. He worked at ease with the middling landowners, who soon came to control the state legislature.[9]

McDougall and Clinton were alike in some ways. Both had been early critics of British policies and supporters of independence; both persevered in their wartime responsibilities against great odds; both were loyal to the ideals of republican government. They had worked reasonably well together when McDougall commanded the Highland defenses, each agreeing in his own way on the need for great sacrifices to save the state from its enemies.

Wartime cooperation, however, did not guarantee a political association in peacetime. Although McDougall had been raised on a farm and had acquired modest landholdings by the time of his death, he never considered himself a landowner or landed gentleman. McDougall's life was in trade and commerce; he had captained a privateer, not a plow; he was an urban dweller, his attitudes were those of a city man. These mercantile-urban influences were revealed in McDougall's politics, and all served to clarify his differences with Clinton. In three sessions of the Senate, therefore, McDougall's voting record showed him aligning the least often with men like John Williams and Alexander Webster from the northeast, William Whiting, Jacob Kloch, and Abraham Yates from the northwest, and Ephriam Paine, John Haring, and Joseph Gasherie from the middle counties, who were Clinton's principal supporters in the Senate. McDougall opposed the Clintonian party on two issues: the need to strengthen the national Congress and a legislative emission of paper currency. In all other instances, McDougall practiced the "politics of opportunity" no less than the Clintonians, promoting the best interests of the city he represented, just as senators from upstate counties followed the interests and wishes of their rural constituencies.[10] The interests of New York City were commercial and financial and national in scope; so too were McDougall's.

The mainstay of New York City's economy—seaborne commerce— was in a shambles following the evacuation of the British. A few Loyalist merchants had remained behind, but the city's once grand merchant fleet was gone. Its wharves and warehouses were crumbling, and capital was scarce. To make matters worse, English creditors demanded payment of prewar debts, and the old pre-1776 trade with the West Indies, so profitable to merchants and farmers alike, was closed to American shipping. Other economic activities in the city suffered as well. Artisans and tradesmen—the mechanics who aspired to better things—were unable to compete against the flood of low-priced English manufactured goods.[11]

McDougall sought to promote the economic recovery and development of New York City in several ways. When Governor Clinton recommended in his opening speech to the 1784 Legislature that something be done about the exclusion of New York shipping from West Indian trade, McDougall responded by offering amendments to a public auction bill that would impose discriminatory duties upon British products entering the state.[12] His proposal had no other purpose than to retaliate against British restrictions upon American ships and products in the West Indies. Senators from rural counties, however, were unwilling to give up inexpensive English merchandise in order to promote commerce, and McDougall's amendments failed to pass.[13] The Senate did agree to a tonnage duty that gave a slight advantage to New York vessels in the whaling and coastwise traffic, thereby promoting ship-building, and to a schedule of specific duties on foreign manufactured items, which offered some protection to local craftsmen. But in both cases, the bills were intended primarily as revenue measures, not as acts to stimulate the economic recovery of southern New York. McDougall continued to urge a protective state tariff, even during the next year when merchant sentiment was shifting toward a system of national commercial regulation. Although he favored national regulation too, and supported a bill in 1785 empowering the national congress to impose duties on trade,[14] the need to encourage commerce and manufacturing in his senatorial district was more urgent and required more immediate assistance. When the Council of Revision vetoed the modestly protective state impost act of 1785 on the grounds that commercial regulation more appropriately belonged to the national Congress, McDougall therefore joined rural senators in overriding that veto.[15] In McDougall's mind, it was necessary for the state to provide protection to craftsmen, merchants, and shipbuilders until such time as the Articles of Confederation could be amended to give the central government the power to establish a uniform commercial and revenue system.

Outside the Senate, McDougall was instrumental in the establishment of the city's first commercial banking enterprise. He thought of it also as a means of promoting a business revival. Several factors converged in early 1784 to make the creation of a bank possible. Despite the huge wartime emissions of paper currency and public securities, the state as a whole was suffering from a money shortage. Old issues had become worn and had been recalled and destroyed, and the public lacked confidence in the bills that still circulated. Simple business transactions were difficult and frequently were reduced to a system of barter. Commodity prices and real estate values were low, hurting farmer and businessman alike; debtors at all levels found themselves hard-pressed to meet their obligations.

For the merchant community, the shortage of specie was particularly distressing. International accounts were hard to settle and business expansion was slowed by the exportation of the state's meager stock of specie.[16] In the public clamor for relief, several remedies were proposed. McDougall sponsored a Senate bill prohibiting the exportation of gold and silver. To some rural New Yorkers, the answer lay in a return to the prewar loan office system, by which bills of credit were issued upon farm mortgages, and legislation was introduced in the early days of the 1784 Assembly session to revive the old practice. To Chancellor Robert R. Livingston, a Hudson Valley land magnate, an incorporated bank of issue with a third of its assets in specie and the remainder in improved real estate was the solution for the state's monetary problems. Livingston's proposal, Alexander Hamilton commented caustically, "would be the philosopher's stone that was to turn all their rocks and trees into gold." [17]

Neither state loan office bills nor notes issued by Livingston's "land bank" interested McDougall. They reminded him of the wartime paper issues which had quickly depreciated and victimized the holders.[18] Apparently imbued with the monetary ideas of Robert Morris and the successful operations of the Bank of North America, both of which he had observed first hand during his visits to Philadelphia, McDougall saw a specie bank of discount and deposit as the best method of collective self-help for New York's merchant community. By pooling metallic resources in a bank offering short-term loans and issuing notes redeemable in gold and silver, the city's merchants could make the greatest use of their dwindling supply of specie. Certainly, bank stockholders would expect a return on their investment, and the dividend record of the Philadelphia bank was an attractive inducement. Primarily for that reason, John Church and Jeremiah Wadsworth, stockholders in Robert Morris' Bank of North America, were already promoting the idea of a specie bank in New York City, hoping to capitalize upon favorable merchant sentiment.[19] But as far as McDougall could see, the benefits to the city's commercial economy by the expansion of the money supply and stabilization of short-term credit transactions would far outweigh the advantages of private gain.

When a prospectus for Livingston's land-banking project appeared in the New York Packet on February 12, 1784, mercantile forces quickly gathered behind the alternative idea of a specie bank. After reminding the public of the disadvantages of a banking operation based on real estate, as Livingston proposed, several merchants—with William Maxwell, Comfort Sands, Henry Remsen, Samuel Franklin, and McDougall among them—issued a call for a public meeting at the

Merchants' Coffee House to consider an alternative. Heavily attended and presided over by McDougall, the initial meeting adjourned for several days after appointing a special committee to draft articles of association for a specie bank. When McDougall opened a second meeting on February 26, agreement was easily obtained to establish a bank with a capitalization of $500,000 in gold and silver, and by March 15, sufficient pledges, including McDougall's of $1250, were received to make it possible to assemble the stockholders and elect bank officers and directors.

McDougall thus became the first president of the Bank of New York.[20] A trusted hard money man, McDougall had a record of military service that would hopefully balance unfavorable public reaction to the presence of a number of Loyalist merchants on the Board of Directors and to the employment of William Seton, who had remained in the city throughout the British occupation, as the Bank's first cashier. McDougall's place in the Senate was also no doubt viewed an asset in attaining legislative incorporation and thus limiting liability for the stockholders.

But if the Bank's promoters expected that McDougall's presence in the Senate would count for much in gaining incorporation, they under-estimated the extent of rural opposition to such a merchant-oriented institution. Upstate senators preferred paper money over a conservative banking institution designed to meet the needs of the merchant community, a fact which McDougall discovered when he carried a petition to the Senate and drafted a bill incorporating the Bank of New York in March, 1784. The bill never got beyond a first reading. A second bill offered in November, 1784, was buried in the committee of the whole, and it was not until April 9, 1785, that a vote was taken. McDougall's bank bill was rejected by a two to one margin.[21] But the credit and specie needs of the merchants remained, and the Bank of New York opened for business in June, 1784. Even without incorporation, it was a success. Supported by the Chamber of Commerce and accepted by merchants and traders generally, the Bank aided the commercial rehabilitation of New York City.[22]

McDougall was also aware of the need to extend economic relief to mechanics and common laborers in his constituency. The problems of economic adjustment—housing, establishing old trades or finding new jobs, paying debts—were as onerous to the lower classes as to the merchants. Artisans and laborers experienced as much difficulty sup-

porting themselves and satisfying their creditors as did any other seg-
ment of society, but with an additional danger: they could be and
frequently were thrown into debtor's prison for small amounts.
McDougall proposed several forms of assistance. One of his earliest
acts in the 1784 Senate session was to introduce a bill abolishing imprisonment for debts of £10 or less.[23] The entire state would have
benefited from the bill's provisions, but McDougall's particular concern was to lighten the load of members of New York City's lower
class, many of whom were veterans struggling to support themselves.
Ironically, it was the Clintonian senators who defended the sacredness
of contracts and debts and who insisted that judgment should be made
against a debtor's person when he lacked other means of payment. In
the end, amendments so drastically altered the intent of McDougall's
bill that he joined other senators in rejecting it.[24] Imprisonment for
debt remained unchanged in New York until the nineteenth century.

McDougall also favored a form of tax relief to promote the economic interest of the laboring class as well as others in his district.
When the Senate considered tax revenues for 1784, a provision was
included in the £100,000 bill which authorized apportionment in the
Southern District according to the individual's circumstances and
ability to pay taxes upon real and personal property. The provision
was designed to shift the tax burden from individuals of little property
and low incomes to persons of greater wealth in the war-ravaged
southern part of the state and to that extent the tax bill represented a
departure from the established practice of a flat-rate assessment applied equally to all levels of property.[25] The 1784 tax measure passed,
despite the spirited opposition of some country members who argued
that the exemption granted to the people of the Southern District was
unfair to their own constituents, who had willingly paid large wartime
taxes, however burdensome upon the poor, while the Southern District contributed nothing to the state treasury. The issue was revived
the next year by upstate senators who pushed a bill prohibiting the
Court of Chancery from issuing injunctions, staying the forcible collection of taxes from persons in the Southern District pleading an inability to pay and thus nullifying the liberalized assessment and collection policy.[26] On that ground McDougall voted to have the bill
rejected, but it was in vain. The anti-injunction measure passed the
Senate and became law, and equality of property assessment and tax
payment became a reality once more.[27]

In yet another way, McDougall sought to promote the economic well-being of the ordinary man, especially the veteran reestablishing himself in civilian life. When provisions were made in 1784 for the sale of forfeited Tory estates in the Southern District and for the sale of unappropriated state lands, McDougall argued that depreciation certificates issued on military pay to all New York soldiers should be included among the ten other types of wartime certificates acceptable in payment for land. Rural senators disagreed. While they were willing to allow the use of certificates issued for cattle and horses seized by the army and other forms of bills easily accumulated by speculators, they objected to one of the most widespread forms of public securities, depreciation certificates. This exclusion of thousands of veterans from the benefits of the bill prompted McDougall to vote against all legislation disposing of public and confiscated lands.[28]

Promoting the economic recovery of New York City through the interests of merchants and mechanics was not the only element of McDougall's short postwar government service. He also stood on the side of religious liberty, and urged political moderation toward Loyalists. Little remains to permit a careful examination of McDougall's attitude on the proper role to be played by Loyalists in New York's postwar society. It can be said that he was not ready to forgive all of the state's former enemies, particularly not those who had worked actively to defeat independence. When it was proposed to allow the return of certain persons already under legislative banishment, he voted against the measure because they had supported Britain's war effort.[29] In general, he favored confiscation of Loyalist property when he could identify the particular individuals as notorious opponents of American liberty. His vote against the confiscatory act of 1784 was not anti-Loyalist but based solely on the grounds that veterans could not use their depreciation certificates to make purchases. Later, in 1785, he himself purchased a Queen's County farm forfeited by the Loyalist Daniel Kissam.[30]

On the other hand, he resisted the anti-Tory emotion that swept the state and New York City in the months following evacuation. He could not endorse a general banishment of all persons who had stayed within British lines during the war; perhaps he felt it made a mockery of those libertarian principles for which the war was fought. Nor did he approve a general disfranchisement of Loyalists, as proposed by Abraham Yates, Jr., of Albany. Yates would have required the testimony of only one witness, given to an election official, as evidence sufficient to disqualify a suspected individual from voting or holding an elective office. A majority in the Senate accepted the provision, but it was too much for McDougall. He voted against Yates.[31] He refused to participate in blind political revenge.

The treatment of former Loyalists was probably more a matter of expediency than principle for McDougall, since he associated with many of them in his economic activities. But the issue of freedom of conscience aroused his ideological ire. Religious freedom was an old question in New York, involving the incorporation of religious bodies and the collection of taxes to support an established ministry. In the years before independence, only one group, the Anglicans of Trinity Church, had received a charter from the crown permitting it to own and dispose of property and otherwise to govern itself. Both the Wall Street Presbyterian Church, of which McDougall originally was a member, and the Dutch Reformed Church had petitioned George III for similar incorporation, but the pleas had been denied on the grounds that chartering non-Anglican churches would violate a statute of Queen Anne obligating the monarch to promote the Church of England.[32] A New York law imposing a tax levy upon the people in the southern counties to maintain an Anglican ministry had also stirred a controversy. In 1775, when royal control was declining daily in the colony, McDougall and William Goforth had discussed the possibility of raising the issue of freedom of worship, particularly the right of co-religionists to organize on an equal legal footing with any other church. Goforth, apparently expressing the sentiments of other men, wanted immediate action, while McDougall feared that religious debate would complicate the already uncertain division between patriots and Loyalists which plagued the Provincial Congress. The matter was therefore postponed.[33] The question was again raised in 1777 in the convention drafting the state's first constitution, and Article 38 of the final document guaranteed freedom of worship. There the matter rested, for little could be done to disestablish Anglicanism in the state while the British held southern New York.

As soon as the war ended, however, McDougall was ready to act. On February 17, 1784, he initiated an effort to separate church and state in New York and to implement the principle of freedom of worship. At the heart of his religious concern was the right of any denomination to appoint trustees to serve as a corporate body to care for a congregation, even to the extent of allowing a faction to split off and take a just proportion of the church's property. The Senate accepted the principle of uniform church incorporation, including a £1,500 limit on church property holdings and a requirement that a property inventory be filed every three years. But it rejected the legalization of corporate subdivisions when unity and harmony no longer existed within a congregation. Over the objections of Senate Anglicans led by James Duane, Trinity Church of New York City was included in the provisions of McDougall's bill. The Legislature also repealed the old colonial law requiring a property tax for the support of an established ministry, and the prewar charter of Trinity Church was modified to conform with the declarations of liberty of conscience expressed in the state constitution.[34] With that, McDougall's goal of separating church and state was fully realized.

Public affairs claimed most of McDougall's time and energy during his first year back in New York City. His activities outside the Senate appeared to be limited by the state of his health, and it was apparent that his old business aggressiveness was gone. He showed only a passing interest in land speculation in forfeited estates, acquiring a small farm in Queen's County, and there is no evidence that he added to his holdings in the northern part of the state. Until May, 1785, he gave time to his responsibility as president of the Bank of New York, where he chaired the quarterly meetings of stockholders and reviewed the discount decisions of William Seton, bank cashier, who actually managed the bank's operations. Although the bank's success was gratifying (as was the dividend on its stock), McDougall declined to serve a second term as president. The work was simply too tedious. For a time he thought of reviving his West Indian trading connections, and solicited from an old friend the names of prospective molasses dealers in the Caribbean.[35] But even that failed to claim his full attention, for his wartime ailments of rheumatism and kidney stone had worked their toll on his vitality. By the fall of 1785, he admitted that his condition had worsened. Perhaps sensing that he had little time left, he put his personal affairs in order. In September he sent his elderly sister to live with an upstate relative. The next month, he sought to settle an old account with Peter R. Livingston and Isaac Sears, involving Hampden Hall of prewar days. As he told Livingston, "My constitution fails me much and I am very anxious to *settle* EVERY matter that I have any connection with." [36]

Perhaps he should have quietly retired from public life in late 1785. He certainly could have done so comfortably, and his health demanded that he find a cure. But despite his sinking condition, McDougall was on hand for the opening of the Senate's ninth session on January 6, 1786. Unfinished business required attention, and the state's sluggish economy, marked by slow trade and a severe money shortage, was its most pressing problem. Merchants demanded relief from insistent British creditors, who threatened legal action unless accounts were settled; and since the previous legislature had postponed a decision, further delay did not seem possible.[37] The money shortage plagued everyone, and once more the advocates of paper currency proposed a large emission as the only equitable way to promote the economic well-being of farmers and merchants. The arguments were thoroughly aired in the state's newspapers, and petitions favoring paper money continued to pour into the legislature. In the preceding two years, the Senate had resisted by narrow margins the paper currency bills passed by the Assembly, with most of the anti-paper senators, including McDougall, representing the southern counties and New York City. In early 1786, the money shortage was so acute and the personal hardships as a result of that scarcity so great that even the New York Chamber of Commerce had to admit that it might be necessary to issue paper money, though not to designate it as legal tender.[38]

The initiative for issuing paper money was taken in the Assembly, while the Senate gave its time to routine matters. But there was no doubt that paper money would be the major issue to come before the Senate in that session. At first, McDougall's health held up, but by the first week of March, 1786, when the Assembly finally completed a paper currency bill, he was ill and bed-ridden. After ten days of rest and medication, he recovered sufficiently to resume his seat and join the discussion on the Assembly's proposal.[39] Through the second and third weeks of March, the debate passed back and forth without a vote. If McDougall spoke on the question, his arguments are not known, but he was certainly opposed to paper money. He could not forget the havoc and anguish caused by the huge wartime emissions, or the bitter letters of protest and complaint about the runaway inflation which had victimized the army. Nor could he have forgotten the strenuous political efforts necessary to obtain depreciation adjustments for soldiers and officers. Altogether it had been a near-disas-

trous experience for the country, and he feared the danger would return if the Legislature succumbed to the paper mania practiced in
other states. To make matters worse, the bill as drafted in the Assembly provided that military depreciation certificates could not be exchanged for the new currency.

McDougall's illness forced him to miss the closing days of debate,
but when the Senate got down to voting the currency bill on March
29, he rose from his sick bed to go on record for the last time against
paper money. Carried into the Senate chamber on a stretcher, he arrived in time to vote against the bill's most important clause, a proposal to make paper money legal tender in all public and private transactions. Though anti-paper money senators were successful on that
issue, it was evident that they lacked the votes to defeat the entire
measure. But McDougall did not witness the final passage of the
paper money bill on March 29. Too ill to remain, he left before the
day was out. It was to be his last day of public service.[40]

After ten weeks of fever, Alexander McDougall died on June 9,
1786. Amid eulogies by his fellow citizens hailing him as a patriot and
republican who gave himself to his country's welfare, McDougall's
death was a sign that the older members of New York's and America's
revolutionary generation were passing. A few of the early group of
New York leaders were still active in public affairs—Clinton, Schuyler, Jay, Duane—and a number of the old Sons of Liberty—Willett,
Lamb, Goforth—were still around. But most others were passing
away. When George Washington learned of McDougall's death, and
that of Nathanael Greene's as well, he wondered who would take the
place of the fallen "pillars of the revolution." While some were dying,
Washington wrote Thomas Jefferson, others were "mouldering by in-
sensible degrees. May our country never want props to support the
glorious fabrick!" [41] McDougall had now reached in death that higher
place and reputation as revolutionary and soldier which he had sought
throughout his life.

# Chapter Fifteen
# An Appraisal

If Alexander McDougall was regarded as a "pillar of the revolution" by his contemporaries, what then is the measure of his contribution to the making of the "glorious fabrick" of the American Revolution? Mc-Dougall unquestionably conceived of himself as a disinterested patriot, fighting in the cause of liberty. Unselfish devotion to higher principle was clearly present in his life, as it was indeed in the lives of many other men of his time. But patriotic virtue only partly explains McDougall's revolutionary activities. There was also a human side. McDougall was clearly an ambitious man, desirous of rising above his humble origins to participate in the deference-based society in which he grew to manhood. That ambition was a basic element in Mc-Dougall's ultimate climb to importance in the Revolution. The characterization of him as a pretentious busy-body was only slightly overdrawn by his critics and it remains a particularly believable portrait of his early public life. The fact that McDougall restlessly sought a higher place in society to match the wealth he acquired in the Great War for Empire, indicated that he differed little from other men of his age in gratifying his social aspirations. The extraordinary political ferment of the prerevolutionary decade provided occasions in which to demonstrate his leadership qualities; after 1776, military life offered fresh opportunities to climb still higher. This combination of wealth, ability, and opportunity resulted in McDougall's meteoric rise in society. The psychological impact of this social transformation upon Mc-Dougall is difficult to measure. One development, however, may be noted. Throughout his long involvement in public affairs—from waterfront obscurity to modest national reputation—McDougall was intensely loyal to those men of higher status who accepted him. But he was far from the obsequious fellow his critics said he was; he was always his own man and quick to protect his own accomplishments.

His loyalty to others was more like that of a man who remembers and values those who befriend him. At first it was the Livingston party leaders to whom he paid partisan homage. Then during seven years of war it was George Washington. From these leaders, McDougall acquired his political skills and social graces and won a degree of recognition and friendship; to all of them, McDougall returned a steadfast loyalty.

As a revolutionary leader, however, McDougall was motivated by more than a calculating social aspiration. Under the early tutelage of Livingston Whigs, as well as through self-education in the literature of radical English Whiggery, McDougall came to be concerned with the larger meaning inherent in America's resistance to imperial authority. In the beginning, that resistance meant nothing more than the preservation of those political and economic patterns within which his fellow countrymen lived and worked. Colonial society was well suited to self-made men, and McDougall's own rise from milkboy to merchant of modest fortune and finally to public leader gave ample testimony to the opportunities open to ambitious young men. But British policies after 1763 appeared to narrow the circumference of opportunity. It seemed less easy to strike off on one's own, and harder to attain that freedom necessary to control one's own destiny. The political consequences of British policies were particularly upsetting. Like many others of his time, McDougall believed that British measures were the work of politicians corrupted by the power of their offices and guided by the ambition to acquire greater power at the expense of the liberty of others. Under the circumstances, the "people" had to resist the designs of the power-hungry office-holders, those in London as well as those in the colonies. McDougall thus struck out not only at imperial officials but also at the nearest symbols of political corruption, the De Lanceys of New York. Their partisan activities in 1769 and 1770, like those of British ministers, demonstrated in McDougall's mind the corroding influence of political ambition and power. Here, especially, McDougall proved capable of treading the narrow line between his own aspirations and those Whig principles which condemned ambition in public leaders. The guide he followed in distinguishing between hypocrisy and idealism was his belief in the superiority of the people's rights and interests. Thus the legislative action of the De Lanceys, he believed, was reprehensible because, as elected representatives of the people, they had been entrusted with power to protect the public interest, a trust they betrayed when they submitted to the Quartering Act while the people demanded that it be resisted. The result was a diminution of the public's freedom and happiness.

McDougall never fully elaborated what he meant by liberty and freedom. As a coffee-house strategist and street leader, he had little time and perhaps less patience for constructing a theoretical base upon which to build colonial resistance to British rule before 1776. He accepted, as others did, the English constitution as the basis of the freest political system in the world, and he believed that New York's own political institutions were an extension of that English constitutional system. But it was through street activity rather than in legitimate political involvement that he articulated his radical Whig principles, and his political action contributed substantially to the revolutionary impulse toward independence and change. He acted upon his belief that "the people" as a mass were the ultimate checks upon the tyrannical and irresponsible use of power. If the political system went sour, if leaders could not be trusted because of evidence of their greed and corruption, only the people could be relied upon to purify the government. Appeals to the people for support were more than commonplace tactics of local politics; they were now an acknowledgement that the people were the best and final judges in all matters involving the general happiness of society. And for all of his wartime pessimism, he continued to believe that virtue and rationality among people were the surest guardians of liberty and freedom and the foundation upon which society's well-being was founded.

But independence itself would not guarantee the preservation of "virtue and rationality." Independence would provide a freeing of existing areas of opportunity from the restraints of British and colonial authority. In a sense, McDougall saw freedom of opportunity as the ultimate form of self-fulfillment of a people. But that freedom and opportunity also imposed obligations of restraint upon the individual, so that one man's liberty did not encroach upon and destroy the freedom of another. On a higher level, the greatest obligations were carried by those who occupied seats of authority in government. Men in positions of power had to be responsive to the wishes of those living under the rule of government (which only a republican political structure would assure). All men might not be qualified to become rulers— wealth was still a fairly good measure of a man's place in society and a reasonably accurate yardstick of his personal capabilities. Yet all men had a fundamental right to know what their representatives did in the management of public affairs. Liberty and representative government really required both private and public virtue, a willingness of each person—private citizen and officeholder—to subordinate personal interests to the higher demands of the general welfare. Thus independence became to McDougall more than an act of political rebellion against Britain's imperial authority; it was something like a crusade, an act of moral regeneration. Its objectives transcended the immediate interests of individuals, and fulfillment of those objectives demanded sacrifice from every person for the common good of all.

The ideal of a new order of freedom, controlled by and for the people, never lost its appeal to McDougall. But the belief that the people and their representatives possessed the virtue, wisdom, and patriotism necessary to realize that ideal weakened during the war years. McDougall's faith in the people was shaken by his military experiences. He concluded that most men had a greater concern for their personal interests than they did for supporting a war for their own liberation. According to his view of the war period, the people at home, now freed from British rule, pursued property, while the patriot-soldiers endured hardships and fought the battles. A deep rift had appeared in American society, McDougall concluded. Self-interest was threatening to overpower republican idealism. Without abandoning his belief in republican government but convinced that contradictory thrusts in society had to be brought into harmony to avoid disaster, McDougall came to accept the necessity of a national authority strong enough to transcend the localism of the states. Only then could independence and the general happiness of all be assured.

By the end of the war, McDougall had lost his visionary zeal but not his belief in republicanism. His conception of representative government was illustrated during his brief years in the New York Senate. It was his belief that he should work for those public policies his constituents wanted and needed. If those policies did not necessarily coincide with the objectives of other senators, it was not the result of a conflict of principle so much as a reflection of the diverse social and economic interests and needs within a large population. Thus, McDougall was not by conviction or sentiment a conservative, as some historians have described him, especially not in his opposition to paper money or other agrarian goals. He was simply a businessman, serving an urban center whose need for a circulating medium was of a different order. Indeed, his support of two measures—the abolition of imprisonment for small debts and the changes in the assessment of local taxes according to ability to pay—suggests that he stood on the side of expanding opportunity that would benefit the ordinary man, and not merely those in commerce and banking. In any case, the needs of small farmers were not always those of the artisans and shopkeepers whom McDougall represented and served in government.

McDougall's role in the American Revolution was a blend of personal ambition, practical politics, and idealism. He was preoccupied with the tactics of shaping and directing community action against Britain, sometimes in quite devious ways; but he did not lose sight of the general principles upon which that opposition was founded. He saw himself fighting a heroic battle against tyranny, but he was ever mindful of the politics of decision-making during wartime. Thus he played a far greater part in moving the colonies toward independence and then fighting to defend it than in organizing the resulting society. In one way or another he gave nearly half of his life to what he considered a higher cause. It was this fact, his patience and perseverance in the face of personal tribulation, that gives significance to McDougall as a revolutionary leader. Having few grand plans for the postwar period, he would probably have quickly agreed that achieving the full meaning of the Revolution was a task for succeeding generations. It was enough that he had helped to establish a new nation upon the principles of liberty.

# Notes

## INTRODUCTION

1. Examples of popular leaders in other colonies would include such figures as Samuel Adams of Boston, Charles Thomson of Philadelphia, Christopher Gadsden of Charleston, Cornelius Harnet of North Carolina, Patrick Henry and Richard Henry Lee of Virginia, and Samuel Chase of Baltimore. The designation "popular leaders" is used here in preference to other labels because it conveys more fully the nature of their involvement in local politics as well as their unyielding opposition to British imperial policies. A general discussion of the popular leaders is in Merrill Jensen, *The Founding of a Nation: A History of the American Revolution 1763–1776* (New York, 1968), 374–76. Bernard Mason has surveyed how historians have viewed the Revolution in New York in, "The Heritage of Carl Becker: The Historiography of the Revolution in New York," *New-York Historical Society Quarterly*, LIII (1969), 127–47.

2. See Carl L. Becker, *The History of Political Parties in the Province of New York, 1760–1776* (Madison, 1909). A variant of Becker's "radicals" is in Bernard Friedman, "The Shaping of the Radical Consciousness in Provincial New York," *Journal of American History*, LVI (1970), 781–801. For a defense of the term "radical" see Pauline Maier, *From Resistance to Revolution: Colonial Radicals and the Development of American Opposition to Britain, 1765–1776* (New York, 1972), xii–xiii.

3. Maier, *From Resistance to Revolution*, xv.

4. Patricia U. Bonomi, *A Factious People: Politics and Society in Colonial New York* (New York, 1971), 279–86. The restrictive pattern of office-holding in New York City is analyzed in Bruce M. Wilkenfeld, "The New York City Common Council, 1689–1800," *New York History*, LII (1971), 249–73.

5. James Kirby Martin, *Men in Rebellion: Higher Governmental Leaders and the Coming of the American Revolution* (New Brunswick, N.J., 1973).

## CHAPTER ONE: THE EARLY YEARS

1. Geneology, McDougall Papers, Oversize Folder, New-York Historical Society [NYHS].

2.  For a general statement of Campbell's colonizing activity, see William Smith, Jr., *The History of the Province of New York*, Michael Kammen, ed. (2 vols., Cambridge, Mass., 1972), I, 195; George Prydie, "Scottish Colonization in the Province of New York," *New York History*, XVI (1935), 138–57; Ian C. C. Graham, *Colonists from Scotland: Emigration to North America, 1707–1783* (Ithaca, N.Y., 1956), 48, 77–80.

3.  E. B. O'Callaghan, "Early Highland Immigration to New York," *Historical Magazine*, V (1861), 301–03.

4.  Cadwallader Colden to William Smith, Jr., Jan. 15, 1759; Smith to Colden, Feb. 5, 1759, *The Letters and Papers of Cadwallader Colden*, New-York Historical Society *Collections* (9 vols., New York, 1918–37), V, 283–86, 289–92.

5.  Lt. Gov. George Clarke to Duke of Newcastle, June 15, 1739, E. B. O'Callaghan, ed., *Documents Relative to the Colonial History of the State of New York* (15 vols., New York, 1856–87), VI, 145; *New York Assembly Journal*, Oct. 10, 13, 1738. The Assembly appointed a committee to investigate Campbell's enterprise but never made a formal report.

6.  Clarke to Newcastle, June 15, 1739, *New York Colonial Documents*, VI, 145.

7.  Thomas Jones, *History of New York During the Revolutionary War* . . . , Edward Floyd De Lancey, ed. (2 vols., New York, 1879), I, 24–25.

8.  For a general description of New York City, see George W. Edwards, *New York as an Eighteenth Century Municipality, 1731–1776* (New York, 1917).

9.  Jones, *History of New York During the Revolutionary War*, I, 25, is critical of McDougall, but it is one of the few published accounts of McDougall's early life. Sister Anna Madeleine Shannon, "General Alexander McDougall, Citizen and Soldier, 1732–1786" (Ph.D. diss., Fordham University, 1957) is a full biographic study.

10.  "To the Public," a manuscript broadside critical of McDougall's background, dated June 4, 1777, apparently written by Henry Beekman Livingston. George Washington Papers, Series 4, Reel 42, Library of Congress [LC]. All references to the Washington Papers are to the microfilm edition of the Library of Congress.

11.  *Ibid.*

12.  Statement of Reverend J. McVicar, July 11, 1751; Stephen McDougall to Alexander McDougall, Glasgow, Mar. 19, 1752, McDougall Papers, Box 1, NYHS.

13.  "Naval Office Lists," Public Record Office, Colonial Office, 5/1227 (microcopy, NYHS); *New York Mercury*, Nov. 13, 1752; July 1, 1754, May 12, 1755. McDougall was already trading to the West Indies by 1753. Stephen McDougall to Gov. George Thomas (Antigua), Glasgow, Oct. 2, 1753, McDougall Papers, Box 1, NYHS.

14.  "To the Public," June 4, 1777, Washington Papers, Series 4, Reel 42, LC.

15.  Lists of crew members and letters of marque are in McDougall Papers,

Box 1 and Oversize Folder, NYHS. For a report on privateering out of New York City in 1757, see I. N. Stokes, comp., *The Iconography of Manhattan Island.* . . . (6 vols., New York, 1915–28), IV, 688.

16. McDougall's father-in-law in Scotland heard of his successes and advised him to quit while he was ahead. Stephen McDougall to Alexander McDougall, Aug. 29, 1758, April 7, 1760, McDougall Papers, Box 1, NYHS.

17. Jones, *History of New York During the Revolutionary War*, I, 25.

18. The principal statement of McDougall's wealth is in a surviving "Waste Book, 1767–1771," W. Wright Hawkes Collection of Revolutionary War Documents, Schaffer Library, Union College, Schenectady, N.Y.

19. McDougall Papers, Box 1, NYHS.

20. "Waste Book, 1767–1771," Hawkes Collection, Union College; McDougall Papers, Box 1, NYHS.

21. McDougall's father-in-law may have influenced him to send his boys to college. To McDougall, May 27, Sept. 4, 1766, *ibid.*

22. "Waste Book, 1767–1771," Hawkes Collection, Union College; New York Treasurer, Manifest Books, XXXVI, Jan. 11, 1759 entry, New York State Library [NYSL], Albany; Erastus C. Knight, comp., *New York in the Revolution as Colony and State: A Supplement* (Albany, 1901), 96–97.

23. The option was with John Edsall of Orange County, New York. McDougall Papers, Box 1, NYHS.

24. Alice Hanson Jones, "Wealth Estimates for the American Middle Colonies, 1774," *Economic Development and Cultural Change*, XVIII (1970), 119.

25. "Waste Book," May 20, 1769 entry, Hawkes Collection, Union College.

26. "To the Public," June 4, 1777, Washington Papers, Series 4, Reel 42, LC; *New York Journal*, Mar. 1, 1770.

## CHAPTER TWO: IMPERIAL POLICIES AND PARTISAN POLITICS

1. This interaction is discussed in Gordon S. Wood, "Rhetoric and Reality in the American Revolution," *William and Mary Quarterly*, 3rd ser., XXIII (1966), 3–32.

2. Virginia D. Harrington, *The New York Merchant on the Eve of the American Revolution* (New York, 1935), 316–17; Jesse Lemisch, "Jack Tar in the Streets: Merchant Seamen in the Politics of Revolutionary America," *William and Mary Quarterly*, 3rd Ser., XXV (1968), 371–407; Patricia U. Bonomi, *A Factious People: Politics and Society in Colonial New York* (New York, 1971), 178–228; Roger J. Champagne, "Family Politics versus Constitutional Principles: The New York Assembly Elections of 1768 and 1769," *William and Mary Quarterly*, 3rd Ser., XX (1963), 57–79.

3. Maier, *From Resistance to Revolution*, 51–76; Roger J. Champagne, "Liberty Boys and Mechanics of New York City, 1764–1774," *Labor History*, VIII (1967), 115–35.

4. General Thomas Gage, headquartered in New York City, reported to London that the city's mob consisted primarily of seamen who were called out by their merchant-employers. To Secretary of State Henry Conway, Dec. 21, 1765, Clarence E. Carter, ed., *The Correspondence of General Thomas Gage with the Secretaries of State, 1763–1775* (2 vols., New Haven, 1931–33), I, 78–79. For the role of Newspaper polemics in arousing the public see Michael D'Innocenzo and John J. Turner, "The Role of New York Newspapers in the Stamp Act Crisis, 1764–1766," *New-York Historical Society Quarterly*, LI (1967), 215–31, 345–65.

5. *New York Gazette or Weekly Post-Boy*, Nov. 7, 1765; Colden to Conway, Nov. 5, 1765, *Colden Letter Books*, New-York Historical Society *Collections*, (2 vols., New York, 1876–77), II, 54–56.

6. Roger J. Champagne, "The Military Association of the Sons of Liberty," *New-York Historical Society Quarterly*, XLI (1957), 338–50. See also Maier, *From Resistance to Revolution*, 77–112.

7. The politics of the triumvirate may be found in Dorothy Dillon, *The New York Triumvirate: A Study of the Legal and Political Careers of William Livingston, John Morin Scott, and William Smith, Jr.* (New York, 1949); Milton M. Klein, "William Livingston's *A Review of the Military Operations in North America*," Lawrence H. Leder, ed., *The Colonial Legacy*, (4 vols., New York, 1971–73), II, 107–40. McDougall's involvement in the Wall Street Church, along with the principal Livingston family leaders, is in Hugh Hastings, comp., *Ecclesiastical Records of the State of New York* (7 vols., Albany, 1901–06), VI, 4046–48, 4081, 4083–84, 4095–96.

8. Livingston described conditions in the city to the absent Governor Robert Monckton, Nov. 8, 1765. *Aspinwall Papers*, Massachusetts Historical Society *Collections*, 4th Series (2 vols., Boston, 1871), II, 562–63. The acceptance of the mob as an extralegal effort to redress grievances when legal remedies failed is analyzed in Pauline Maier, "Popular Uprisings and Civil Authority in Eighteenth Century America," *William and Mary Quarterly*, 3rd Ser., XXVII (1960), 3–35.

9. *New York Gazette or Weekly Post-Boy*, Nov. 28, 1765. William Smith apparently wrote the "instructions" to the city's Assembly representatives. See William Smith, Jr. Papers, Folder 197, NYPL. The division of sentiment among the Sons of Liberty is analyzed in Jesse Lemisch, "New York's Petitions and Resolves of December 1765: Liberals vs. Radicals," *New-York Historical Society Quarterly*, XLIX (1965), 313–26.

10. As late as 1769, Isaac Sears and John Lamb vigorously denied that McDougall had been involved in the resistance to parliamentary taxation in 1765. *New York Journal*, Mar. 1, May 3, 1770.

11. A full discussion of the elections of 1768 and 1769 is in Champagne, "Family Politics versus Constitutional Principles." A different view is in Bernard Friedman, "The New York Assembly Elections of 1768 and 1769: The Disruption of Family Politics," *New York History*, XLVI (1965), 3–24. The role of personality in New York's politics is in Milton M. Klein, "Politics and

Personalities in Colonial New York," *ibid.*, XLVII (1966), 3–16.

12.   Bonomi, *A Factious People*, 232–36.

13.   The question of party labels is always a troublesome problem. One recent view argues that the political rivals are best seen as Whigs of different shadings, one being "moderate" (Livingstons) and the other "popular" (De Lanceys) in their Whigism, *Ibid.*, 237–39. The way the politicians viewed themselves and the style of their campaign literature, however, gives a far greater importance to the ambitions and interests of the rival families and their supporters. For the Whiggism of the De Lanceys, see Leopold Launitz-Schurer, Jr., "Whig-Loyalists: The De Lanceys of New York," *New-York Historical Society Quarterly*, LVI (1972), 179–98.

14.   The election issues are summarized in Champagne, "Family Politics versus Constitutional Principles," 56–57, 73–74.

15.   Bonomi, *A Factious People*, 239–40, 241, 245.

16.   *New York Journal*, Mar. 16, 23, 1769, Mar. 1, April 26, 1770; *New York Mercury*, April 30, 1770.

17.   *New York Journal*, Mar. 1, 1770.

18.   Election results are in Champagne, "Liberty Boys and Mechanics," 132; Patricia U. Bonomi, "Political Patterns in Colonial New York City: The General Assembly Election of 1768," *Political Science Quarterly*, LXXXI (1966), 432–47. Isaac Sears was rewarded with the inspectorship of potash. *Journal of the Legislative Council of the Colony of New York* (2 vols., Albany, 1861), II, 1700; *The Colonial Laws of New York from the Year 1664 to the Revolution* (5 vols., Albany, 1894), IV, 1090–94; *New York Journal*, May 3, 1770.

19.   A general survey of the Quartering Act is in John Shy, *Toward Lexington, The Role of the British Army in the Coming of the American Revolution* (Princeton, 1965). New York's reluctance to support the royal troops, which resulted in the suspension of the Assembly in 1767, is in Nicholas Varga, "The New York Restraining Act: Its Passage and Some Effects, 1766–1768," *New York History*, XXXVII (1956), 233–58. See also *New York Mercury*, June 11, 1770 for a list of appropriations for the army.

20.   Livingston to Philip Schuyler, Feb. 27, 1769, Philip Schuyler Papers, Box 23, NYPL.

21.   *New York Gazette*, Feb. 12, 1770.

22.   *Smith Historical Memoirs*, 68; Evert and Gerard Bancker, Barrack Master Accounts, 1768–1774, NYPL; New York Miscellaneous Manuscripts, 1767–1770, NYHS. McDougall's attendance at Assembly meetings is in *New York Gazette*, Feb. 12, 1770.

23.   *New York Assembly Journal*, May 20, 1769; Moore to Lord Hillsborough, May 29, 1769, *New York Colonial Documents*, VIII, 169–70.

24.   Colden to Lord Hillsborough, Dec. 4, 1769, *Colden Letter Books*, II, 193–94, and Oct. 4, 1769 and Jan. 6, 1770, *New York Colonial Documents*, VIII, 189, 199–200.

25.   *New York Assembly Journal*, Nov. 4, 1769.

26. For the expulsion of other Livingston men, see Lawrence H. Leder, "The New York Elections of 1769: An Assault on Privilege," *Mississippi Valley Historical Review*, XLIX (1963), 675–82.

27. *New York Assembly Journal*, Dec. 15, 1769; Colden to Lord Hillsborough, Dec. 16, 1769, *Colden Letter Books*, II, 194–95; Colden to Lord Hillsborough, Jan. 6, 1770; *New York Colonial Documents*, VIII, 199–200; McDougall to the Public, *New York Journal*, Feb. 15, 1770.

28. "The Paper signed a Son of Liberty contains the following assertions," n.d., McDougall Papers, Box 1, NYHS.

29. *To the Betrayed Inhabitants of the City and Colony of New York* (December 16, 1769) [New York, 1769].

30. There is a striking similarity between McDougall's broadside and entries in William Smith's diary, especially "Notes of Proceedings in Assembly 1769." *Smith Historical Memoirs*, 59–71.

31. The "Sources and Traditions" of revolutionary thinking are discussed in Bernard Bailyn, *The Ideological Origins of the American Revolution* (Cambridge, Mass., 1967), 22–54. See also Caroline Robbins, *The Eighteenth Century Commonwealthman* (Cambridge, Mass., 1959); Maier, *From Resistance to Revolution*, 27–48. A listing of books and pamphlets in McDougall's possession may be found in "Inventory of all the goods, chattles and credits, which were of Alexander McDougall Esqr deceased," McDougall Papers, Oversize Folder, NYHS. The influence of Trenchard and Gordon is discussed in Milton M. Klein, ed., *The Independent Reflector* (Cambridge, Mass., 1963), 20–23. McDougall's respect for the political views of the senior Robert R. Livingston is in George Brancroft Transcripts: Livingston Papers, NYPL.

32. "The Paper signed a Son of Liberty contains the following assertions," n.d., McDougall Papers, Box 1, NYHS.

33. *Ibid.*

34. Certainly Peter R. Livingston's view of the Quartering Act was self-serving. Livingston to Philip Schuyler, Feb. 6, 27, 1769, Philip Schuyler Papers, Box 23, NYPL. One public writer stressed the partisan nature of the controversy over the Quartering Act, claiming that it sprang from the ambitions of disappointed office-seekers who wanted only a return to power. *A Citizen's Address to the Public* (December 18, 1769) [New York, 1769].

35. *New York Journal*, Dec. 28, 1769; Colden to Lord Hillsborough, Jan. 6, 1770, *New York Colonial Documents*, VIII, 199–200.

36. *New York Journal*, Dec. 28, 1769; *New York Assembly Journal*, Dec. 18, 19, 1769; Stokes, *Iconography of Manhattan*, IV, 800. On Wednesday after the meeting, John Lamb appeared before the Assembly for questioning, but he admitted nothing. Peter R. Livingston to Robert Livingston, Dec. 23, 1769, Livingston-Redmond Papers, Roll 6, Franklin D. Roosevelt Library [FDRL].

37. Peter R. Livingston to Robert Livingston, Dec. 25, 1769, *ibid.; To the Public* (December 28, 1769) [New York, 1769]; *New York Journal*, Jan. 4, 1770; *New York Assembly Journal*, Dec. 22, 1769.

38. "J.W. a squinter on public affairs," *A Mode of Elections Considered* (December 29, 1769) [New York, 1769]; *To the Independent Freeholders and Freemen of this City and County* (January 4, 1770) [New York, 1769]; *New York Mercury*, Jan. 8, 22, 29, 1770; *New York Journal*, Jan. 11, 1770. On January 9 the house rejected Thomas' ballot bill. *New York Assembly Journal*, Jan. 9, 1770. See also Peter R. Livingston to Robert Livingston, February 5, 1770, Livingston-Redmond Papers, Roll 6, FDRL.

39. Shy, *Toward Lexington*, 210–11, 217–23, 279.

40. Money was extremely scarce, debts were difficult to collect, trade was very slow, and land values were depressed. James Beekman to Thomas Harris, July 22, 1769, To Robert and Nathan Hyde, June 6, 1769, to Fludyer, July 22, Oct. 7, 1769, Philip L. White, ed., *The Beekman Mercantile Papers, 1746–1799* (4 vols., New York, 1956), II, 720–21, 731–32, 804, 840; Anthony Lispenard Bleecker to John Relfe, Jan. 22, 1770, to Simon Cooley, April 14, 1770, Bleecker Letter Book 1767–1787, NYHS.

41. *New York Journal*, Jan. 18, and Supplement, Mar. 1, 1770.

42. "Brutus," *To the Public* (January 15, 1770) [New York, 1770]. McDougall later used the pseudonym Brutus in his private correspondence, and it seems reasonable to guess that he used it at this earlier date.

43. *New York Journal*, Jan. 18, 25, Mar. 1, 1770; broadside in manuscript form, dated Jan. 17, 1770, New York Misc. Mss. 1767–1770, NYHS.

44. *To the Public* [New York, 1770].

45. The most detailed description of the "Battle of Golden Hill" is in *New York Journal*, Supplement, Mar. 1, 1770. See also Henry B. Dawson, *The Sons of Liberty in New York* (Poughkeepsie, N.Y., 1859), 112–17.

46. Peter R. Livingston to Robert Livingston, Jan. 22, 1770, Livingston-Redmond Papers, Roll 6, FDRL; *New York Journal*, Mar. 1, 1770.

47. Mayor Hicks' proclamation of January 20 is in Stokes, *Iconography of Manhattan*, IV, 804. See also *New York Mercury*, Feb. 5, 1770.

48. Benjamin Young Prime to Dr. Peter Tappen, April 12, 1770, New York Misc. Mss., NYHS.

49. *To the Sons of Liberty in this City* (February 3, 1770) [New York, 1770]; *New York Mercury*, Feb. 5, 1770. The evidence is not entirely clear that Sears purchased the land. A search of the title records in 1915–17 suggests that Sears bought the land on which the last Liberty Pole was erected. Stokes, *Iconography of Manhattan*, IV, 805–06. For other evidence, see Peter R. Livingston, Feb. 5, 1770, Livingston-Redmond Papers, Roll 6, FDRL.

50. *New York Journal*, Feb. 8, 1770.

CHAPTER THREE: "THE WILKES OF AMERICA"

1. George Rude, *Wilkes and Liberty: A Social Study of 1763–1774* (Oxford, 1960) is the standard account of Wilkes' political activities. American interest in John Wilkes is discussed in Maier, *From Resistance to Revolution*, 162–69, and

in "John Wilkes and American Disillusionment with Britain," *William and Mary Quarterly*, 3rd Ser., XX (1963), 379–95. See also Jack P. Greene, "Bridge to Revolution: The Wilkes Fund Controversy in South Carolina, 1769–1775," *Journal of Southern History*, XXXIX (1963), 19–52.

2.  *New York Gazette*, Feb. 12, 1770; "The Dougliad, No. 3," *New York Mercury*, April 23, 1770; *Smith Historical Memoirs*, 73–75; "Substance of the Evidence against Capt. McDougall," McDougall Papers, Box 1, NYHS.

3.  John Wilkes' offense in the 45th issue of the *North Briton* was a criticism of the king's speech to parliament in 1763, the last straw in a series of attacks upon George III and his ministers. See George Nobbe, *The North Briton: A Study in Political Propaganda* (New York, 1939).

4.  *New York Journal*, Feb. 15, Mar. 22, 1770. As soon as it was reported that "45 virgins" had visited McDougall, an indignant citizen wrote to John Holt that the story was the work of a "false and impious wretch." *Ibid.*, Mar. 29, 1770; *New York Mercury*, April 2, 1770.

5.  *Out-Lines* [New York, 1770]: *New York Journal*, Mar. 29, 1770.

6.  *Ibid.*, Mar. 1, 1770.

7.  *New York Mercury*, April, May, and June, 1770 issues.

8.  Jonathan Landon to Robert Morris, Mar. 24, 1770, quoted in Bonomi, *A Factious People*, 272.

9.  *New York Journal*, Feb. 15, 22, 1770.

10.  *Ibid.*, Mar. 22, 29, April 5, 12, 1770.

11.  Leonard W. Levy, *Legacy of Suppression: Freedom of Speech and Press in Early American History* (Cambridge, Mass., 1960), 10–21.

12.  "The Paper signed a Son of Liberty contains the following assertions to wit," n.d. McDougall Papers, Box 1, NYHS.

13.  *New York Journal*, Feb. 22, Mar. 1, 8, 15, 1770; *New York Gazette*, Feb. 19, Mar. 5, 12, 19, April 2, 16, 1770; *New York Mercury*, April 9, 1770; Jones, *New York During the Revolutionary War*, I, 28–29.

14.  Copy of Council Minute, Feb. 14, 1770, James Duane Papers, Box 1766–1771, NYHS; *New York Gazette*, May 7, 1770; Dillon, *New York Triumvirate*, 108; *Smith Historical Memoirs*, 75; Jones, *New York During the Revolutionary War*, I, 30–32.

15.  *New York Gazette*, April 16, May 7, 1770.

16.  "The King Against Alexander McDougall," John Tabor Kempe Papers, Sorted Legal Papers, NYHS; "Substance of the Evidence Against Capt. McDougall," McDougall Papers, Box 1, NYHS. The *New York Gazette*, May 7, 1770, contains the fullest account of McDougall's trial. See also *New York Journal*, May 3, 1770; *New York Mercury*, April 30, 1770.

17.  "Information against Alexander McDougall, filed with Supreme Court, April 27, 1770," McDougall Papers, Box 1, NYHS.

18.  Jones, *New York During the Revolutionary War*, I, 30; *New York Gazette*, May 7, 1770.

19.   William Smith to Philip Schuyler, April 29, 1770, Philip Schuyler Papers, Box 23, NYPL.

20.   *New York Gazette*, May 7, 1770; *New York Journal*, May 3, 1770; *New York Mercury*, April 30, 1770; Dillon, *New York Triumvirate*, 113.

21.   McDougall Papers, Box 1, NYHS.

22.   Arthur M. Schlesinger, *The Colonial Merchants and the American Revolution 1763–1776* (New York, 1918), 113–16, 124–25, 160–72, 186–90; *New York Journal*, Mar. 4, May 7, 1770; Thomas Harris (London) to James Beekman, Mar. 8, 1770, *Beekman Mercantile Papers*, II, 808–09.

23.   *New York Journal*, Mar. 22, 29, 1770.

24.   Alexander Colden to Anthony Todd, July 11, 1770, *New York Colonial Documents*, VIII, 218–20; "Brutus," *To the Inhabitants* [New York, 1770]; "Political Memoranda, 1770," McDougall Papers, Box 1, NYHS; Schlesinger, *Colonial Merchants*, 220; *New York Journal*, May 24, 1770.

25.   *Ibid.*, June 7, 28, 1770; "Political Memoranda, 1770," McDougall Papers, Box 1, NYHS.

26.   Schlesinger, *Colonial Merchants*, 221–22; *New York Journal*, June 21, July 5, 1770; *Boston Gazette*, June 25, 1770.

27.   Colden to Lord Hillsborough, July 7, 1770; *Colden Letter Books*, II, 222–24; *New York Journal*, June 21, July 12, 1770; subscription papers in favor of non-importation, dated June 12, 1770, McDougall Papers, Box 1, NYHS.

28.   *New York Mercury*, June 25, 1770.

29.   *New York Journal*, April 12, 19, 26, May 3, 10, 17, 24, 31, June 7, 1770.

30.   *Ibid.*, June 21, 28, July 5, 12, 1770; *New York Mercury*, June 18, 1770; "Political Memoranda, 1770," McDougall Papers, Box 1, NYHS.

31.   *New York Journal*, Aug. 2, 1770; *Boston Gazette*, July 16, 1770; "Political Memoranda, 1770," McDougall Papers, Box 1, NYHS; Schlesinger, *Colonial Merchants*, 225.

32.   *Advertisement* (July 7, 1770) [New York, 1770].

33.   Alexander Colden to Anthony Todd, July 11, 1770, *New York Colonial Documents*, VIII, 218–20; "Political Memoranda, 1770," McDougall Papers, Box 1, NYHS.

34.   *Boston Gazette*, July 16, 1770; *New York Mercury*, July 23, 1770.

35.   *New York Mercury*, July 23, 1770.

36.   Colden to Lord Hillsborough, n.d., *Colden Letter Books*, II, 224; *New York Mercury*, July 16, 1770; *New York Journal*, July 19, 26, Aug. 2, 1770; *Boston Gazette*, July 23, 1770; copies of the "Protest" are in McDougall Papers, Box 1, NYHS.

37.   For an interpretation of the De Lanceys as "popular Whigs," see Bonomi, *A Factious People*, 238–39; and Launitz-Schurer, "Whig-Loyalists: The De Lanceys of New York," 179–98.

## CHAPTER FOUR: THE TEA ACT

1. Colden to Lord Hillsborough, Oct. 5, 1770, *Colden Letter Books*, II, 229; *Smith Historical Memoirs*, 82.

2. *A Letter to the Celebrated Patriot of New York* [New York, 1770].

3. "Swaney," *Paradise Regain'd. To all the Great and Glorious Patriots in New York throughout America,—and around the Globe* [New York, 1770].

4. *New York Mercury*, July 9, 1770; Jones, *New York During the Revolutionary War*, I, 32–33. On April 27, 1771, the Supreme Court discharged McDougall from the indictment. *New York Gazette*, May 6, 1771; Dillon, *New York Triumvirate*, 120–21.

5. McDougall's account of his appearance before the Assembly is in *New York Gazette*, Dec. 24, 1770. Self-incrimination is discussed in Leonard W. Levy and Lawrence H. Leder, "Exotic Fruit: The Right Against Compulsory Self-Incrimination in Colonial New York," *William and Mary Quarterly*, 3rd ser., XX (1963), 3–33.

6. *New York Gazette*, Dec. 24, 1770.

7. *New York Assembly Journal*, Dec. 13, 14, 1770; *New York Gazette*, Dec. 24, 1770.

8. *Ibid.*, Dec. 24, 1770, Jan. 26, 1771.

9. *New York Assembly Journal*, Jan. 19, 22, Feb. 16, 1771; *New York Mercury*, Feb. 25, Mar. 11, 1771; *New York Gazette*, Feb. 18, Mar. 11, 1771.

10. Levy, *Freedom of Speech and Press in Early American History*, 86.

11. *Ibid.*, 43–49.

12. The background to the Tea Act is in Benjamin W. Labaree, *The Boston Tea Party* (New York, 1964).

13. *New York Journal*, Oct. 14, 21, Nov. 4, 1773.

14. *Ibid.*, Oct. 21, 1773; *Rivingston's Gazetteer*, Nov. 11, 18, 1773; *Smith Historical Memoirs*, 147–48, 151–55.

15. *New York Journal*, Dec. 2, 1773; *Rivingston's Gazetteer*, May 12, 1774.

16. *The Association of the Sons of Liberty*. . . . [New York, 1773]; *Rivington's Gazetteer*, May 12, 1774.

17. *New York Journal*, Dec. 2, 1773; *Smith Historical Memoirs*, 157.

18. Papers of Boston Committee of Correspondence, Minute Books, NYPL.

19. *Smith Historical Memoirs*, 157–58; McDougall to Boston, Dec. 13, 1773, Boston Committee of Correspondence, NYPL; Isaac Q. Leake, *Memoir of the Life and Times of General John Lamb* (Albany, 1850), 78–79.

20. *Smith Historical Memoirs*, 158–59.

21. *Ibid.*, 158.

22. *Advertisement of the Committee of the Association* (December 16, 1773) [New York, 1773]; *Rivington's Gazetteer*, May 12, 1774; Leake, *Life of John Lamb*, 79; *Smith Historical Memoirs*, 159–60; *New York Journal*, Dec. 22, 1773.

23. *Smith Historical Memoirs*, 162.

24. *Ibid.*, 163; *Rivington's Gazetteer*, May 12, 1774; Tryon to Lord Dartmouth, Jan. 3, 1774, *New York Colonial Documents*, VIII, 407–08.

25. McDougall to Boston, Dec. 13, 1773, Boston Committee of Correspondence, NYPL.

26. Samuel Adams to New York, Dec. 17, 1773, *ibid.*; *Smith Historical Memoirs*, 163.

27. *New York Journal*, Mar. 17, 1774.

28. New York Committee of Correspondence to Boston, Feb. 28, 1774, Boston Committee of Correspondence NYPL.

29. Boston to New York Committee of Correspondence, Mar. 24, 1774, *Ibid.*; Paul Revere to John Lamb, Mar. 28, 1774, John Lamb Papers, Box 1, NYHS; *New York Journal*, Mar. 24, 1774; *Rivington's Gazetteer*, April 21, 28, 1774.

30. *Ibid.*, April 28, 1774.

31. Colden to Lord Dartmouth, May 4, 1774, *Colden Letter Books*, II, 334–35.

32. The work of the "Mohawks" is in *Rivington's Gazetteer*, April 28, 1774.

33. *Ibid.*; *Smith Historical Memoirs*, 184–85.

34. *Rivington's Gazetteer*, April 28, 1774.

35. *Ibid.*, May 12, 1774.


CHAPTER FIVE: THE COMMITTEE OF FIFTY-ONE

1. Capt. Lawson arrived in the evening of May 11, 1774. "Political memorandums relative to the Conduct of the Citizens on the Boston Port Bill," McDougall Papers, Box 1, NYHS.

2. *Ibid.*, May 12, 1774.

3. *Ibid.*, May 13, 1774.

4. *Ibid.*, May 13–15, 1774. It is possible that planning for a defense of Boston began as early as May 11. A broadside, dated May 11, called for a meeting of the "Mechanics" that evening "on business of the utmost importance."

5. "Political memorandums," May 15, 1774; McDougall and Sears to Boston, May 15, 1774, Boston Committee of Correspondence, Other Colonies, NYPL.

6. Colden to William Tryon, Aug. 2, 1774, *Colden Letter Books*, II, 352.

7. "Agricola," *To the Inhabitants of the City and County of New York* [New York, 1774]; Van Schaack to Peter Silvester, May 21, 1774, Henry C. Van Schaack, *Life of Peter Van Schaack* (New York, 1842), 16–17.

8. "Political memorandums," May 16, 1774, McDougall Papers, Box 1, NYHS; *New York Mercury*, May 23, 1774; *Committee of Correspondence. . . .* (May 16, 1774) [New York, 1774].

9. "Political memorandums," May 17–18, 1774, McDougall Papers, Box 1, NYHS; Boston to New York, May 13, 1774, Boston Committee of Correspondence, NYPL; Thomas Young to John Lamb, May 13, 1774, Lamb Papers, Box 1, NYHS; *Rivington's Gazetteer*, May 19, 1774; *To the Public* (May 18, 1774) [New York, 1774]; Carl L. Becker, *The History of Political Parties in the Province of New York, 1760–1776* (Madison, 1909), 112–13; *Smith Historical Memoirs*, 186. For a different view of the Mechanics Committee, see Staughton Lynd, "The Mechanics in New York Politics, 1774–1788," *Labor History*, V (1964), 225–46.

10. Peter Force, comp., *American Archives*, Fourth Series (6 vols., Washington, 1837–43), I, 294–95; "Political memorandums," May 19, 1774, McDougall Papers, Box 1, NYHS; *Smith Historical Memoirs*, 187; *New York Mercury*, May 23, 1774; Jones, *New York During the Revolutionary War*, I, 35.

11. "Political memorandums," May 20, 1774, McDougall Papers, Box 1, NYHS; *Smith Historical Memoirs*, 187.

12. "Political memorandums," May 25, 1774, McDougall Papers, Box 1, NYHS.

13. *Ibid.*, May 23, 24, 1774; Committee of 51, May 23, 1774, Force, *American Archives*, 4 ser. I, 295–96; New York to Boston, May 23, 1774, *Ibid.*, 296–98; *New York Journal*, May 26, 1774.

14. "Political memorandums," May 28, 1774, McDougall Papers, Box 1, NYHS.

15. *Boston Gazette*, May 23, 1774. The letter was misdated the 14th. David Colden to William Tryon, June 1, 1774, *Colden Letter Books*, II, 343, *New York Journal*, June 2, 1774.

16. Boston to New York, May 30, 1774, Boston Committee of Correspondence, Minute Books, NYPL; New York to Boston, June 7, 1774, Force, *American Archives*, 4 ser. I, 303–04.

17. McDougall to Charles Thomson, June 1, 1774, McDougall Papers, Box 1, NYHS.

18. McDougall and Sears to Samuel Adams, June 20, 1774, *Ibid.*

19. McDougall to Adams, June 26, 1774, Samuel Adams Papers, Box 2, NYPL.

20. *New York Journal*, June 30, 1774. John Holt began using the divided snake device, inscribed "Unite or Die." For opposition to the Intolerable Acts in other colonies, see Labaree, *Boston Tea Party*, 217–35.

21. Committee of 51, June 27, 1774, Force, *American Archives*, 4 ser. I, 307.

22. The specific arguments were printed in both the newspapers and broadsides after McDougall made his motion on June 27, but they were undoubtedly also expressed at that time. *New York Journal*, June 30, 1774; *Rivington's Gazetteer*, June 30, 1774; *To the Inhabitants of the City and Colony of New York* (July 5, 1774) [New York, 1774]; Force, *American Archives*, 4 ser. I, 307, 309–11.

23. Colden to William Tryon, July 6, 1774, *Colden Letter Books*, II, 348–49.

24.  Committee of 51, July 4, 1774, Force, *American Archives*, 4 ser. I, 308; Colden to Lord Dartmouth, July 6, 1774, *New York Colonial Documents*, VIII, 469–70.

25.  *To the Inhabitants of the City and County of New York* (July 5, 1774) [New York, 1774].

26.  "Proceedings in the Fields," July 6, 1774, *New York Journal*, July 7, 1774; McDougall and Sears to Samuel Adams, July 25, 1774, Adams Papers, Box 2, NYPL.

27.  Committee of 51, July 7, 1774, Force, *American Archives*, 4 ser. I, 309–12.

28.  *Ibid.*

29.  *Rivington's Gazetteer*, July 14, 1774.

30.  *Ibid.*

31.  *To the Freeholders, Freemen and Inhabitants of the City and County of New York* (July 9, 1774) [New York, 1774].

32.  Smith to Schuyler, July 9, 1774, Philip Schuyler Papers, Box 24, NYPL.

33.  McDougall and Sears to Adams, July 25, 1774, Adams Papers, Box 2, NYPL.

34.  Committee of 51, July 13, 1774, Force, *American Archives*, 4 ser. I, 315; Committee of Correspondence, July 13, 1774 [New York, 1774]; Stokes, *Iconography of Manhattan*, IV, 784.

35.  *Rivington's Gazetteer*, July 21, 1774, and *Ibid.*, Aug. 4, 1774, reprinting a letter from New York originally in the *Boston Gazette*, July 25, 1774.

36.  Committee of 51, July 19, 1774, Force, *American Archives*, 4 ser. I, 315–17; McDougall and Sears to Adams, July 25, 1774, Adams Papers, Box 2, NYPL.

37.  *New York Journal*, July 21, 1774.

38.  *On Tuesday the 19th Day of July, 1774, the Inhabitants of the City of New York met at the Coffee House* . . . [New York, 1774]; *To the Inhabitants of the City and County of New York* (July 23, 1774) [New York, 1774].

39.  *Committee of Correspondence, July 25, 1774* [New York, 1774]; *Rivington's Gazetteer*, July 28, 1774; Committee of 51, July 27–28, 1774, Force, *American Archives*, 4 ser. I, 319–20.

40.  *Rivington's Gazetteer*, Aug. 11, 1774.

41.  The broadsides of "Agricola" were particularly strong. *To the Inhabitants of the City and County of New York* (July 12, and July 20, 1774) [New York, 1774]; see also "Ebenezer Snuffle, Secretary," *At a meeting of the true Sons of Liberty, in the City of New York* . . .[New York, 1774].

42.  *Debates at the Robin-Hood Society, in the city of New York, on Monday night 19th of July, 1774* [New York, 1774].

43.  Morris to Mr. Penn, May 20, 1774, Jared Sparks, *The Life of Gouverneur Morris* (3 vols., Boston, 1832), I, 23–26. For a different interpretation of Mor-

ris' letter, see Friedman, "Shaping of the Radical Consciousness in Provincial New York," 781–82; Lynd, "Mechanics in New York Politics," 225–46.

## CHAPTER SIX: THE CONTINENTAL ASSOCIATION

1.  McDougall to John Sullivan, Nov. 17, 1774, *Letters and Papers of Major-General John Sullivan* . . . , New Hampshire Historical Society *Collections* (3 vols., Concord, N.H., 1930–39), I, 49.

2.  Adams also received courtesy calls from the Fifty-One and New York's delegates to Congress. Diary entries, Aug. 20–26, 1774, L. H. Butterfield, ed., *Diary and Autobiography of John Adams* (4 vols., Cambridge, Mass., 1961), II, 102–11.

3.  *New York Journal*, Sept. 8, 1774.

4.  *Diary and Autobiography of John Adams*, II, 135, 146. Becker, *New York Political Parties*, Chapter VI, is still one of the most perceptive accounts of the issues and debates in the Congress. See also, "Minutes of Congress of 1774" and a copy of Galloway's Plan of Union endorsed in Duane's handwriting, "Seconded and supported by the New York delegates," in James Duane Papers, Box 1772–74, NYHS.

5.  Van Schaack to John Jay, Oct. 12, 1774, *Life of Peter Van Schaack*, 21–22.

6.  Colden to Lord Dartmouth, Oct. 5, Dec. 7, 1774, *New York Colonial Documents*, VIII, 492–94, 512–14.

7.  Committee of 51, Nov. 7, 14, 15, 1774, Force, *American Archives*, 4 ser. I, 328–30; *The mechanicks of this city are earnestly requested to meet* . . . (November 18, 1774) [New York, 1774]; *New York Journal*, Nov. 17, 24, 1774; William Smith to Schuyler, Nov. 22, 1774, Philip Schuyler Papers, Box 24, NYPL; Colden to Lord Dartmouth, Dec. 7, 1774, *New York Colonial Documents*, VIII, 512–14. For a different view of the situation in the fall of 1774, see Bernard Mason, *The Road to Independence: The Revolutionary Movement in New York, 1773–1777* (Lexington, Ky., 1966), 34–41.

8.  The criticism of the popular leaders may be traced in the issues of the *New York Mercury*, *New York Journal*, and *Rivington's Gazetteer* during the later summer, fall, and early winter months. Especially important are the pamphlets written by Reverend Samuel Seabury, under the name of "A West Chester Farmer." *Free Thoughts, on the Proceedings of the Congress at Philadelphia, & c.* (November 16, 1774) [New York, 1774]; *The Congress Canvassed: or an Examination into the Conduct of the Delegates, & c.* (November 28, 1774) [New York, 1774]; *A View of the Controversy, & c. in a Letter to the Author of A Full Vindication, & c.* (December 24, 1774) [New York, 1774]; *An Alarm to the Legislature, & c.* (January 27, 1775) [New York, 1775]. Pamphlets by Myles Cooper, President of King's College, and Thomas Bradbury Chandler, a New Jersey Anglican clergyman, are also important. *The American Querist: Or, Some Questions proposed relative to the present disputes between Great Britain and her American Colonies* [New York, 1774]; *A Friendly Address to all Reasonable Americans, on*

*the subject of our political confusions* . . . [New York, 1774]; *What Think Ye of the Congress? Or, an Enquiry, How Far the Americans are Bound to Abide by, and execute the decisions of, the late Congress* [New York, 1775].

9. Friedman, "Shaping of the Radical Consciousness in Provincial New York," 784–86.

10. *Free Thoughts, on the Proceedings of the Congress at Philadelphia*, 18.

11. The Whig position can be traced in the *New York Journal*, Nov. 10, 24, Dec. 1, 22, 1774, Jan. 5, 1775; [Alexander Hamilton], *A Full Vindication of the Measures of Congress from the Calumnies of Their Enemies, in Answer to a Letter under the Signature of a Westchester Farmer, & c.* [New York, 1774], and *The Farmer Refuted; or, A More comprehensive and impartial view of the disputes between Great Britain and the Colonies* [New York, 1775]; [Philip Livingston], *The Other Side of the Question: or, a defence of the liberties of North America* . . . [New York, 1774]; Force, *American Archives*, 4 ser. I, 821–27, 1074–75, 1188–90.

12. Hugh Hughes to John Lamb, Nov. 23, 1774, Lamb Papers, Box 1, NYHS.

13. Thomas Young to John Lamb, Nov. 19, 1774, *ibid.;* William Hooper to James Duane, Nov. 22, 1774, Duane Papers, Box 1772–74, NYHS.

14. McDougall to Samuel Adams, Jan. 29, 1775, McDougall Papers, Box 1, NYHS; Colden to Lord Dartmouth, Dec. 7, 1774, *New York Colonial Documents*, VIII, 512–14.

15. Colden to William Tryon, Dec. 7, 1774, *Colden Letter Books*, II, 375; to Lord Dartmouth, Nov. 2, Dec. 7, 1774, *New York Colonial Documents*, VIII, 510–11, 512–14.

16. *New York Assembly Journal*, Jan. 26, 1775; Colden to Thomas Gage, Jan. 29, 1775, *Colden Letter Books*, II, 381–82; *New York Journal*, Jan. 26, 1775.

17. McDougall to Samuel Adams, Jan. 29, 1775, McDougall Papers, Box 1, NYHS.

18. Committee notes, Jan. 30, 1775, *ibid.*

19. McDougall to William Cooper, Feb. 9, 1775, *ibid.*

20. McDougall to Samuel Adams, Jan. 29, 1775, *ibid.*

21. Colden to Capt. Montagu, Feb. 8, 9, 1775, to Thomas Gage, Feb. 20, 1775, *Colden Letter Books*, II, 384–85, 387; Schlesinger, *Colonial Merchants*, 490.

22. *New York Journal*, Feb. 23, 1775; Peter R. Livingston to Robert Livingston, Feb. 19, 1775, Livingston-Redmond Papers, Roll 6, FDRL.

23. Colden to Thomas Gage, Feb. 20, 1775, and to Lord Dartmouth, March 1, 1775, *Colden Letter Books*, II, 387, 390.

24. John Murray made a full confession to the Committee of Inspection. Committee notes, March 13, 16, 20, 1775, McDougall Papers, Box 1, NYHS.

25. McDougall to Josiah Quincy, Jr., April 6, 1775, *ibid.*

26. Colden to Lord Dartmouth, March 1, 1775, *New York Colonial Documents*, VIII, 543–44.

27. McDougall to William Cooper, Feb. 9, 1775, McDougall Papers, Box 1, NYHS.

28. *New York Assembly Journal*, Feb. 23, 1775; Colden to Lord Dartmouth, March 1, 1775, and to William Tryon, April 5, 1775, *Colden Letter Books*, II, 388–89, 398–99.

29. For example, see McDougall to Josiah Quincy, Jr., March 2, 1775, McDougall Papers, Box 1, NYHS.

30. Force, *American Archives*, 4 ser. I, 1269, II, 4; Committee notes, March 1, 1775, McDougall Papers, Box 1, NYHS.

31. Force, *American Archives*, 4 ser. II, 49–50; John Thurman, *To the Freemen and Freeholders* (March 4, 1775) [New York, 1775].

32. *New York Journal*, March 9, 1775; *To the Friends of American Liberty* (March 4, 1775) [New York, 1775]; *Smith Historical Memoirs*, 211; Jones, *New York During the Revolutionary War*, 1, 37–38.

33. *New York Journal*, March 9, 1775; *Smith Historical Memoirs*, 211.

34. Isaac Low, *To the Public* (March 9, 1775) [New York, 1775]; Committee notes, March 15, 1775, McDougall Papers, Box 1, NYHS.

35. Lord Dartmouth to American Governors, Jan. 4, 1775, *New York Colonial Documents*, VIII, 527–28; *Smith Historical Memoirs*, 212–13.

36. Force, *American Archives*, 4 ser. II, 137–38.

37. Committee notes, March 27, 1775, McDougall Papers, Box 1, NYHS; Force, *American Archives*, 4 ser. II, 255, 283–84, 347–48, 349; John Thurman, *To the Inhabitants of the City and County of New York* (April 15, 1775) [New York, 1775].

38. Mason, *Road to Independence*, 85–88, and Becker, *New York Political Parties*, 186–92, provide the fullest account of the first provincial convention.

CHAPTER SEVEN: THE PROVINCIAL CONGRESS

1. Committee notes, April 24, 1775, McDougall Papers, Box 1, NYHS.

2. *Smith Historical Memoirs*, 222; Jones, *New York During the Revolutionary War*, I, 39–40; Force, *American Archives*, 4 ser. II, 364; Robert R. Livingston to Robert Livingston, April 22 and 24, 1775, Robert R. Livingston Papers, Box 2, NYHS; Marinus Willett, *A Narrative of the Military Actions of Colonel Marinus Willett* (New York, 1969 edition), 30–31.

3. *Smith Historical Memoirs*, 222; Robert R. Livingston to Robert Livingston, April 22 and 24, 1775, Robert R. Livingston Papers, Box 2, NYHS; Stokes, *Iconography of Manhattan*, IV, 884; Colden to Lord Dartmouth, June 7, 1775, *Colden Letter Books*, II, 421–22; Force, *American Archives*, 4 ser. II, 547–48.

4. *Smith Historical Memoirs*, 222, Colden to Lord Dartmouth, May 3, 1775, *New York Colonial Documents*, VIII, 571–72; Force, *American Archives*, 4 ser. II, 25, 445–46; Robert R. Livingston to his wife, May 3, 1775, Livingston Family Papers, NYPL.

5. Quoted in Stokes, *Iconography of Manhattan*, IV, 896.

6. Committee notes, April 24, 1775, McDougall Papers, Box, 1, NYHS; Becker, *New York Political Parties*, 194; *The following persons are recommended to the public, as proper to be elected for a General Committee* . . . (April 27, 1775) [New York, 1775]; *The Following persons are nominated by the Sons of Liberty, to represent them in the committee* . . . (April 28, 1775) [New York, 1775]; *Smith Historical Memoirs*, 223; Force, *American Archives*, 4 ser. II, 459.

7. *New York Journal*, May 4, 1775; Jones, *New York During the Revolutionary War*, I, 41–45.

8. Robert R. Livingston to his wife, May 3, 1775, Livingston Family Papers, NYPL.

9. Colden to Lord Dartmouth, May 3, 1775, *Colden Letter Books*, II, 402–03; Beekman to Pierce and Brown, May 6, 1775, *Beekman Mercantile Papers*, II, 898–99; Christopher Smith to John Alsop, May 12, 17, 1775, John Alsop Papers, NYHS.

10. Force, *American Archives*, 4 ser. II, 468–69, 470–71, 481, 529–30, 531, 534–35, 617–18, 670–71.

11. *Ibid.*, 470–71, 636–37; General Committee to Colden, May 11, 1775, *New York Colonial Documents*, VIII, 583–85.

12. Force, *American Archives*, 4 ser. II, 468, 529.

13. *Ibid.*, 471, 480, 482, 530, 532; Christopher Smith to John Alsop, May 26, and Peter Kettelas to John Alsop, May 27, 1775, John Alsop Papers, NYHS.

14. Eliphalet Dyer to Joseph Trumbull, June 3, 1775, Edmund C. Burnett, ed., *Letters of Members of the Continental Congress* (8 vols., Washington, 1921–36), I, 109.

15. The Albany request was heard in the city committee on May 15, Force, *American Archives*, 4 ser. II, 605–06.

16. Details were learned from the Albany committee. *Ibid.* McDougall knew what was coming. Joseph Warren to McDougall, April 30, 1775, *ibid.*, 450.

17. *Ibid.*, 605, 637, 671.

18. From May 22 to July 8, 1775, both men were named to sixteen committees. Richard Montgomery, deputy from Dutchess County and soon to be commissioned a Continental brigadier, was next with eleven assignments. Most other deputies, including those from the capital, served on six or seven committees. For a view of the Provisional Congress primarily in terms of the Whig-Tory political division, see Mason, *Road to Independence*, 63–99.

19. *Journals of the Provincial Congress, Provincial Convention, Committee of Safety and Council of Safety of the State of New York* (2 vols., Albany, 1842), I, 9.

20. Land deeds, McDougall Papers, Box 1, NYHS. James Duane was one of the most active speculators in this area. Edward P. Alexander, *A Revolutionary Conservative: James Duane of New York* (New York, 1938), 54–55.

21. As late as March, 1774, Governor Tryon at the urging of the Assembly,

and influenced by Duane's lobby, had ordered the arrest of Allen and Warner for molesting settlers with New York land titles. *Ibid.*, 83–85.

22. *New York Provincial Congress*, I, 9.

23. *Ibid.*, I, 9–10, 12, 20–21.

24. *Ibid.*, I, 14–15, 18–20.

25. *Ibid.*, I, 10, 21, 26, 41, 45, 47; Robert C. Livingston to Robert Livingston, May 29, 1775, Livingston-Redmond Papers, Roll 6, FDRL.

26. *New York Provincial Congress*, I, 11, 28, 35, 37, 51, 60, 65.

27. To Robert R. Livingston, Jr., May 5, 1775, Brancroft Transcripts: Livingston Papers, NYPL.

28. Minute of Council meeting, May 1, 1775, *Letters and Papers of Cadwallader Colden*, VII, 287–89.

29. *New York Provincial Congress*, I, 8–9, 20, 26, 46, 50, 52–53.

30. *Ibid.*, I, 35, 37–38.

31. *Ibid.*, I, 41, 48.

32. *Ibid.*, I, 52–54, 57–58. For an interesting popular account, which is critical of provincial military policies, see Bruce Bliven, Jr., *Under the Guns: New York 1775–1776* (New York, 1972).

33. Eliphalet Dyer to Joseph Trumbull, June 3, 1775, Burnett, *Letters of Members of Congress*, I, 109.

34. *New York Provincial Congress*, I, 20, 30, 36–37, 41, 47, 49, 51, 56; Force, *American Archives*, 4 ser. II, 967; *Calendar of Historical Manuscripts Relating to the War of the Revolution in the Office of the Secretary of State* (2 vols., Albany, 1868), I, 97.

35. Captaincies were given to Marinus Willett, William Gofroth, and Gershom Mott, and several weeks later John Lamb's artillery company was included in McDougall's regiment. The regiment's second in command was Rudolphus Ritzema, a graduate of King's College and a Dutch clergyman. *Ibid.*, 62, 114; Francis B. Heitman, *Historical Register of Officers of the Continental Army during the War of the Revolution . . .* (New York, 1914), 43–44, 368; Force, *American Archives*, 4 ser. III, 23–25.

36. McDougall's men were uniformed in blue shortcoats with crimson cuffs and facing, but there is no record that they actually wore them. *New York Provincial Congress*, I, 59, 66–67, 75–76, 83, 86, 94; List of muskets taken from City Hall, July 8, 1775, McDougall Papers, Box 1, NYHS; Loan receipts, Oversized Folder, 1775, *ibid.* By the end of July, New York had spent nearly £60,000. P.V.B. Livingston to New York Delegates in Congress, July 31, 1775, James Duane Papers, Box 1775–79, NYHS.

37. The first court martial in McDougall's regiment was held on July 25, 1775, and involved drunkenness. On desertion, see Elias Dayton to McDougall, Sept. 2, 1775, McDougall Papers, Box 1, NYHS.

38. Washington to Philip Schuyler, June 25, 1775, Force, *American Archives*, 4 ser. II, 1084–85; Christopher Smith to John Alsop, June 26, 1775, John

Alsop Papers, NYHS; Douglas S. Freeman, *George Washington* (7 vols., New York, 1948–57), III, 462–66.

39. *New York Provincial Congress*, I, 64–65; McDougall to Philip Schuyler, Aug. 9, 1775, McDougall Papers, Box 1, NYHS.

40. McDougall to Philip Schuyler, Nov. 14, 1775, Schuyler to McDougall, Nov. 28, 1775, *ibid.*

41. McDougall sponsored the request of the capital's clergymen to open the day's work with prayer. *New York Provincial Congress*, I, 9, 11. By August 15, the secretary merely noted each day, "No prayers." On the absence of members, see the vote of Aug. 17, 1775, *ibid.*, 109.

42. Tryon to Lord Dartmouth, Aug. 7, 1775, *New York Colonial Documents*, VIII, 597; *New York Provincial Congress*, I, 81, 97–98, 102.

43. Force, *American Archives*, 4 ser. III, 15; *New York Provincial Congress*, I, 100–01; Sears to the New York Congress, Aug. 8, 1775, Emmet Collection, NYPL.

44. *New York Provincial Congress*, I, 91; *New York Journal*, Aug. 24, 1775.

45. Becker, *New York Political Parties*, 226–27; Tryon to Lord Dartmouth, Sept. 5, 1775, *New York Colonial Documents*, VIII, 631–32; Force, *American Archives*, 4 ser. III, 550.

46. *New York Council of Safety*, I, 149, 156–57; Force, *American Archives*, 4 ser. III, 795; *New York Provincial Congress*, I, 184.

47. Hugh Hughes to McDougall, Nov. 2, 1775, McDougall Papers, Box 1, NYHS.

48. Duane to McDougall, Nov. 5, 1775, *ibid.*

49. McDougall to Schuyler, Nov. 14, 1775, Schuyler to McDougall, Nov. 28, 1775; Rudolphus Ritzema to McDougall, Nov. 9, 1775, *ibid.*

## CHAPTER EIGHT: WHIGS VERSUS TORIES

1. *New York Provincial Congress*, I, 197; McDougall to Schuyler, Dec. 7, 1775, McDougall Papers, Box 1, NYHS.

2. McDougall to Schuyler, Nov. 14, 1775, *ibid.*

3. Sears wanted to seize Governor Tryon, but when his plans were frustrated by other Whig leaders who feared a naval bombardment of the city, he moved to Connecticut. *New York Colonial Documents*, VIII, 638, 639, 645; Becker, *New York Political Parties*, 225–26; John Patterson to Robert Livingston, Nov. 6, 1775, Livingston-Redmond Papers, Roll 6, FDRL.

4. Force, *American Archives*, 4 ser. II, 1707–08; IV, 185–86, 393, 400–01, 422–23, 1033–34; Jones, *New York During the Revolutionary War*, I, 65–67; Tryon to Lord Dartmouth, Dec. 6, 1775, *New York Colonial Documents*, VIII, 645–46; McDougall to Jay, Dec. 14, 1775, John Jay Papers, Special Collections, Columbia University Library [CUL].

5.  John Jones to Duane, Dec. 7, 1775, James Duane Papers, Box 1775–79, NYHS.

6.  McDougall to Jay, Nov. 15, 26, and Dec. 24, 1775, Jay Papers, CUL; Jay to McDougall, Dec. 8, 1775, McDougall to Charles Lee, Dec. 20, 1775, McDougall Papers, Box 1, NYHS; Force, *American Archives*, 4 ser. III, 795.

7.  Tryon to Lord Dartmouth, Feb. 7, 1776, *New York Colonial Documents*, VIII, 663; Jones, *New York During the Revolutionary War*, I, 108–09; W. C. Ford, ed., *The Journals of the Continental Congress*, 1774–1789 (34 vols., Washington, 1904–37), IV, 25–28; McDougall to Stamford Committee of Inspection, Dec. 30, 1775, McDougall Papers, Box 1, NYHS.

8.  *New York Provincial Congress*, I, 236; McDougall to Schuyler, Dec. 7, 1775, McDougall Papers, Box 1, NYHS.

9.  Force, *American Archives*, 4 ser. IV, 173–74.

10.  *Smith Historical Memoirs*, 252–53; *New York Provincial Congress*, I, 210–11, 217, 217–18, 219; McDougall to Jay, Dec. 18, 1775, Jay Papers, CUL.

11.  William Smith to Tryon, Dec. 17, 1775, *New York Colonial Documents*, VIII, 653–54; *Smith Historical Memoirs*, 255–56; Force, *American Archives*, 4 ser. IV, 1020–21; McDougall to Charles Lee, Dec. 29, 1775, McDougall Papers, Box 1, NYHS; Alexander Hamilton to Jay, n.d., Jay Papers, CUL; Hugh Hughes to Samuel Adams, Jan. 8, 1776, Samuel Adams Papers, NYPL.

12.  *Smith Historical Memoirs*, 255–57; James Duane to Robert Livingston, Jan. 5, 1776, Duane Papers, Box 1775–79, NYHS; McDougall to Schuyler, Jan. 17, 1776, McDougall Papers, Box 1, NYHS; Becker, *New York Political Parties*, 242.

13.  Charles Lee to McDougall, Oct. 26, 1775, *The Lee Papers*, New-York Historical Society *Collections* (3 vols., New York, 1872–74), 1, 214–16; McDougall to Lee, Dec. 20, 1775, McDougall Papers, Box 1, NYHS. The standard biography of Lee is John R. Alden, *General Charles Lee, Traitor or Patriot* (Baton Rouge, La., 1951).

14.  Charles Lee to Robert Morris, Jan. 3, 1776, Bancroft Transcripts, Revolutionary Papers, 1, NYPL; Lee to Washington, Jan. 5, Washington to Lee, Jan. 8, 1776, Lee to McDougall, Oct. 26, 1775, *Lee Papers*, I, 214–16, 234–37; Lee to McDougall, Jan. 28, 1776, Hawkes Collection, Union College; *New York Provincial Congress*, I, 190.

15.  Tryon to Lord Dartmouth, Feb. 7, 1776, *New York Colonial Documents*, VIII, 663; Jones, *New York During the Revolutionary War*, I, 108–09; Force, *American Archives*, 4 ser. IV, 595–96, 683–84, 1145.

16.  *New York Provincial Congress*, I, 258–59, 266, 270; New York Committee of Safety to Lee, Jan. 21, Lee to New York Committee of Safety, Jan. 23, Lee to Washington, Jan. 24, 1776, *Lee Papers*, I, 242–44, 256–58, 259; Force, *American Archives*, 4 ser. IV, 1145.

17.  *Ibid.*, 807–08, 1062.

18.  Lee to John Hancock, Jan. 22, Hancock to Lee, Jan. 26, 1776, *Lee*

*Papers*, I, 247–51, 262; Lee to Robert Morris, Bancroft Transcripts, Revolutionary Papers, I, NYPL; Force, *American Archives*, 4 ser. IV, 1091; *Journal of the Continental Congress*, IV, 92.

19.  *New York Provincial Congress*, 1, 258–59, 266, 270; Force, *American Archives*, 4 ser. IV, 1096, 1098, 1100.

20.  Charles Lee to McDougall, Oct. 26, 1775, Jan. 31, 1776, *Lee Papers*, I, 214, 16, 269–70; Lee to McDougall, Jan. 28, 1776, Hawkes Collection, Union College.

21.  Force, *American Archives*, 4 ser. IV, 943.

22.  *Ibid.*, 942; Tryon to Lord Dartmouth, Feb. 8, 1776, *New York Colonial Documents*, VIII, 666–67; Charles Inglis to Colden, Feb. 5, 1776, John McKesson Papers, NYHS; John Henry Livingston to Robert R. Livingston, Jr., Feb. 13, 1776, Bancroft Transcripts, Livingston Papers, NYPL; John Alsop to McDougall, Feb. 12, 1776, William Goforth to McDougall, April 6, 1776, McDougall Papers, Box 1, NYHS.

23.  Becker, *New York Political Parties*, 248. In response to the flight from New York City, the Poughkeepsie Committee ruled that visitors could not remain longer than three days unless they had a certificate testifying to their support of the Association and Congress. *New York Mercury*, Feb. 26, 1776.

24.  "Report on the Defence of New York, March, 1776," *Lee Papers*, I, 354–57. See also, Lee to Washington, Feb. 5, 19, to Hancock, Feb. 9, 1776, *ibid.*, 271–72, 309, 279–80.

25.  "Report on the Defence of New York," *ibid.*, 354–57.

26.  Force, *American Archives*, 4 ser. V, 75; *New York Provincial Congress*, I, 333, 335, 343, 355; Sears to Lee, March 7, 1776, Isaac Sears Papers, NYHS; Jones, *New York During the Revolutionary War*, I, 572.

27.  Jay to McDougall, March 13, 1776, Hawkes Collection, Union College; McDougall to Jay, March 20, 1776, Jay Papers, CUL.

28.  *New York Provincial Congress*, I, 283, 284, 286, 291; Lee to New York Congress, Feb. 16, 1776, and New York Congress to Lee, Feb. 24, March 6, 1776, *Lee Papers*, I, 301, 349–50. See also Lee to Joseph Reed, Feb. 28, 1776, *ibid.*, 333–34.

29.  *New York Provincial Congress*, I, 282, 283, 288, 294.

30.  *Ibid.*, 246, 280, 356.

31.  John C. Fitzpatrick, *The Writings of George Washington* (39 vols., Washington, 1931–44), IV, 208, 229, 237, 266, 293, 351, 378, 389–90, 391–92; Council of General Officers, March 13, 1776, Washington Papers, Ser. 4, Reel 35, LC.

32.  *New York Provincial Congress*, I, 357, 360–61; "Regulations agreed to for the defence of the City of New York . . . ," William Alexander Papers, NYHS.

33.  Henry Livingston to Robert Livingston, March 26, 1776, Livingston-Redmond Papers, Roll 6, FDRL; Major Nicholas Fish to Richard Varick,

April 9, 1776, Henry P. Johnston, *The Campaign of 1776 Around New York and Brooklyn*, Long Island Historical Society *Memoirs* (New York, 1878), Part II, 127–28; "Diary of Revn. Mr. Shewkirk," Feb. 11, April 8, 1776, *ibid.*, 106, 107; "Genuine Extract of a letter by the last mail from New York, April 12, 1776," *Maryland Gazette*, Sept. 19, 1776.

34. Lord Stirling to Washington, March 15, 20, April 1, 1776, Washington Papers, Ser. 4, Reel, 35 LC. The arrival of continental regiments is noted in the *New York Mercury*, April 1, 8, 15, 1776. See also Freeman, *George Washington*, IV, 78; *Maryland Gazette*, Sept. 19, 1776; Stokes, *Iconography of Manhattan*, IV, 924, 925, Orderly Books, First New York Regiment, Feb. 9–June 11, 1776, NYHS.

35. *Maryland Gazette*, Sept. 19, 1776; Stokes, *Iconography of Manhattan*, IV, 923; Johnston, *Campaign of 1776*, Part II, 66–67, 127–28; Henry Livingston to Robert Livingston, March 6, 1776, Livingston-Redmond Papers, Roll 6, FDRL; McDougall to Schuyler, March 3, 1776, McDougall Papers, Box 1, NYHS.

36. McDougall to Schuyler, March 14, 1776, *ibid.*

37. Jay to McDougall, March 23, 1776, *ibid.;* McDougall to Jay, March 20, 1776, Jay Papers, CUL.

38. Ritzema to McDougall, Nov. 19, 1775, Capt. Fred Weissenfels to McDougall, Feb. 12, 1776, McDougall to Schuyler, Feb. 7, 1776, McDougall Papers, Box 1, NYHS.

39. Schuyler to McDougall, Feb. 15, 1776, *ibid.*

40. McDougall to James Duane, Feb. 13, 1776, *ibid.; Journal of Continental Congress*, IV, 190.

41. Freeman, *George Washington*, IV, 89; *Smith Historical Memoirs*, 270.

42. Becker, *New York Political Parties*, 256–58; McDougall to Schuyler, March 14, 1776, McDougall Papers, Box 1, NYHS.

43. Jay to McDougall, April 27, 1776, *ibid.*

44. John Sullivan to John Adams, May 4, 1776, *Letters and Papers of John Sullivan*, I, 194–96.

## CHAPTER NINE: DEFENDING NEW YORK

1. Regimental returns and recruiting report of Capt. Cornelius Stienrod, McDougall Papers, Oversized Folder, NYHS; McDougall to Schuyler, April 26, 1776, Box 1, *ibid;* McDougall to Washington, May 6, June 15, 1776, Washington Papers, Ser. 4, Reel 36, LC. See also *Writings of George Washington*, V, 1.

2. Barrack guard report, June 22, 1776, McDougall Papers, Box 1, NYHS, Court martial, July 7, 1776, Force, *American Archives*, 5 ser. I, 225; Joseph Reed to Congress, *ibid.*, 576; Freeman, *George Washington*, IV, 85; General Orders, June 8, 1776, *Writings of George Washington*, V, 100.

3.   Force, *American Archives*, 4 ser. V, 4071; General Orders, May 25, July 1, 1776, *Writings of George Washington*, V, 81, 208; Morning sickness reports, McDougall Papers, Oversized Folder, NYHS; John Sullivan to John Hancock, Aug. 5, 1776, *Letters and Papers of John Sullivan*, I, 291.

4.   *Journal of Continental Congress*, V, 641. McDougall's new brigade command consisted of his old regiment, the Third New York, the 19th Connecticut, and the Corp of Artificers. *Writings of George Washington*, V, 422–23.

5.   *Ibid.*, 490; Ira D. Gruber, *The Howe Brothers and the American Revolution* (New York, 1972), 108–10; Johnston, *Campaign of 1776*, Part I, 130; Force, *American Archives*, 5 ser. I, 1112. McDougall's camp was in the Bowery. *New York Mercury*, Aug. 26, 1776.

6.   Col. William Douglas to wife, Aug. 26, 1776, Johnston, *Campaign of 1776*, Pt. 11, 69; Court martial of Herman Zedwitz, Washington Papers, Ser. 4, Reel 37, LC; Asa Stone to Ben Stone, Aug. 24, 1776, Misc. Mss., NYSL.

7.   Freeman, *George Washington*, IV, 169; Col. Gold S. Silliman to wife, Aug. 29, 1776, Johnston, *Campaign of 1776*, Part II, 54; Force, *American Archives*, 5 ser. I, 1214. A return of the New York Third, dated Oct. 17, 1776, showed ten killed, four missing and three prisoners in the action of August 28. Washington Papers, Ser. 4, Reel 38, LC. Accounts of the Battle of Long Island are in Christopher Ward, *The War of the Revolution* (2 vols., New York, 1952), I, 216–30; Don Higginbotham, *The War of American Independence: Military Attitudes, Policies, and Practice, 1763–1789* (New York, 1971), 152–58.

8.   John Morin Scott to John Jay, Sept. 6, 1776, Johnston, *Campaign of 1776*, Part II, 36–39; Council of War, Aug. 29, 1776, Washington Papers, Ser. 4, Reel 38, LC; Washington to Congress, Aug. 31, 1776, *Writings of George Washington*, V, 506–09; Col. Joseph Reed to William Heath, Augs. 30, 1776, *William Heath Papers*, Massachusetts Historical Society *Collections* (3 vols., Boston, 1898–1905), II, 20–21; Force, *American Archives*, 5 ser. I, 1233.

9.   General Orders, Aug. 29, 1776, Johnston, *Campaign of 1776*, Part II, 31; also *ibid.*, Part I, 218–19.

10.   *Ibid.*, Part I, 221–23; Part II, 78–79; George A. Billias, *John Glover and His Marblehead Mariners* (New York, 1960), 100–04.

11.   McDougall's brigade, now including William Smallwood's Marylanders, was part of Joseph Spencer's center division. General Orders, Aug. 31, Sept. 1, 1776, *Writings of George Washington*, V, 501, VI, 4. See also Greene to Washington, Sept. 6, 1776, Washington Papers, Ser. 4, Reel 38, LC; Freeman, *George Washington*, IV, 184; Washington to Congress, Sept. 8, 1776, *Writings of George Washington*, VI, 30–31.

12.   McDougall to Heath, Sept. 10, 1776, Force, *American Archives*, 5 ser. II, 275–76.

13.   Putnam to Washington, Sept. 3, 1776, Washington Papers, Ser. 4, Reel 38, LC; Council of War, Sept. 12, 1776, McDougall Papers, Box 1, NYHS; Heath to Washington, Sept. 13, 1776, *Heath Papers*, II, 22–24.

14.  Bruce Bliven, Jr., *Battle for Manhattan* (New York, 1964 edition), 27–43; Gruber, *Howe Brothers*, 120–24.

15.  Col. Smallwood to Maryland Convention, Oct. 12, 1776, Force, *American Archives*, 5 ser. II, 1011–14; General Orders, Sept. 16, 18, 26, 1776, *Writings of George Washington*, VI, 56–57, 71, 120; Ward, *War of the Revolution*, I, 238–45.

16.  Force, *American Archives*, 5 ser. II, 855, 869, 907; Johnston, *Campaign of 1776*, Part II, 98–99. On September 22, Lieutenant Governor Colden died at the age of 88, symbolizing the passing of the old order. *New York Mercury*, Sept. 28, 30, 1776; Force, *American Archives*, 5 ser. II, 503; Tryon to Lord Germain, Sept. 24, 1776, *New York Colonial Documents*, VIII, 685. McDougall could draw personal elation from the newspaper account that his surviving son, Ronald Stephen, who had been taken captive in action near Montreal, had arrived aboard a British prison ship. *New York Mercury*, Sept. 28, 1776.

17.  Freeman, *George Washington*, IV, 205–06; General Orders, Sept. 27, Oct. 9, 1776, Washington to Lund Washington, Sept. 30, 1776, *Writings of George Washington*, VI, 124–25, 137–38, 190–91; Return of Oct. 5, 1776, Force, *American Archives*, 5 ser. II, 907.

18.  Col. Smallwood to Maryland Convention, Oct. 12, 1776, Thomas Ewing to Maryland Convention, Oct. 13, 1776, Joseph Reed to Heath, Oct. 13, 1776, Heath to John Nixon, Oct. 14, 1776, Force, *American Archives*, 5 ser. II, 1011–14, 1024–25, 1026, 1035; General Orders, Oct. 14, 15, 1776, *Writings of George Washington*, VI, 206, 207–08; Freeman, *George Washington*, IV, 215.

19.  Council of War, Oct. 16, 1776, Washington Papers, Ser. 4, Reel 38, LC; Gruber, *Howe Brothers*, 127, 32.

20.  *New York Mercury*, Oct. 19, 1776, General Orders, Oct. 15, 1776, *Writings of George Washington*, VI, 207–08; Tench Tilgham to William Duer, Oct. 15, 1776, William Duer Papers, NYHS; *Maryland Gazette*, Dec. 5, 1776.

21.  Johnston, *Campaign of 1776*, Part II, 137–38; Freeman, *George Washington*, IV, 221, 224–26; Gruber, *Howe Brothers*, 132.

22.  Johnston, *Campaign of 1776*, Part II, 56–57, 72, 139; William H. W. Sabine, ed., *Historical Memoirs from 12 July 1776 to 25 July 1778 of William Smith Historian of the Province of New York . . .* (New York, 1958), 37–38.

23.  Ward, *War of the Revolution*, I, 260–66; Johnston, *Campaign of 1776*, Part II, 56–57, 72, 79–81, 139; "Letter from the Army, North of White Plains, Nov. 1, 1776," *Connecticut Courant*, Nov. 11, 1776; Col. John Haslet to Caesar Rodney, Nov. 12, 1776, George H. Ryden, ed., *Letters to and from Caesar Rodney, 1756–1784* (Philadelphia, 1933), 142–43.

24.  Haslet to Rodney, Nov. 12, 1776, *ibid.*, 142–43; Johnston, *Campaign of 1776*, Part II, 81; *Smith Historical Memoirs 1776–1778*, 49; Ward, *War of the Revolution*, I, 264–65; Force, *American Archives*, 5 ser. II, 1284.

25.  Ward, *War of the Revolution*, I, 265; Haslet to Rodney, Nov. 12, 1776, *Letters to and from Caesar Rodney*, 142–43.

26. *Smith Historical Memoirs 1776–1778*, 49; Johnston, *Campaign of 1776*, Pt. 1, 275; Part II, 139.

27. Lee to Benjamin Rush, Nov. 2, 1776, *Lee Papers*, II, 262.

28. Brigade return, Nov. 28, 1776, Washington Papers, Ser. 4, Reel 38, LC; Court martial proceedings, Oct. 30 to Nov. 1, 1776, *ibid.;* General Orders, Oct. 29, 1776, *Writings of George Washington*, VI, 232.

29. Ward, *War of the Revolution*, I, 267–68; Gruber, *Howe Brothers*, 132.

30. Council of War, Nov. 6, 1776, Washington Papers, Ser. 4, Reel 38, LC. Ice formed November 2. Edward H. Tatum, Jr., *The American Journal of Ambrose Serle, Secretary to Lord Howe 1776–1778* (San Marino, Calif., 1940), 136, 140.

31. Freeman, *George Washington*, IV, 241–57; Gruber, *Howe Brothers*, 134–36.

32. Freeman, *George Washington*, IV, 260–70; *Lee Papers*, II, 291, 299, 304, 305, 313–14, 326. Lee's division began crossing the Hudson on December 2 at Peekskill. Heath to Washington, *Heath Papers*, II, 34. McDougall's remark was repeated by Israel Evans, chaplain in the 1st New York Regiment. *Smith Historical Memoirs 1776–1778*, 37. For moves in New Jersey, see Higginbotham, *War of American Independence*, 162–64.

33. Washington to Congress, Dec. 20, 1776, Washington to McDougall, Dec. 21, 1776, *Writings of George Washington*, VI, 408, 419.

34. McDougall to Washington, Dec. 19, 1776, Washington Papers, Ser. 4, Reel 39, LC.

35. The most thorough discussion of the Hudson's place in American strategy is Dave Richard Palmer's excellent book, *The River and the Rock: The History of Fortress West Point, 1775–1783* (New York, 1969). British strategy and the Hudson is in Piers Mackesy, "British Strategy in the War of American Independence," *Yale Review*, LII (1963), 539–57.

36. Until he returned to Peekskill, McDougall defended Morristown against local Tories and British foraging parties. His experience in New Jersey influenced his actions in the months ahead. McDougall to Washington, Dec. 19, 22, 30, 1776, March 7, 1777, Washington Papers, Ser. 4, Reels 39, 40, LC.

37. Washington to Congress, Jan. 9, 1777, to McDougall, Feb. 20, March 6, 1777, *Writings of George Washington*, VII, 29–30, 179–80, 257–58; McDougall to Washington, Feb. 16, 1777, Washington Papers, Ser. 4, Reel 40, LC.

38. Heath to Washington, Jan. 19, 24, Feb. 7, 1777, William Duer to Washington, Jan. 28, March 2, 1777, David Wooster to Washington, Feb. 21, March 2, 1777, McDougall to Washington, March 7, 1777, Washington Papers, Ser. 4, Reels 39, 40, LC; Washington to Heath, Feb. 3, March 23, 1777, *Writings of George Washington*, VII, 94–96, 314–15; William Duer to McDougall, and to New York Convention, Feb. 25, 1777, McDougall Papers, Box 2, NYHS.

39. Washington to Heath, March 13, 1777, *Writings of George Washington*, VII, 282–83; Hamilton to McDougall, March 10, 1777, McDougall to Wash-

ington, March 12, 1777, Washington Papers, Ser. 4, Reel 40, LC; Washington to McDougall, March 15, 1777, Hawkes Collection, Union College; McDougall to New York Convention, March 22, 1777, McDougall Papers, Box 2, NYHS.

40.   McDougall to Washington, March 29, 1777, Washington Papers, Ser. 4, Reel 40, LC; George Clinton to A. Hawkes Hay, March 24, 1777, Hugh Hastings and J. A. Holden, eds., *Public Papers of George Clinton, First Governor of New York* (10 vols., Albany, 1898–1914), I, 679–80; *Calendar of Historical Manuscripts*, II, 153–59; Willett, *Narrative*, 39–42.

41.   Clinton to Jay, March 24, 1777, *Clinton Public Papers*, I, 679–80; Washington to Congress, March 29, to Heath, March 29, 30, to George Clinton, March 31, to Governor Jonathan Trumbull, March 29, 1777, *Writings of George Washington*, VII, 328, 333, 335, 340; McDougall to Washington, March 29, 1777, Washington Papers, Ser. 4, Reel 40, LC.

42.   Washington to McDougall, April 2, 1777, Hawkes Collection, Union College.

43.   "Proceedings of a General Court Martial," June 1, 1777, *Calendar of Historical Manuscripts*, II, 153–59.

44.   [Henry Beekman Livingston], "To the Public," June 4, 1777, Washington Papers, Ser. 4, Reel 42, LC.

45.   To Lewis Morris, Feb. 26, 1776, Emmet Collection, NYPL.

46.   Dec. 6, 1775, Jay Collection, CUL.

47.   Livingston to Washington, Feb. 15, 1777, Washington Papers, Ser. 4, Reel 40, LC. Washington replied that Livingston must make his recommendation to the New York authorities, *Writings of George Washington*, VII, 181–82.

48.   [Henry Beekman Livingston], "To the Public," June 4, 1777, Washington Papers, Ser. 4, Reel 42, LC.

49.   McDougall to Clinton, June 18, 1777, *Clinton Public Papers*, II, 37–38.

50.   McDougall to Robert Yates, Oct. 21, 1776, *Calendar of Historical Manuscripts*, II, 10.

51.   McDougall to New York Convention, March 22, to Navy Board of War, May 16, 1777, McDougall Papers, Box 2, NYHS.

52.   Washington to S. B. Webb, April 7, to Heath, April 10, to Clinton, April 20, to Congress, April 28, to Heath, May 10, to Joseph Trumbull, May 12, to S. H. Parsons, May 25, 1777, *Writings of George Washington*, VII, 370, 384, 444, 491; VIII, 38–39, 54–55, 124; George Clinton to Col. Woodhull, to Col. Hasbrouck, April 26, 1777, *Clinton Public Papers*, I, 732, 734; Heath to Washington, March 28, 1777, Washington Papers, Ser. 4, Reel 40, LC; McDougall to Jonathan Trumbull, April 19, 1777, McDougall Papers, Box 2, NYHS.

53.   McDougall to New York Convention, April 21, 1777, *ibid.*

54.   Washington to McDougall, April 10, 23, 26, 1777, *Writings of George*

*Washington*, VII, 387, 454–55, 477; McDougall to Clinton, April 21, to James Clinton, April 23, George Clinton to New York Convention, April 26, 1777, *Clinton Public Papers*, I, 724–25, 729, 735–36; *Smith Historical Memoirs 1776–1778*, 123; Gruber, *Howe Brothers*, 179–86, 199–200.

55. The relief force covered eighteen miles in one day, a respectable marching pace for the time. Freeman, *George Washington*, IV, 410; McDougall to Clinton, April 27, 1777, Council of War, April 28, 1777. McDougall Papers, Box 2, NYHS; McDougall to Washington, April 27, 29, 1777, Washington Papers, Ser. 4, Reel 41, LC.

56. Washington to McDougall, May 1, 1777, *Writings of George Washington*, VIII, 1–2.

57. McDougall to Washington, May 5, 1777, Washington Papers, Ser. 4, Reel 41, LC.

58. Washington to McDougall, May 7, 11, 16, 1777, *Writings of George Washington*, VIII, 25–27, 45, 67–68.


CHAPTER TEN: DEFENDING THE HIGHLANDS

1. Orderly Book, McDougall's Brigade, April 9–August 28, 1777, NYHS; *Writings of George Washington*, VII, 415.

2. Washington to McDougall, April 17, to Putnam, June 12, to Clinton and to Putnam, July 1, 1777, *ibid.*, 423–28, VIII, 234–35, 325, 327; Freeman, *George Washington*, IV, 427–34.

3. McDougall to Heath, June 13, 1777, *Heath Papers*, II, 106–08.

4. McDougall to Clinton, June 18, 1777, *Clinton Public Papers*, II, 37–38; Washington to Putnam, June 20, to McDougall, Aug. 1, 2, 1777, *Writings of George Washington*, VIII, 276, IX, 4, 5–6; McDougall to Washington, June 21, Putnam to Washington, July 31, 1777, Washington Papers, Ser. 4, Reels 42, 43, LC.

5. Orderly Book, McDougall's Brigade, April 9–August 28, 1777, NYHS; Putnam to Washington, June 28, and to Henry Beekman Livingston, July 4, 1777, Washington Papers, Ser. 4, Reel 42, LC; McDougall to Washington, Aug. 20, 1777, *ibid.*, Reel 43; McDougall to Gates, Aug. 17, 21, 1777, Horatio Gates Papers, NYHS.

6. Putnam to Washington, Sept. 14, 16, 1777, McDougall to Washington, Sept. 17, 1777, Washington Papers, Ser. 4, Reel 44, LC.

7. Washington to Putnam, and to McDougall, Sept. 14, 19, 22, 1777, *Writings of George Washington*, IX, 218, 221, 239, 246–47; McDougall to Washington, Sept. 20, 1777, Washington Papers, Ser. 4, Reel 44, LC; Washington to McDougall, Hawkes Collection, Union College.

8. Council of War, Sept. 28, 1777, *Writings of George Washington*, IX, 278–79.

9. Freeman, *George Washington*, IV, 504.

10.  General Orders, Oct. 3, 1777, *Writings of George Washington*, IX, 307–08.

11.  Clothing Return, Oct. 13, 1777, Papers of the Continental Congress, Reel 168, National Archives[NA](microfilm edition); Adam Stephen to Washington, Oct. 9, 1777, Washington Papers, Ser. 4, Reel 44, LC.

12.  Freeman, *George Washington*, IV, 512–16, 535–36; Adam Stephen to Washington, Oct. 9, 1777, Washington to Congress, Oct. 5, 1777, Washington Papers, Ser. 4, Reel 44, LC; Higginbotham, *War of American Independence*, 186.

13.  There is no satisfactory account of the action at Germantown, especially the involvement of Greene's wing. Greene encouraged McDougall to collect materials and write a history of the battle, but McDougall never did. Greene to McDougall, Feb. 5, and McDougall to Greene, Feb. 28, 1778, McDougall Papers, Box 2, NYHS.

14.  Washington to Congress, Oct. 5, 1777, Washington Papers, Ser. 4, Reel 44, LC; Henry A. Muhlenberg, *The Life of Major-General Peter Muhlenberg* (Philadelphia, 1849), 110–13; Ward, *War of the Revolution*, I, 368–69; Higginbotham, *War of American Independence*, 187.

15.  Freeman, *George Washington*, IV, 529–30; Washington to Congress, Oct. 7, 1777, *Writings of George Washington*, IX, 321–22.

16.  *Journal of Continental Congress*, IX, 823; John Hancock to McDougall, Oct. 27, 1777, McDougall Papers, Oversized Folder, NYHS; General Orders, Oct. 10, 11, 1777, *Writings of George Washington*, IX, 347, 352; Court of Inquiry, Oct. 10–12, 1777, *Letters and Papers of John Sullivan*, I, 482–532; Freeman, *George Washington*, IV, 535.

17.  General Orders, Oct. 11, 24, Nov. 1, 1777, Washington to James Potter, Oct. 21, 1777, *Writings of George Washington*, IX, 353, 380, 421–22, 492–93, 408.

18.  *Connecticut Courant*, Dec. 2, 1777; *Smith Historical Memoirs 1776–1778*, 262, 269; Ward, *War of the Revolution*, I, 376–77; Freeman, *George Washington*, IV, 551–53.

19.  McDougall to Greene, Feb. 14, to Heath, Mar. 12, 1778, McDougall Papers, Box 2, NYHS.

20.  Freeman, *George Washington*, IV, 545–51, 555–63.

21.  Greene to McDougall, Jan. 25, Feb. 5, 1778, Address to Congress, Jan. 6, Varnum to McDougall, Feb. 7, 1778, McDougall Papers, Box 2, NYHS.

22.  McDougall to Greene, Feb. 4, 1778, *ibid.*

23.  McDougall to Greene, Feb. 28, 1778, *ibid.*

24.  McDougall to Greene, Feb. 14, to Varnum, Feb. 26, 1778, *ibid.*; John Clark to Greene, Jan. 10, "1777"[1778], Nathanael Greene Papers, I, William L. Clements Library, Ann Arbor, Mich.

25.  Freeman, *George Washington*, IV, 582–83, 594–95, 605, 608.

26.  Lafayette to McDougall, Feb. 5, Greene to McDougall, Feb. 5, McDougall to Lafayette, Feb. 18, McDougall to Greene, Feb. 28, 1778, Mc-

Dougall Papers, Box 2, NYHS; Washington to Congress, and to McDougall, Feb. 12, Mar. 16, 1778, *Writings of George Washington*, X, 429, 451–52, XI, 95–97.

27. Washington to Clinton, and to Robert R. Livingston, Mar. 12, 1778, *ibid.*, XI, 68–70.

28. Washington to Putnam, and to McDougall, Mar. 16, Instructions, Mar. 17, 1778, *ibid.*, 94–95, 95–97, 100–01.

29. McDougall to Greene, Feb. 28, 1778, McDougall Papers, Box 2, NYHS.

30. McDougall began a rough journal on March 21 when he received Washington's order to take command in the Highlands; it covers the period of his second assignment on the Hudson. *Ibid.*

31. Visitors are mentioned in McDougall's journal, *ibid.; Smith Historical Memoirs 1776–1778*, 335.

32. McDougall to Washington, Mar. 29, 1778, Washington Papers, Ser. 4, Reel 48, LC.

33. Washington to Clinton, Mar. 17, 1778, *Writings of George Washington*, XI, 101–02.

34. Journal, Mar. 30, April 5, 1778; Report of the Court of Enquiry, McDougall Papers, Box 2, NYHS.

35. Clinton to McDougall, Nov. 13, 1778, Hawkes Collection, Union College.

36. Journal, April 4–6, 1778, McDougall Papers, Box 2, NYHS.

37. McDougall to Parsons, April 2, to Thomas Conway, April 4, 1778, *ibid.;* McDougall to Parsons, April 4, 1778, Charles S. Hall, *Life and Letters of Samuel Holden Parsons* (Binghamton, N.Y., 1905), 171–72; McDougall to Clinton, April 5, 1778, *Clinton Public Papers*, III, 131–33.

38. Clinton to McDougall, April 6, 1778, *ibid.*, 133.

39. Palmer, *River and the Rock*, 157–59; Parsons to McDougall, Mar. 28, 1778, Journal, April 7–8, 1778, McDougall Papers, Box 2, NYHS; McDougall to Clinton, April 7, 1778, *Clinton Public Papers*, III, 146–47.

40. Palmer, *River and the Rock*, 142–44, 150–55, 157, 161; Journal, April 8, 10, 11, 1778, McDougall Papers, Box 2, NYHS; McDougall to Parsons, April 11, 1778, Misc. Mss. 7525, NYSL.

41. Clinton to Gates, April 8, 1778, *Clinton Public Papers*, III, 151.

42. Journal, April 9, 1778, McDougall Papers, Box 2, NYHS; McDougall to Washington, April 13, 1778, Washington Papers, Ser. 4, Reel 48, LC.

43. McDougall to Clinton, April 13, 1778, *Clinton Public Papers*, III, 166.

44. McDougall to Clinton, April 15, 19, 29, May 6, Clinton to McDougall, April 18, May 10, McDougall to Conway, April 21, 1778, *ibid.*, 169–70, 186–87, 194–95, 200–02, 233, 274, 293–94; McDougall to Congress, April 23, 1778, McDougall Papers, Box 2, NYHS; Washington to McDougall, Mar. 25, 1778, *Writings of George Washington*, XI, 146.

45. Clinton to Jonathan Trumbull, May 1, 1778, *Clinton Public Papers*, III, 346–47.

46. Journal, April 25, 1778, McDougall Papers, Box 2, NYHS; Washington to McDougall, April 22, 1778, *Writings of George Washington*, XI, 297–98.

47. Clinton to McDougall, April 29, to Gouverneur Morris, May 14, 1778, *Clinton Public Papers*, III, 232–33, 310.

48. McDougall to Clinton, May 11, 1778, *ibid.*, 294; Clinton to McDougall, May 10, 1778, McDougall Papers, Box 2, NYHS.

49. To McDougall, June 13, 1778, *ibid.*, Oversized Folder.

50. Journal, April 26–27, May 2, 1778, *ibid.*, Box 2; Washington to Congress, May 1, 1778, *Writings of George Washington*, XI, 332. The celebration continued the next day at West Point. Palmer, *River and the Rock*, 163.

51. Journal, May 11–16, 1778, McDougall Papers, Box 2, NYHS; Palmer, *River and the Rock*, 164.

52. McDougall to Washington, May 21, 1778, Washington Papers, Ser. 4, Reel 49, LC.

53. To Henry Laurens, June 30, 1778, Papers of Continental Congress, Item 159, ff. 135–36, NA.

54. Washington to McDougall, July 12, Sept. 15, Oct. 23, 24, 25, 1778, Hawkes Collection, Union College; Council of War, July 25, Washington to Gates, Sept. 31, to McDougall, Oct. 2, General Orders, Oct. 19, 22, 1778, *Writings of George Washington*, XII, 230–31, 527–28, XIII, 7–8, 107, 130; McDougall to Washington, Oct. 9, 1778, Washington Papers, Ser. 4, Reel 52, LC.

55. McDougall left for Hartford on November 13 and remained there until at least November 23. McDougall to Washington, Nov. 13, 1778, *ibid.*, Reel 54; Washington to Jedediah Huntington, Nov. 22, and to McDougall, Nov. 24, 1778, *Writings of George Washington*, XIII, 308, 320–22.

## CHAPTER ELEVEN: MISSION TO PHILADELPHIA

1. See two letters of McDougall to Clinton, Dec. 15, 1778, *Clinton Public Papers*, IV, 377, 383–87, for a description of conditions in the Highlands; Clinton to McDougall, Dec. 15, 1778, *ibid.*, 387–89.

2. Higginbotham, *War of American Independence*, 205–08, 213–16, 400–02; John Shy, "The American Revolution: The Military Conflict Considered as a Revolutionary War," Stephen G. Kurtz and James H. Hutson, eds., *Essays on the American Revolution* (Chapel Hill, 1973), 121–56; McDougall to Egbert Benson, Feb. 9, 1779, McDougall Papers, Box 3, NYHS.

3. Palmer, *River and the Rock*, 185–86, 189–90.

4. McDougall to Clinton, Dec. 15, 1778, *Clinton Public Papers*, IV, 383–87.

5. McDougall to Greene, Nov. 12, 1778, Greene Papers, II, Clements Library.

6.  McDougall to Washington, Dec. 10, 1778, McDougall Papers, Box 2, NYHS.

7.  Washington to McDougall, Feb. 9, 1779, *Writings of George Washington*, XIV, 81–87.

8.  McDougall to Clinton, Dec. 15, 1778, *Clinton Public Papers*, IV, 377, 383–87; McDougall to Clinton, Jan. 20, to John Sullivan, March 7, 1779, McDougall Papers, Box 3, NYHS.

9.  McDougall to Greene, March 24, 1779, *ibid.*

10.  McDougall to Egbert Benson, Feb. 9, 1779, *ibid.*

11.  McDougall to Benson, May 12, 1779, *ibid.*

12.  McDougall to John McKesson, Jan. 24, 1779, *ibid.*

13.  McDougall to Benson, May 12, 1779, *ibid.*

14.  McDougall to Benson, Feb. 9, 1779, *ibid.*

15.  *Ibid.*

16.  McDougall to Clinton, March 1, 1779, *ibid.*

17.  McDougall to Joseph Reed, March 25, 1779, Joseph Reed Papers, Box 5, NYHS.

18.  McDougall to Speaker of New York Assembly, and to Clinton, March 1, 1779, McDougall Papers, Box 3, NYHS; McDougall to Speaker of New York Senate, March 1, 1779, Legislative Papers, X, Box 2, NYSL; Walter Livingston to McDougall, March 1779, McDougall Papers, Box 3, NYHS; Governor Clinton's message to the legislature, Jan. 28, 1779, *Clinton Public Papers*, IV, 525–26.

19.  McDougall to Washington, Jan. 19, 1779, Washington Papers, Ser. 4, Reel 55, LC; McDougall to Samuel Holden Parsons, Jan. 9, and to Clinton, Jan. 20, 1779, McDougall Papers, Box 3, NYHS.

20.  *Connecticut Courant*, Jan. 26, 1779; McDougall to Capt. Merely, March 2, and James Reed to McDougall, March 8, 1779, *Clinton Public Papers*, IV, 622–24.

21.  McDougall to Clinton, April 3, 1779, *ibid.*, 687–89.

22.  McDougall to Clinton, April 22, Udny Hay to Clinton, April 23, 1779, *ibid.*, 745–46, 750; McDougall to Gates, April 26, 1779, Horatio Gates Papers, Box 11, NYHS, Udny Hay to McDougall, May 26, 1779, McDougall Papers, Box 3, NYHS.

23.  McDougall to Clinton, April 3, 1779, *Clinton Public Papers*, IV, 687–89.

24.  James Reed to Clinton, March 14, 1779, *ibid.*, 622–24.

25.  McDougall to Clinton, March 14, 1779, *ibid.*, 630–33.

26.  McDougall to Clinton, Dec. 28, 1778, *ibid.*, 430–33; Clinton to McDougall, Jan. 14, 1779, *ibid.*, 483–84.

27.  McDougall to Clinton, Jan. 27, Feb. 6, 1779, *ibid.*, 520–21, 547–48.

28.  McDougall to Clinton, March 14, 1779, *ibid.*, 630–33. The legislature, Clinton replied, had done nothing to curb horse stealing or to facilitate the

work of court-martials. To McDougall, March 18, 1779, *ibid.*, 644–45.

29. McDougall to John Sullivan, March 7, 1779, McDougall Papers, Box 3, NYHS.

30. McDougall to Clinton, Jan. 20, 1779, *ibid.*; Palmer, *River and the Rock*, 182–86.

31. McDougall to Washington, March 4, 21, 22, 31, May 13, 1779, Washington Papers, Ser. 4, Reels 56, 57, 58, LC; Washington to McDougall, March 3, 22, 25, 28, 1779, *Writings of George Washington*, XIV, 182, 278, 291–92, 304. As early as April 18, McDougall suspected the British were preparing to attack the Highlands. To John Nixon, April 18, 1779, McDougall Papers, Box 3, NYHS. See also, Washington to McDougall, May 24, 1779, *Writings of George Washington*, XV, 141–42; McDougall to Washington, May 25, 29, 1779, Washington Papers, Ser. 4, Reel 59, LC; McDougall to Clinton, May 25, 1779, *Clinton Public Papers*, IV, 666–67.

32. Clinton to Udny Hay, and McDougall to Clinton, May 31, 1779, *ibid.*, 870–71; McDougall to Parsons, May 31, to Washington, June 1, 11, Parsons to McDougall, June 1, 4, 1779, McDougall Papers, Box 3, NYHS; Capt. Thomas Armstrong to McDougall, June 1, 1779, Washington Papers, Ser. 4, Reel 59, LC; Washington to McDougall, June 2, 1779, *Writings of George Washington*, XV, 213–14; Hall, *Life and Letters of Parsons*, 245–46; *Connecticut Courant*, June 8, 1779.

33. Washington to McDougall, June 19, General Orders, July 19, 1779, *Writings of George Washington*, XV, 285–86, 436–38; Palmer, *River and the Rock*, 197–202.

34. Freeman, *George Washington*, V, 133, 142.

35. *Ibid.*, IV, 614.

36. Edmund C. Burnett, *The Continental Congress* (New York, 1964 edition), 311–16; Higginbotham, *War of American Independence*, 401–02; Freeman, *George Washington*, V, 78. See also Washington's letter of Jan. 20, 1779, to a congressional committee urging a settlement for the officer corps. *Writings of George Washington*, XIV, 26–32.

37. *Journal of Continental Congress*, XI, 502–03, XIV, 638–39, 720–21, 908, 946–49, 973–76, 977–78; Burnett, *Continental Congress*, 391–92.

38. "The Memorial of the General Officers serving in the Army of the United States," McDougall Papers, Oversize Folder, NYHS; Washington to Robert Howe, Sept. 27, 1779, *Writings of George Washington*, XVI, 345–46.

39. McDougall to Washington, Nov. 6, 1779, Washington Papers, Ser. 4, Reel 62, LC; Washington to McDougall, Nov. 13, 17, 21, 1779, *Writings of George Washington*, XVII, 100–02, 120, 154; McDougall to Washington, Nov. 16, 21, Heath to McDougall, Dec. 4, 1779, McDougall Papers, Box 4, NYHS.

40. The winter of 1779–80 proved to be quite severe in the Hudson Valley. George Weedon to Nathanael Greene, Feb. 15, 1780, Greene Papers, VI, Clements Library; McDougall to Washington, March 16, 1780, Washington

Papers, Ser. 4, Reel 64, LC; McDougall to Clinton, Jan. 27, 1780, McDougall Papers, Box 4, NYHS.

41. McDougall to John McKesson, Feb. 10, 1780, *ibid.*

42. Greene to McDougall, n.d., *ibid.*

43. McDougall to Greene, May 29, 1780, *ibid.*

44. McDougall to Greene, March 21, 1780, Greene Papers, VI, Clements Library.

45. Washington to McDougall, June 15, to Robert R. Livingston, June 29, 1780, *Writings of George Washington,* XIV, 12–13, 90–91. McDougall took command at West Point on June 21, and found 1,200 out of 1,900 men in the five brigades fit for duty. Orderly Books, Capt. Jonathan Titus, 1780, NYSL; Garrison Return, July 2, 1780, McDougall Papers, Oversize Folder, NYHS.

46. Washington to McDougall, July 2, 1780, Hawkes Collection, Union College; Freeman, *George Washington,* V, 179; Report on New York City Harbor, July 7, 1780, McDougall Papers, Oversize Folder, NYHS; McDougall to Washington, July 24, 1780, Washington Papers, Ser. 4, Reel 68, LC.

47. Greene to his wife, July 11, Robert Howe to Greene, July 14, 1780, Greene Papers, VII, Clements Library; General Officers to McDougall, July 11, 1780, McDougall Papers, Box 4, NYHS.

48. Memorial of General Officers, July 11, 1780, *ibid.*

49. McDougall to Greene, Aug. 8, 1780, and Disbursement of Expenses, *ibid.;* Committee at Headquarters to Congress, July 23, 1780, Burnett, *Letters of Members of Continental Congress,* V, 288–89.

50. John Armstrong to William Irvine, Aug. 3, 1780, *ibid.,* 307.

51. *Journal of Continental Congress,* XVII, 689; McDougall to Greene, Aug. 8, 1780, McDougall Papers, Box 4, NYHS.

52. Notes delivered to the committee of Congress, August, 1780, *ibid.*

53. Henry Laurens to Richard Henry Lee, Aug. 1, 1789, Burnett, *Letters of Members of Continental Congress,* V, 306; Burnett, *Continental Congress,* 461–67.

54. *Journal of Continental Congress,* XVII, 725.

55. *Ibid.,* 770–73, 811.

56. McDougall to Congress, Sept. 15, 1780, Papers of Continental Congress, 116, ff. 115–19, Reel 179, NA.

57. McDougall to Greene, Aug. 15, 28, 1780, McDougall Papers, Box 4, NYHS; Washington to Congress, Aug. 20, 1780, *Writings of George Washington,* XIX, 403–13; Burnett, *Continental Congress,* 393.

58. McDougall to Congress, Aug. 14, Oct. 25, 1780, with an account of his expenses to September 15. Papers of Continental Congress, 161, ff. 107–08, 123–28, Reel 179, NA; *Journal of Continental Congress,* XVIII, 1005, XIX, 341, XXI, 900; Higginbotham, *War of American Independence,* 400–01.

CHAPTER TWELVE: DELEGATE TO CONGRESS

1.  McDougall to Greene, August 15, 1780, McDougall Papers, Box 4, NYHS.

2.  Washington to McDougall, and to Lamb, September 27, 1780, *Writings of George Washington*, XX, 99; Instructions to Officer Commanding West Point, September 27, 1780, Ms. 1338, U.S. Military Academy Library, West Point, New York.

3.  Pierre Van Cortlandt to McDougall, Oct. 6, 1780, McDougall Papers, Box 4, NYHS.

4.  McDougall to Washington, Oct. 30, 1780, Washington Papers, Ser. 4, Reel 72, LC.

5.  Henry Knox said that it was McDougall's off-repeated axiom. To McDougall, March 4, 1781, McDougall Papers, Box 4, NYHS.

6.  New York Assembly Speaker to McDougall, Oct. 10, and McDougall to Washington, Oct. 30, 1780, Washington Papers, Ser. 4, Reel 72, LC.

7.  Washington to McDougall, Oct. 24, 1780, *Writings of George Washington*, XX, 254.

8.  For two weeks McDougall held temporary command at West Point until William Heath, Greene's replacement, arrived. Washington to McDougall, Oct. 14, 1780, *ibid.*, 181. Heath had arrived by October 28, when McDougall wrote a long letter of advice. To Heath, Oct. 28, 1780, *Heath Papers*, III, 120–22.

9.  Greene to McDougall, Oct. 30, 1780, McDougall Papers, Box 4, NYHS.

10.  John Sullivan to Washington, Jan. 29, 1781, Burnett, *Letters of Members of Continental Congress*, V, 548.

11.  James Duane to Washington, Jan. 29, 1781, *ibid.*, 551–53.

12.  Burnett, *Continental Congress*, 489–93.

13.  *Ibid.*, 473–76, 479–80; James Duane to Washington, Dec. 9, 1780, Burnett, *Letters of Members of Continental Congress*, V, 477–80. The problems of wartime finance are covered in E. James Ferguson, *The Power of the Purse; A History of American Public Finance, 1776–1790* (Chapel Hill, 1961).

14.  James Duane to Clinton, Nov. 14, 1780, Burnett, *Letters of Members of Continental Congress*, V, 444–45; *Journal of Continental Congress*, XIX, 64.

15.  *Ibid.*, 78, 86, 90, 91, 104, 115, 121, 135, 142, 179, 185.

16.  *Ibid.*, 110–11, 156; Burnett, *Continental Congress*, 480–81; John Sullivan to Washington, March 6, 1781, Burnett, *Letters of Members of Continental Congress*, VI, 12.

17.  *Journal of Continental Congress*, XIX, 203; McDougall to Clinton, March 12, 1781, Burnett, *Letters of Members of Continental Congress*, VI, 25–26.

18.  McDougall to Congress, March 9, 1781, McDougall Papers, Box 4, NYHS.

19.  *Ibid.*

20. *Journal of Continental Congress*, XIX, 253, 326, 327, 332–34.

21. Richard Platt to McDougall, April 15, 1781, McDougall Papers, Box 4, NYHS; McDougall to John Laurance, April 20, 1781, John Laurance Papers, NYHS; *Journal of Continental Congress*, XIX, 420; Petition of Alexander McDougall, April 19, 1781, Papers of Continental Congress, 42, V. f. 255, Reel 179, NA.

22. McDougall to William Malcolm, April 21, 1781, *ibid.*, 161, I, ff. 131–32; Washington to McDougall, May 13, 1781, Washington Papers, Ser. 4, Reel 77, LC. McDougall left Philadelphia on May 23, 1781, McDougall Papers, Box 4, NYHS.

23. Greene to McDougall, May 17, 1781, *ibid.*; Freeman, *George Washington*, V, 277–80, 290; Washington to McDougall, March 31, 1781, *Writings of George Washington*, XXI, 400.

24. Higginbotham, *War of American Independence*, 379–80.

25. General Orders, June 18, 1781, *Writings of George Washington*, XXII, 232; Washington to McDougall, June 21, 1781, McDougall Papers, Box 4, NYHS.

26. Washington to McDougall, Aug. 19, to Lafayette, July 30, 1781, *Writings of George Washington*, XXII, 434, XXIII, 19–20; Heath to McDougall, Aug. 24, 1781, *Heath Papers*, III, 226–27; Freeman, *George Washington*, V, 310; Palmer, *River and the Rock*, 308–09.

27. McDougall to Washington, July 17, 30, Aug. 3, 1781, Washington Papers, Ser. 4, Reels 79, 80, LC; Washington to McDougall, Aug. 10, 1781, *Writings of George Washington*, XXII, 489–90.

28. McDougall to Heath, Nov. 7, 10, 17, 20, 21, 29, 1781, and to Hugh Hughes, Nov. 26, 1781, McDougall Papers, Box 4, NYHS; Palmer, *River and the Rock*, 334.

29. The exchange of numerous letters between the two generals may be followed in the McDougall Papers, Box 4, NYHS.

30. Freeman, *George Washington*, IV, 384.

31. McDougall to Heath, Dec. 16, 1781, McDougall Papers, Box 4, NYHS.

32. Heath to McDougall, Dec. 19, 1781, *ibid.*, is a good example.

33. Orderly Book, Christopher Marshall, Jan. 4, 1782, U.S. Military Academy Library, West Point; John Crane's order of Jan. 7, 1782, McDougall Papers, Box 5, NYHS.

34. Nathan Goodale to McDougall, Jan. 23, Rufus Putnam to McDougall, Jan. 26, James Mellius to McDougall, Jan. 27, Heath to McDougall, Jan. 18, 1782, *ibid.*

35. Heath to Washington, Jan. 18, McDougall to Washington, Jan. 27, 1782, Washington Papers, Ser. 4, Reel 82, LC. See also Heath to McDougall, Jan. 24, 1782, McDougall Papers, Box 5, NYHS; General Orders, Jan. 29, 1782, *Writings of George Washington*, XXIII, 471.

36. Washington to McDougall, Feb. 3, 1782, *ibid.*, 482–83.

37.  Heath to Stirling, Feb. 21, March 17, to Richard Varick, March 12, to Washington, March 13, Varick to Heath, March 14, 1782, *Heath Papers*, III, 347–48, 352–53, 355, 355–56, 357; Washington to Heath, March 4, 1782, *Writings of George Washington*, XXIV, 40; Lord Stirling to Heath, Feb. 19, 1782, McDougall Papers, Box 5, NYHS; McDougall to Washington, Feb. 8, 1782, Washington Papers, Ser. 4, Reel 83, LC.

38.  Washington to Stirling, April 4, and General Orders, April 7, 1782, *Writings of George Washington*, XXIV, 102–03, 104; Lord Stirling to McDougall, Aug. 30, Dec. 4, McDougall to Stirling, Nov. 12, Dec. 14, 1782, McDougall Papers, Box 5, NYHS.

39.  McDougall to Thomas Edwards, March 21, 1782, *ibid.*

40.  McDougall to Washington, April 1, 1782, *ibid.;* Washington to Heath, April 16, General Orders, April 12, 15, 1782, *Writings of George Washington*, XXIV, 117, 120, 125; Heath to Washington, April 18, 1782, *Heath Papers*, III, 365–66.

41.  On April 4 McDougall sent his defense to New York's delegates in Congress requesting them to forward the papers to Roberdeau. McDougall Papers, Box 5, NYHS.

42.  The full trial proceedings, including evidence, are in the McDougall Papers, NYHS.

43.  Washington to Congress, Aug. 3, General Orders, Aug. 28, 1782, *Writings of George Washington*, XXIV, 450, 454, XXV, 76–84; *Journal of Continental Congress*, XXIII, 468.

44.  James Duane to McDougall, Aug. 28, 1782, McDougall Papers, Box 5, NYHS.

45.  McDougall to Washington, June 15, Aug. 23, 26, 1782, Washington Papers, Ser. 4, Reel 85, LC.

46.  Washington to McDougall, Aug. 28, General Orders, Aug. 29, 1782, *Writings of George Washington*, XXV, 73–74, 85; McDougall to Washington, Sept. 4, 1782, Washington Papers, Ser. 4, Reel 87, LC.


## CHAPTER THIRTEEN: PHILADELPHIA AND NEWBURGH

1.  Washington to Robert Morris, May 17, to Benjamin Lincoln, May 1, 28, 1782, *Writings of George Washington*, XXIV, 192–93, 287–90, 295–96.

2.  Washington to Robert Morris, June 16, to Benjamin Lincoln, June 17, Oct. 2, 1782, *ibid.*, 348–51, 352–54, XXV, 226–29.

3.  Washington to Bejamin Lincoln, Oct. 2, 1782, *ibid.*, XXV, 226–29; North Carolina Delegates to Alexander Martin, Oct. 22, 1782, Burnett, *Letters of Members of Continental Congress*, VI, 518.

4.  Samuel Holden Parsons to McDougall, Aug. 12, 1781, McDougall Papers, Box 4, NYHS, mentions that Lincoln, Knox, Glover, Paterson, and Huntington agreed with McDougall's view.

5.  McDougall to Philip Van Cortlandt, Feb. 6, 1782, *ibid.*, Box 5.

6.  Fourth Session, Chapter VII, *Laws of the State of New York* (Poughkeepsie, 1782), 152–54.

7.  McDougall to Clinton, March 28, 1782, McDougall Papers, Box 5, NYHS.

8.  To McDougall, Aug. 12, 1781, *ibid.*, Box 4.

9.  Report of John Paterson to McDougall, Dec. 15, Petition of Massachusetts Regiments, Dec. 18, Paterson to McDougall, Dec. 18, 1781, *ibid.*; McDougall to Washington, Jan. 2, 1782, Washington Papers, Ser. 4, Reel 82, LC.

10.  Parsons to McDougall, Aug. 12, 1781, McDougall Papers, Box 4, NYHS; Hatch, *Administration of the American Revolutionary Army*, 144–46.

11.  The mission to Massachusetts is discussed in Hatch, *Administration of the American Revolutionary Army*, 144.

12.  Washington to Joseph Jones, Dec. 14, 1782, *Writings of George Washington*, XXV, 430–31; *Journal of Continental Congress*, XXII, 451–53; Madison to Edmund Randolph, Oct. 22, 1782, Burnett, *Letters of Members of Continental Congress*, VI, 514.

13.  Washington to Benjamin Lincoln, Nov. 6, 1782, *Writings of George Washington*, XXV, 321–23; Madison to Edmund Randolph, Oct. 29, 1782, Burnett, *Letters of Members of Continental Congress*, VI, 528; Hatch, *Administration of the American Revolutionary Army*, 148–49.

14.  To Benjamin Lincoln, Dec. 20, 1782, Francis S. Drake, *Life and Correspondence of Henry Knox, Major-General in the American Revolutionary Army* (Boston, 1873), 77.

15.  Hatch, *Administration of the American Revolutionary Army*, 147, 149; Washington to Joseph Jones, Dec. 14, 1782, *Writings of George Washington*, XXV, 430–31.

16.  Instructions to the Committee from the Army, Dec. 7, 1782, McDougall Papers, Box 5, NYHS.

17.  Richard H. Kohn, "The Inside History of the Newburgh Conspiracy: America and the Coup d'Etat," *William and Mary Quarterly*, 3rd ser., XXVII (1970), 187–220, is the fullest discussion of the Newburgh affair. For a reply and defense of Horatio Gates, see Paul David Nelson, "Horatio Gates at Newburgh, 1783: A Misunderstood Role," *ibid.*, XXIX (1972), 143–58. Knox to Benjamin Lincoln, Dec. 20, 1782, Drake, *Life and Correspondence of Henry Knox*, 77; McDougall to Knox, Jan. 9, 1782, McDougall Papers, Box 6, NYHS; James Madison, "Notes of Debates," Jan. 10, 1783, *Journal of Continental Congress*, XXV, 850.

18.  Memorial to Congress, December, 1782, Papers of Continental Congress, 42, VI, ff. 59–64, NA.

19.  Ferguson, *Power of the Purse*, 148–54; Burnett, *Continental Congress*, 532–33.

20.   Arthur Clairy to McDougall, Ogden, and Brooks, Jan. 5, 1783, Mc-
Dougall Papers, Box 6, NYHS.

21.   McDougall to Knox, Jan. 9, 1783, *ibid.;* Kohn, "Newburgh Conspiracy," 192.

22.   The army's memorial is endorsed with the names of the committee
members appointed on January 6: Philip White, Samuel Osgood, Jonathan
Arnold, Oliver Wolcott, Alexander Hamilton, Silas Condict, Richard Peters,
Philemon Dickinson, Daniel Carroll, James Madison, Abner Nash, and John
Rutledge. Papers of the Continental Congress, 42, VI, ff. 59–64, NA. James
Madison, "Notes of Debates," Jan. 6, 7, 1783, *Journal of Continental Congress,*
XXV, 847, 850.

23.   *Ibid.,* 851–53; Madison to Edmund Randolph, Jan. 16, 1783, Burnett,
*Letters of Members of Continental Congress,* VII, 19.

24.   James Madison, "Notes of Debates," Jan. 24, 25, 1783, *Journal of Continental Congress,* XXV, 862–66; *ibid.,* XXIV, 93–95; Kohn, "Newburgh Conspiracy," 194.

25.   James Madison, "Notes of Debates," Jan. 24, 1783, *Journal of Continental
Congress,* XXV, 863–64.

26.   Jan. 25, 1783, *ibid.,* 865–66.

27.   Arthur Lee to Samuel Adams, Jan. 29, 1783, Burnett, *Letters of Members
of Continental Congress,* VII, 28.

28.   McDougall and Ogden to Knox, Feb. 8, 1783, McDougall Papers, Box
6, NYHS.

29.   *Ibid.*

30.   Gouverneur Morris to Knox, Feb. 7, 1783, Burnett, *Letters of Members of
Continental Congress,* VII, 34–35.

31.   Hamilton to Washington, Feb. 7, 1783, *ibid.,* 33–35.

32.   McDougall to Knox, Feb. 8, 1783, McDougall Papers, Box 6, NYHS.

33.   "Brutus" [McDougall] to Knox, Feb. 12, 1783, Henry Knox Papers, XI,
Massachusetts Historical Society. For a different interpretation of this letter,
see Kohn, "Newburgh Conspiracy," 197. Higginbotham, *War of American Independence,* 408, mistakenly has McDougall returning to Newburgh with
Ogden about this time.

34.   Knox to Robert Morris, Feb. 21, 1783, Drake, *Life and Correspondence of
Henry Knox,* 77–78.

35.   Knox to McDougall, Feb. 21, 1783, McDougall Papers, Box 6, NYHS;
McDougall to Knox, Feb. 19, 1783, Burnett, *Letters of Members of Continental
Congress,* VII, 50.

36.   Kohn, "Newburgh Conspiracy," 204–05; James Madison, "Notes of
Debates," Feb. 27, 28, 1783, *Journal of Continental Congress,* XXV, 916–18.

37.   "Brutus" [McDougall] to Knox, Feb. 27, 1783, Henry Knox Papers, XI.
Massachusetts Historical Society. On the other hand, Baron von Steuben
predicted that the army would be kept together five or six months longer.

Von Steuben to Greene, March 9, 1783, Greene Papers, LXXV, Clements Library.

38. Kohn, "Newburgh Conspiracy," 198–204; Joseph Hones to Washington, Feb. 27, 1783, Burnett, *Letters of Members of Continental Congress*, VII, 61. For a defense of Horatio Gates, see Nelson, "Horatio Gates at Newburgh, 1783," 143–58. The army's mood is described in Knox to Benjamin Lincoln, March 3, 1783, Drake, *Life and Correspondence of Henry Knox*, 79.

39. McDougall to Knox, March 15, 1783, McDougall Papers, Box 6, NYHS. Massachusetts had swung over to commutation by February 26, but New Hampshire, Rhode Island, and New Jersey remained in opposition; Connecticut was divided. *Journal of Continental Congress*, XXIV, 149–51, 178–79.

40. McDougall to Knox, March 15, 1783, McDougall Papers, Box 6, NYHS. William Floyd reported to Governor Clinton that commutation "was lost by the vote of one single person." March 12, 1783, Burnett, *Letters of Members of Continental Congress*, VII, 72.

41. The documents associated with the Newburgh Conspiracy, including the army memorial of December, 1782, are in *Journal of Continental Congress*, XXIV, 291–311, as part of a congressional report to the states. The "conspirators" accused John Brooks of tipping their hand to Washington. John Armstrong to Horatio Gates, April 29, 1783, Burnett, *Letters of Members of Continental Congress*, VII, 155; Kohn, "Newburgh Conspiracy," 201.

42. General Orders, March 11, 1783, *Journal of Continental Congress*, XXIV, 297–98, 310–11. Ironically, Gates as the ranking major general chaired the officers' meeting of March 15. *Ibid.*, 306–10; Freeman, *George Washington*, V, 433–36; Kohn, "Newburgh Conspiracy," 211.

43. James Madison, "Notes of Debates," March 17, 1783, *Journal of Continental Congress*, XXV, 926. Washington's second report of March 18 was read in Congress the same day as the passage of commutation. *Ibid.* XXIV, 207–10.

44. John Armstrong to Horatio Gates, April 22, May 30, 1783, Burnett, *Letters of Members of Continental Congress*, VII, 150–51, 175; Hatch, *Administration of the American Revolutionary Army*, 179–81; North Callahan, *Henry Knox, George Washington's General* (New York, 1958), 210–12. At a meeting of the New York regiments on June 2, McDougall was elected president of the state society. McDougall Papers, Box 6, NYHS.

45. McDougall to John Vanderbelt, Sept. 8, 1783, *ibid.*

CHAPTER FOURTEEN: END OF A PUBLIC CAREER

1. Margaret Livingston to Robert R. Livingston, April 30, 1783, Robert R. Livingston Papers, Box 11, NYHS; John Morin Scott to James Duane, April 30, 1783, Duane Papers, Box 1782–83, NYHS; McDougall to Washington,

Oct. 5, 1783, Washington Papers, Ser. 4, Reel 93, LC; Washington to Mc-
Dougall, Oct. 15, 1783, *Writings of George Washington*, XXVII, 192.

2.  Sidney I. Pomerantz, *New York, An American City, 1783–1803* (New
York, 1938), 20.

3.  E. Wilder Spaulding, *New York in the Critical Period 1783–1789* (New
York, 1932), 6–12.

4.  Alexander C. Flick, *History of the State of New York* (10 vols., New York,
1933–37), IV, 271–73; Pomerantz, *New York*, 23.

5.  Frederick Haldiman to Schuyler, June 30, and John Lansing, Jr. to
Schuyler, Dec. 26, 1783, Philip Schuyler Papers, Box 35, NYPL; William
Malcom to James Duane, July 20, 1783, Duane Papers, Box 1782–83, NYHS;
Memorial of Refugee Citizens of New York, Sept. 1, 1783, Misc. Ms. 10700,
NYSL; "Further information by Mr. ————," Aug. 19, 1783, *Clinton Public
Papers*, VIII, 244–45; McDougall to Clinton and to Richard Morris, Dec. 25,
Richard Morris to McDougall, Dec. 28, 1783, McDougall Papers, Box 6,
NYHS; Robert R. Livingston to Robert Morris, Dec. 20, 1783, Robert R.
Livingston Papers, Box 13, NYHS.

6.  Alexander Hamilton to James Duane, Aug. 5, 1783, Duane Papers, Box
1782–83, NYHS.

7.  Stokes, *Iconography of Manhatten*, V, 1182; *Pennsylvania Gazette*, Jan. 7,
1784; *Connecticut Courant*, Mar. 3, 1784; Leake, *Life of John Lamb*, 296–97.

8.  "State of M. General McDougall's pay, for a settlement with the State of
New York," Aug. 26, 1783; "A List of Certificates in the hands of Alexander
McDougall," McDougall to John Vanderbelt, Sept. 8, 1783, McDougall Papers, Box 6, NYHS; Robert Troup to James Duane, July 26, and McDougall
to Duane, Oct. 17, 1783, Duane Papers, Box 1782–83, NYHS.

9.  The standard biography of Clinton is E. Wilder Spaulding, *His Excellency
George Clinton* (New York, 1938).

10.  The most penetrating analysis of the Clintonian party, its leaders and its
objectives, is Alfred E. Young, *The Democratic Republicans of New York: The Origins 1763–1797* (Chapel Hill, 1967), 33–58.

11.  Pomerantz, *New York*, 147–48; Petition of New York City Merchants,
April 20, 1784, Legislative Papers, XI, NYSL; Merrill Jensen, *The New Na-
tion: A History of the United States During the Confederation, 1781–1789* (New
York, 1950), 162–64; Spaulding, *New York in the Critical Period*, 14, 25.

12.  Jan. 21, 1784, *Journal of the Senate of the State of New York . . . Seventh
Session* (New York, 1784), 4–6, 7, 9, 10–12.

13.  Feb. 12, 1784, *ibid.*, 27–28. See also, Chapters I, X, *New York State Laws
. . . Seventh Session*, 3–4, 11–17.

14.  April 14, 1785, *Journal of the Senate of the State of New York . . . Eighth
Session* (New York, 1785), 86. Thomas C. Cochran in *New York in the Confederation, An Economic Study* (New York, 1932), 171, has Philip Schuyler of Albany leading the proponents of the measure. Regrettably, Schuyler was not
present in the New York Senate at the time.

15.  March 15, 1785, *Journal of New York Senate . . . Eighth Session*, 47–48.

16.  Jensen, *New Nation*, 24; Spaulding, *New York in the Critical Period*, 18–19; Petition of New York City Merchants, April 20, 1784, Legislative Papers, XI, NYSL.

17.  Jan. 30, 1784, *Journal of New York Senate . . . Seventh Session*, 14; Spaulding, *New York in the Critical Period*, 144; Hamilton to John Church, March 10, 1784, Harold D. Syrett, ed., *The Papers of Alexander Hamilton* (15 vols., New York, 1961–), III, 520–22.

18.  McDougall voted against paper money bills passed by the Assembly. April 30, 1784, *Journal of New York Senate . . . Seventh Session*, 133.

19.  Church to Hamilton, Feb. 7, 1784, *Hamilton Papers*, III, 507.

20.  Henry M. Domett, *History of the Bank of New York*, 1784–1884 (New York, 1884), 4–7; Stokes, *Iconography of Manhatten*, V, 1185; Constitution of the Bank of New York, *Hamilton Papers*, III, 514–18.

21.  March 18, 19, April 9, 1784, *Journal of New York Senate . . . Seventh Session*, 63; Nov. 13, 15, 1784, *ibid.*, Eighth Session, 21, 23; April 9, 1785, *ibid.*, Second Meeting, 79. Only the senators from New York City were in favor of the bank bill.

22.  Domett, *History of the Bank of New York*, 19–21.

23.  Spaulding, *New York in the Critical Period*, 21–22; Petition of Insolvent Debtors, April 18, 1785, Legislative Papers, IX, NYSL; Feb. 3, 1784, *Journal of New York Senate . . . Seventh Session*, 18. A similar bill did pass the legislature in 1783, only to be vetoed by the Council of Revision. Spaulding, *New York in the Critical Period*, 42.

24.  March 5, 1784, *Journal of New York Senate . . . Seventh Session*, 51–52. The legislature did agree to a law relaxing the procedures by which persons in financial trouble could settle with their creditors. *Ibid.*, 115; Spaulding, *New York in the Critical Period*, 42; Chapter XXXIV, *Laws of the State of New York . . . Seventh Session*, 45–51.

25.  That view was expressed in the tax bill preamble. April 26, 1784, *Journal of New York Senate . . . Seventh Session*, 116, 117; Chapter LVIII, *Laws of the State of New York . . . Seventh Session*, 83–89. The same principle of ability to pay was inserted in New York City's municipal tax measure of 1784. Chapter XLIII, *ibid.*, 57–58.

26.  For complaints of tax collectors about their difficulties, see Petition of New York City Tax Collectors, Jan. 1785, Legislative Papers, XI, NYSL.

27.  March 2, 1785, *Journal of New York Senate . . . Eighth Session*, Second Meeting, 30–31.

28.  April 20, 27, May 4, 1784, *ibid.*, Seventh Session, 104–105, 127, 137–38.

29.  April 29, 1784, *ibid.*, 131, 132.

30.  April 20, May 4, 1784, *ibid.*, 106, 137–38; May 13, 1785, Abstract of Sales of Forfeited Lands in the Southern District of New York, NYHS.

31.  April 29, 1784, *Journal of New York Senate . . . Seventh Session*, 132.

32.  Hugh Hastings, comp., *Ecclesiastical Records of the State of New York* (7 vols., Albany, 1901–06), VI, 4046–48, 4081, 4083–84, 4095–96.

33.  William Goforth to McDougall, Feb. 20, 1779, McDougall Papers, Box 3, NYHS.

34.  *Journal of New York Senate . . . Seventh Session*, 31, 45–47; Chapter XXIII, *Laws of the State of New York . . . Seventh Session*, 42–45.

35.  McDougall to Alexander Stewart, n.d., McDougall Papers, Box 6, NYHS.

36.  McDougall to William McDougall, Sept. 17, Peter R. Livingston to McDougall, Oct. 20, McDougall to Peter R. Livingston, Oct. 29, 1785, *ibid.*

37.  April 5, 1785, *Journal of New York Senate . . . Eighth Session*, Second Meeting, 70; Jan. 27, 1786, *ibid.*, *Ninth Session*, 12.

38.  Spaulding, *New York in the Critical Period*, 144–46; March 8, 1786, *Journal of New York Senate . . . Ninth Session*, 40.

39.  Senate Attendance Records, Ninth Session, Legislative Papers, XII, NYSL.

40.  Washington to Jefferson, Aug. 1, 1786, *Writings of George Washington*, XXVIII, 506.

41.  Stokes, *Iconography of Manhatten*, V, 1211; Washington to Jefferson, Aug. 1, 1786, *Writings of George Washington*, XXVIII, 506

# Bibliography

PRIMARY SOURCES

*Manuscript Collections*

Columbia University, Special Collections
  John Jay Papers
Franklin D. Roosevelt
  Livingston-Redmond Papers, microfilm edition
Library of Congress
  George Washington Papers, microfilm edition
Massachusetts Historical Society
  Henry Knox Papers
National Archives
  Papers of the Continental Congress, microfilm edition
New York Historical Society
  William Alexander Papers
  John Alsop Papers
  Anthony Lispenard Bleecker Letter Books, 1767–1787
  James Duane Papers
  Horatio Gates Papers
  John Tabor Kempe Papers
  John Lamb Papers
  Robert R. Livingston Papers
  Alexander McDougall Papers
  John McKesson Papers
  Naval Office Lists, PRO, C.O. 5/1227, microfilm
  New York Miscellaneous Manuscripts, 1767–1770
  Orderly Book, First New York Regiment, 1776
  Orderly Book, Alexander McDougall's Brigade, 1777
  Joseph Reed Papers
  Isaac Sears Papers
  Tavern Keeper's License Book, 1756–1766

New York Public Library
  Samuel Adams Papers
  George Bancroft Transcripts: Livingston Papers and Revolutionary Papers
  Barrack Master Accounts, Evert and Gerard Bancker, 1768–1774
  Boston Committee of Correspondence Papers
  Livingston Family Papers
  Philip Schuyler Papers
  William Smith, Jr. Papers
New York State Library
  Legislative Papers
  Miscellaneous Manuscripts
  New York Treasurer, Manifest Books
  Orderly Book, Captain Jonathan Titus
Union College, Schenectady, New York
  W. Wright Hawkes Collection of Revolutionary War Documents
U. S. Military Academy Library, West Point, New York
  Miscellaneous Manuscripts
  Orderly Book, Christopher Marshall
William L. Clements Library, Ann Arbor, Michigan
  Nathanael Greene Papers

*Public Records and Correspondence*

*American Archives,* Fourth Series. Peter Force, compiler, 6 vols., Washington, D.C., 1837–43.

*Calendar of Historical Manuscripts Relative to the War of the Revolution In the Office of the Secretary of State.* 2 vols., Albany, 1868.

*Colonial Laws of New York from the Year 1664 to the Revolution.* 5 vols., Albany, 1894.

*Documentary History of the State of New York.* Edmund B. O'Callaghan, ed., 4 vols., Albany, 1850.

*Documents Relative to the Colonial History of the State of New York.* Edmund B. O'Callaghan and Berthold Fernow, eds., 15 vols., New York, 1856–87.

*Ecclesiastical Records of the State of New York.* Hugh Hastings, compiler, 7 vols., Albany, 1901–06.

*Historical Register of Officers of the Continental Army during the War of the Revolution.* Francis B. Heitman. New York, 1914.

*Journal of the Legislative Council of the Colony of New York.* 2 vols., Albany, 1861.

*Journal of the Senate of the State of New York . . . Seventh Session.* New York, 1785.

*Journal of the Senate of the State of New York . . . Eighth Session.* New York, 1785.

*Journal of the Senate of the State of New York . . . Ninth Session.* New York, 1786.

*Laws of the State of New York . . . Fifth Session.* Poughkeepsie, 1782.

*Laws of the State of New York . . . Seventh Session.* New York, 1784.

*Journals of the Continental Congress, 1784–1789.* Worthington C. Ford, ed., 34 vols., Washington, D.C., 1904–37.

*Letters of Members of the Continental Congress.* Edmund C. Burnett, ed., 8 vols., Washington, D.C., 1921–36.

*New York in the Revolution as Colony and State: A Supplement.* Erastus C. Knight, compiler, Albany, 1901.

*Public Papers of George Clinton, First Governor of New York.* Hugh Hastings and J. A. Holden, eds., 10 vols., Albany, 1898–1914.

*Votes and Proceedings of the General Assembly of the Colony of New York.* 1766–1775.

*Personal Correspondence, Memoirs, and Diaries*

*Aspinwall Papers.* Massachusetts Historical Society *Collections*, Fourth Series. 2 vols., Boston, 1871.

*American Journal of Ambrose Serle, Secretary to Lord Howe, 1776–1778.* Edward H. Tatum, ed., San Marino, Calif., 1940.

*Beekman Mercantile Papers, 1746–1799.* Philip L. White, ed., 4 vols., New York, 1956.

*Colden Letter Books.* New-York Historical Society *Collections.* 2 vols., New York, 1876–77.

*Correspondence of General Thomas Gage with the Secretaries of State, 1763–1775.* Clarence E. Carter, ed., 2 vols., New Haven, 1931–33.

*Diary and Autobiography of John Adams.* Lyman H. Butterfield, ed., 4 vols., Cambridge, Mass., 1961.

*Historical Memoirs, from 16 March 1763 to 9 July 1776 of William Smith, Historian of the Province of New York. . . .* William H. W. Sabine, ed., New York, 1956.

*Historical Memoirs from 12 July 1776 to 25 July 1778 of William Smith, Historian of the Province of New York. . . .* William H. W. Sabine, ed., New York, 1958.

*Iconography of Manhattan Island . . . .* I. N. Stokes, compiler, 6 vols., New York, 1915–28.

*Lee Papers.* New-York Historical Society *Collections.* 3 vols., New York, 1872–74.

*Letters and Papers of Cadwallader Colden.* New-York Historical Society *Collections.* 9 vols., New York, 1918–37.

*Letters and Papers of Major-General John Sullivan. . . .* New Hampshire Historical Society *Collections.* 3 vols., Concord, N.H., 1930–39.

*Life and Correspondence of Henry Knox, Major-General in the American Revolutionary Army.* Francis S. Drake. Boston, 1873.

*Life and Letters of Samuel Holden Parsons.* Charles S. Hall. Binghamton, 1905.

*Letters to and from Caesar Rodney, 1756–1784.* George H. Ryden, ed., Philadelphia, 1933.

*Narrative of the Military Actions of Colonel Marinus Willett.* Marinus Willett. New York, 1969 edition.

*Papers of Alexander Hamilton.* Harold D. Syrett, et al., eds., 15 vols., New York, 1961– .

*William Heath Papers.* Massachusetts Historical Society *Collections.* 3 vols., Boston, 1898–1905.

*Writings of George Washington.* John C. Fitzpatrick, ed., 39 vols., Washington, D.C., 1931–44.

*Broadsides and Pamphlets*

*Advertisement.* July 7, 1770. New York, 1770.

"Agricoloa," *To the Inhabitants of the City and County of New York.* July 12 and 20, 1774. New York, 1774.

*Association of the Sons of Liberty. . . .* New York, 1773.

*Advertisement of the Committee of the Association.* December 16, 1773. New York, 1773.

"Brutus," *To the Public.* January 5, 1770. New York, 1770.

"Brutus," *To the Inhabitants.* New York, 1770.

*Friendly Address to all Reasonable Americans, on the subject of our political confusions. . . .* New York, 1774.

[Chandler, Thomas Bradbury], *What Think Ye of the Congress? Or, an Enquiry How Far the Americans are Bound to abide by, and execute the decisions of, the late Congress.* New York, 1775.

*Citizen's Address to the Public.* December 18, 1769. New York, 1769.

*Committee of Correspondence. . . .* May 16, 1774. New York, 1774.

*Committee of Correspondence. . . .* July 13, 1774. New York, 1774.

*Committee of Correspondence. . . .* July 25, 1774. New York, 1774.

[Cooper, Myles], *The American Querist: Or, Some Questions proposed relative to the present disputes between Great Britain and her American Colonies.* New York, 1774.

*Debates at the Robin-Hood Society, in the city of New York, on Monday night 19th of July, 1774.* New York, 1774.

"Ebenezer Snuffle, Secretary," *At a meeting of the true Sons of Liberty, in the City of New York. . . .* New York, 1774.

*The following persons are recommended to the public, as proper to be elected for a General Committee. . . .* April 27, 1775. New York, 1775.

*The Following persons are nominated by the Sons of Liberty, to represent them in the committee. . . .* April 28, 1775. New York, 1775.

[Hamilton, Alexander], *The Farmer Refuted; or, A More comprehensive and impartial view of the disputes between Great Britain and the Colonies.* New York, 1775.

[Hamilton, Alexander], *A Full Vindication of the Measures of Congress from the Calumnies of Their Enemies, in Answer to a Letter under the Signature of a Westchester Farmer, &c.* New York, 1774.

"J. W. a squinter on public affairs," *A Mode of Election Considered.* December 29, 1769. New York, 1769.

*Letter to the Celebrated Patriot of New York.* New York, 1770.

*A Letter found on board the sloop Illicit, Captain Perjury, wrecked at Oyster-Bay.* . . . New York, 1773.

[Livingston, Philip], *The Other Side of the Question: or, a defence of the liberties of North America.* New York, 1774.

*The mechanicks of this city are earnestly requested to meet.* . . . November 18, 1774. New York, 1774.

[McDougall, Alexander], *To the Betrayed Inhabitants of the City and Colony of New York.* December 16, 1769. New York, 1769.

*On Tuesday, the 19th Day of July, 1774, the Inhabitants of the City Of New York met at the Coffee House.* . . . New York, 1774.

*Out-Lines.* New York, 1770.

*Paradise Regain'd. To all the Great and Glorious Patriots in New York and throughout America,—and around the Globe.* New York, 1770.

[Seabury, Samuel], *Free Thoughts on the Proceedings of the Congress at Philadelphia, &c.* New York, 1774.

[Seabury, Samuel], *The Congress Canvassed: or an Examination into the Conduct of the Delegates, &c.* New York, 1774.

[Seabury, Samuel], *A View of the Controversy, &c. in a Letter to the Author of a Full Vindication, &c.* New York, 1775.

[Seabury, Samuel], An Alarm to the Legislature, &c. New York, 1775.

Thurman, John. *To the Freemen and Freeholders.* March 4, 1775. New York, 1775.

*To the Public.* December 28, 1769. New York, 1769.

*To the Independent Freeholders and Freemen of this City and County.* January 4, 1770. New York, 1770.

*To the Sons of Liberty in this City.* February 3, 1770. New York, 1770.

*To the Public.* May 18, 1774. New York, 1774.

*To the Inhabitants of the City and Colony of New York.* July 5, 1774. New York, 1774.

*To the Freeholders, Freemen and Inhabitants of the City and County of New York.* July 9, 1774. New York, 1774.

*To the Inhabitants of the City and County of New York,* July 23, 1774. New York, 1774.

*To the Friends of American Liberty.* March 4, 1775. New York, 1775.

*To the Inhabitants of the City and County of New York.* April 15, 1775. New York, 1775.

*Newspapers*

*Boston Gazette.* 1765–1775.
*Connecticut Courant.* 1776–1783.
*Maryland Gazette.* 1776–1778.
*New York Gazette or Weekly Post-Boy.*
*New York Gazette.*
*New York Journal.*
*New York Mercury.*
*Pennsylvania Gazette.*
*Rivington's Gazetteer.* 1773–1775.


SECONDARY SOURCES

*Monographs*

Alden, John R. *General Charles Lee, Traitor or Patriot.* Baton Rouge, 1951.
Alexander, Edward P. *A Revolutionary Conservative: James Duane of New York.* New York, 1938.
Bailyn, Bernard. *The Origins of American Politics.* New York, 1968.
Bailyn, Bernard. *The Ideological Origins of the American Revolution.* Cambridge, Mass., 1967.
Becker, Carl L. *The History of Political Parties in the Province of New York, 1760–1776.* Madison, 1909.
Billias, George A. *John Glover and His Marblehead Mariners.* New York, 1960.
Bliven, Bruce, Jr. *Under the Guns: New York, 1775–1776.* New York, 1972.
Bliven, Bruce, Jr. *Battle for Manhattan.* New York, 1964 edition.
Bonomi, Patricia U. *A Factious People: Politics and Society in Colonial New York.* New York, 1971.
Bridenbaugh, Carl. *Mitre and Sceptre: Transatlantic Faiths, Ideas, Personalities, and Politics, 1689–1775.* New York, 1962.
Burnett, Edmund C. *The Continental Congress.* New York, 1964 edition.
Callahan, North. *Henry Knox: George Washington's General.* New York, 1958.
Cochran, Thomas. *New York in the Confederation: An Economic Study.* Philadelphia, 1932.
Dawson, Henry B. *The Sons of Liberty in New York.* Poughkeepsie, 1859.
Domett, Henry M. *History of the Bank of New York, 1784–1884.* New York, 1884.
Dillon, Dorothy R. *The New York Triumvirate: A Study of the Legal and Political Careers of William Livingston, John Morin Scott, and William Smith, Jr.* New York, 1949.

Edwards, George W. *New York as an Eighteenth Century Municipality, 1731–1776*. New York, 1917.

Ernst, Joseph Albert. *Money and Politics in America, 1755–1775: A Study in the Currency Act of 1764 and the Political Economy of Revolution*. Chapel Hill, 1973.

Ferguson, E. James. *The Power of the Purse: A History of American Public Finance, 1776–1790*. Chapel Hill, 1961.

Flick, Alexander C. *History of the State of New York*. 10 vols., New York, 1933–37.

Flexner, James T. *George Washington*. 4 vols., Boston, 1965–72.

Freeman, Douglas S. *George Washington*. 7 vols., New York, 1948–57.

Graham, Ian C. C. *Colonists from Scotland: Emigration to North America, 1707–1783*. Ithaca, 1956.

Gruber, Ira D. *The Howe Brothers and the American Revolution*. New York, 1972.

Harrington, Virginia D. *The New York Merchant on the Eve of the American Revolution*. New York, 1935.

Higginbotham, Don. *The War of American Independence: Military Attitudes, Policies, and Practice, 1763–1789*. New York, 1971.

Hatch, Louis C. *The Administration of the American Revolutionary Army*. New York, 1904.

Jensen, Merrill. *The New Nation: A History of the United States During the Confederation, 1781–1789*. New York, 1950.

Jensen, Merrill. *The Founding of a Nation: A History of the American Revolution, 1763–1776*. New York, 1968.

Jones, Thomas. *History of New York During the Revolutionary War. . . .* Edward Floyd De Lancey, ed., 2 vols., New York, 1879.

Johnston, Henry P. *The Campaign of 1776 Around New York and Brooklyn*. Long Island Historical Society *Memoirs*. New York, 1878.

Klein, Milton M., ed., *The Independent Reflector*. Cambridge, Mass., 1963.

Labaree, Benjamin W. *The Boston Tea Party*. New York, 1964.

Leake, Isaac Q. *Memoir of the Life and Times of General John Lamb*. Albany, 1850.

Levy, Leonard W. *Legacy of Suppression: Freedom of Speech and Press in Early American History*. Cambridge, Mass., 1960.

Maier, Pauline. *From Resistance to Revolution: Colonial Radicals and the Development of American Opposition to Britain, 1765–1776*. New York, 1972.

Main, Jackson Turner. *The Sovereign States, 1775–1783*. New York, 1973.

Martin, James Kirby. *Men In Rebellion: Higher Governmental Leaders and the Coming of the American Revolution*. New Brunswick, 1973.

Mason, Bernard. *The Road to Independence: The Revolutionary Movement in New York, 1773–1777*. Lexington, 1966.

Muhlenberg, Henry A. *The Life of Major-General Peter Muhlenberg.* Philadelphia, 1849.

Nobbe, George. *The North Briton: A Study in Political Propaganda.* New York, 1939.

Palmer, Dave Richard. *The River and the Rock: The History of Fortress West Point, 1775–1783.* New York, 1969.

Pomerantz, Sidney I. *New York, An American City, 1783–1803.* New York, 1938.

Robbins, Caroline. *The Eighteenth Century Commonwealthman.* Cambridge, Mass., 1959.

Rude, George. *Wilkes and Liberty: A Social Study of 1763–1774.* Oxford, 1960.

Schlesinger, Arthur M. *The Colonial Merchants and the American Revolution 1763–1776.* New York, 1918.

Shy, John. *Toward Lexington: The Role of the British Army in the Coming of the American Revolution.* Princeton, 1965.

Smith, William, Jr. *The History of the Province of New York.* Michael Kammen, ed., 2 vols., Cambridge, Mass., 1972.

Sparks, Jared. *The Life of Gouverneur Morris.* 3 vols., Boston, 1832.

Spaulding, E. Wilder. *His Excellency George Clinton.* New York, 1938.

Van Schaack, Henry C. *Life of Peter Van Schaack.* New York, 1842.

Wallace, Willard M. *Traitorous Hero: The Life and Fortunes of Benedict Arnold.* New York, 1954.

Ward, Christopher. *The War of the Revolution.* New York, 1952.

Wood, Gordon S. *The Creation of the American Republic, 1776–1787.* Chapel Hill, 1969.

Young, Alfred E. *The Democratic Republicans of New York: The Origins 1763–1797.* Chapel Hill, 1967.

*Articles*

Bonomi, Patricia U. "Political Patterns in Colonial New York City: The General Assembly Election of 1768." *Political Science Quarterly,* LXXXI (1966), 432–47.

Champagne, Roger J. "The Military Association of the Sons of Liberty." *New-York Historical Society Quarterly,* XLI (1957), 338–50.

Champagne, Roger J. "Family Politics versus Constitutional Principles: The New York Assembly Elections of 1768 and 1769." *William and Mary Quarterly,* 3rd series, XX (1963), 57–79.

Champagne, Roger J. "Liberty Boys and Mechanics of New York City, 1764–1774." *Labor History,* VIII (1967), 115–35.

D'Innocenzo, Michael and Turner, John L. "The Role of New York Newspapers in the Stamp Act Crisis, 1764–1766." *New-York Historical Society Quarterly,* LI (1967), 215–31, 345–65.

Friedman, Bernard. "The New York Assembly Elections of 1768 and 1769: The Disruption of Family Politics." *New York History*, XLVI (1965), 3–24.

Friedman, Bernard. "The Shaping of the Radical Consciousness in Provincial New York." *Journal of American History*, LVI (1970), 781–801.

Greene, Jack P. "Bridge to Revolution: The Wilkes Fund Controversy in South Carolina, 1769–1775." *Journal of Southern History*, XXXIX (1963), 19–52.

Jones, Alice H. "Wealth Estimates for the American Middle Colonies, 1774." *Economic Development and Cultural Change*, XVIII (1970), 1–172.

Klein, Milton M. "Politics and Personalities in Colonial New York." *New York History*, XLVII (1966), 3–16.

Klein, Milton M. "William Livingston's *A Review of the Military Operations in North America*." Lawrence H. Leder, ed. *The Colonial Legacy*. 4 vols., New York, 1971–73.

Kohn, Richard H. "The Inside History of the Newburgh Conspiracy: America and the Coup d'Etat." *William and Mary Quarterly*, 3rd series, XXVII (1970), 187–220.

Launitz-Schurer, Leopold, Jr. "Whig-Loyalists: The De Lanceys of New York." *New-York Historical Society Quarterly*, LVI (1972), 179–98.

Leder, Lawrence H. "The New York Elections of 1769: An Assault on Privilege." *Mississippi Valley Historical Review*, XLIX (1963), 675–82.

Levy, Leonard W. and Leder, Lawrence H., "Exotic Fruit: The Right Against Compulsory Self-Incrimination in Colonial New York." *William and Mary Quarterly*, 3rd series, XX (1963), 3–33.

Lemisch, Jesse. "New York's Petitions and Resolves of December 1765: Liberals vs. Radicals." *New-York Historical Society Quarterly*, XLIX (1965), 313–26.

Lemisch, Jesse. "Jack Tar in the Streets: Merchant Seamen in the Politics of Revolutionary America." *William and Mary Quarterly*, 3rd series, XXV (1968), 371–407.

Lynd, Staughton. "The Mechanics in New York Politics, 1774–1788." *Labor History*, V (1964), 225–46.

Mackesy, Piers. "British Strategy in the War of American Independence." *Yale Review*, LII (1963), 539–57.

Maier, Pauline. "John Wilkes and American Disillusionment with Britain." *William and Mary Quarterly*, 3rd series, XX (1963), 373–95.

Maier, Pauline. "Popular Uprisings and Civil Authority in Eighteenth Century America." *William and Mary Quarterly*, 3rd series, XXVII (1970), 3–35.

Mason, Bernard. "The Heritage of Carl Becker: The Historiography of the Revolution in New York." *New-York Historical Society Quarterly*, LIII (1969), 127–47.

Nelson, Paul David. "Horatio Gates at Newburgh, 1783: A Misunderstood

Role." *William and Mary Quarterly*, 3rd series, XXIX (1972), 143–51.

O'Callaghan, Edmund B. "Early Highland Immigration to New York." *Historical Magazine*, V (1861), 301–03.

Pryde, George. "Scottish Colonization in the Province of New York." *New York History*, XVI (1935), 138–57.

Scott, William A. "Attitude Change Through Reward of Verbal Behavior." *Journal of Abnormal and Social Psychology*, LV (1957), 72–75.

Scott, William A. "Attitude Change by Response Reinforcement: Replication and Extension." *Sociometry*, XXII (1959), 528–35.

Shalhope, Robert E. "Toward a Republican Synthesis: The Emergence of an Understanding of Republicanism in American Historiography." *William and Mary Quarterly*, 3rd series, XXIX (1972), 49–80.

Shy, John. "The American Revolution: The Military Conflict Considered as a Revolutionary War." Stephen G. Kurtz and James H. Hutson, eds., *Essays on the American Revolution*. Chapel Hill, 1973.

Varga, Nicholas. "The New York Restraining Act: Its Passage and Some Effects, 1766–1768." *New York History*, XXXVII (1956), 233–58.

Wood, Gordon S. "Rhetoric and Reality in the American Revolution." *William and Mary Quarterly*, 3rd series, XXIII (1966), 3–32.

Wilkenfeld, Bruce M. "The New York City Common Council, 1689–1800." *New York History*, LII (1971), 249–73.

*Unpublished Materials.*

Christen, Robert Jay. King Sears: Politician and Patriot in a Decade of Revolution. Unpublished Ph.D. dissertation, Columbia University, 1968.

Shannon, Sister Anna Madeleine. General Alexander McDougall, Citizen and Soldier, 1732–1786. Unpublished Ph.D. dissertation, Fordham University, 1957.

Zaworski, Raymond E. Early State Banking in Massachusetts and New York, 1784–1792. Unpublished masters thesis, Illinois State University, 1968.

# Index